10th Edition

IAS MAINS

25 Years

COMPULSORY ENGLISH

Solved Papers
2001-2025

***for* UPSC & State Civil Services Main Examinations**

Author's Profile

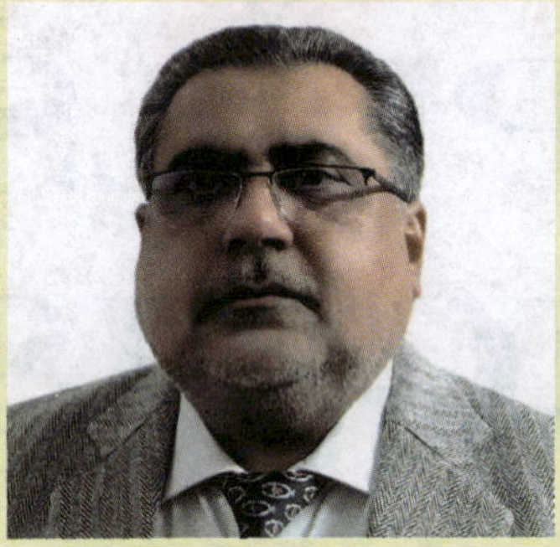

A P BHARDWAJ is a well-known name and an established author of #1 Best-selling books on English and essay papers for IAS MAINS and states' civil and judicial services examinations. He has single-handedly trained and tutored innumerable students to get admission into national law universities and colleges and hence known as CLAT GURU. He has also trained and enabled hundreds of students to score well in English and essay papers in civil and judicial services examinations. He has authored more than a dozen books. He is the author of GKP'S *CONCISE GK & ENGLISH WIZARD*. He is an author with several nationally and internationally acclaimed publishers.

10th Edition

IAS MAINS

25 Years

COMPULSORY ENGLISH

Solved Papers

2001-2025

for UPSC & State Civil Services Main Examinations

A P Bhardwaj

GKP

Title : IAS Mains : Compulsory English - 25 Years Solved Papers 2001-2025, 10th ed

Language : English

Author's Name : A P Bhardwaj

Typeset & Published by :

Career Launcher Infrastructure (P) Ltd.

A-45, Mohan Cooperative Industrial Area, Near Mohan Estate Metro Station,
New Delhi - 110044

Marketed by :

G.K. Publications (A Unit of CL Educate)
14/4, Mathura Road, Faridabad, Haryana-121003

ISBN : **978-93-69140-76-3**

Printer's Details : Printed in India, New Delhi.

Acknowledgements

First and foremost, support from my family members and friends needs to be acknowledged. My wife, Upasna Bhardwaj, and my daughter, Anaadi Asmita Bhardwaj always deserve special mention for their constant support and understanding.

My daughter Anaadi is steadily growing and acquiring technical know- how, and her skills have been of immense help for me to impart finishing touches to my manuscript.

My wife's contributions cannot be reciprocated, but must be acknowledged that without her support, none of this manuscript can take shape.

My sisters' blessings always play a great role. Mentions may be made of **Archana Thakur, Anju, (Nahan), Vandana Negi Bindu, (Paonta Sahib), Prem Didi (Sundernagar), and Sadhna Suri, Neeti (Jalandhar). Kamlesh Thapa (Kamo Didi), (Nahan).**

I am fortunate to have a special niece **Shruti Thakur (Haripur Khol, Nahan),** who has been one of my greatest well-wishers. Her husband **'Luv Thakur'** is a very Bandas (carefree, lion hearted & fun loving) person whose company is enjoyed by everyone around him. My other nieces **Gudiya, Chunna (Rajma)** and **Tanya** have always been inseparable parts of our most cherished and joyful family moments.

The children are considered as living representatives of God, and I feel truly blessed to be surrounded by a galaxy of little stars **like Atharav, Aanvi, Arya Varat ('Arya"/ NANNU), Shayaant,('Shayyu"), Pragun, (Teddy Bear) , Kamakshi, (kamabhakhti, Kamakhya devi)**.

Their innocence, affection, and boundless energy add joy, happiness, and meaning to our lives.

To all of them, I offer my heartfelt gratitude for always being there with me and for me.

A P BHARDWAJ
JUNE 2026
CHANDIGARH

Dedicated To

My Brothers-in -law

Karanveer Chaudhary (kaka Bhai) & Dinesh Chaudhary ('Babli Bhai')

(Haripur Khol, Nahan, Sirmaur, HP)

They are brothers in the truest sense of the word. Kind – hearted, generous, and ever willing to lend a helping hand, they extend their support to everyone irrespective of status, background or relationship. They genuinely deserve and earn respect from genuine people. They exemplify the values of goodwill and brotherhood through their actions and conduct. May they be blessed with good health, prosperity, and lasting happiness.

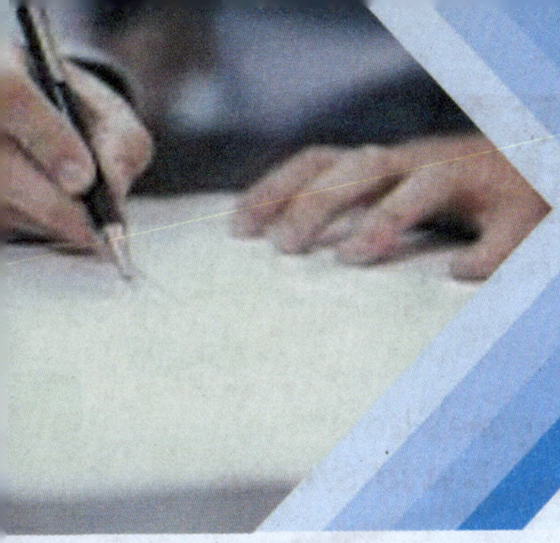

Preface To The Tenth Edition

It gives me immense pleasure to present the revised and updated 10th edition of my book, namely **25 years IAS MAINS COMPULSORY ENGLISH SOLVED PAPERS.** The 10th edition has been updated with 2023, 2024, 2025 papers.

A noteworthy trend has emerged in these recent papers: the nature of essay topics has undergone a significant transformation. Earlier essays primarily revolved around social, economic, political and current themes. But now the topics covered are meant to check the candidates' level of self-motivation, organic personality development, and are designed to assess the overall breadth of general reading, depth of understanding, and their ability to apply ideas in day-to-day life.

To help the students understand these emerging trends, I have chosen and written on topics such as **"Happiness is a state of mind, 'No man is an island,' and East or west, home is the best**.

These essays aim to demonstrate how a seemingly simple topic can be developed into a meaningful, analytical, and well-structured essay.

A close look at these topics reveals the need and demand of the present times and present generation. Today's youth are increasingly engulfed by over digitalization, excessive social media indulgence, and growing self-absorption. Many youngsters have gone almost crazy about social media usage, virtual world is overshadowing the real world, virtual world interactions are mistakenly eclipsing genuine human relationships. Broken homes are becoming a common phenomenon, and inevitable evil and its acceptability among youngsters and their parents is jeopardizing the social institutions of family, and marriage. Consequently, many children from fractured families are growing up emotionally wounded, unevenly developed. This, in turn, contributes to unrest, disorder, and social instability.

The essay topics in recent UPSC examinations appear to encourage introspection and a return to enduring human values such as emotional balance, empathy, family bonding, and meaningful social interactions and relationships.

I sincerely hope that this new edition will not only help aspirants prepare effectively for Compulsory English paper, but also inspire them to think deeply, read widely, and express their ideas with clarity, maturity, and balance.

A P BHARDWAJ
June 2026

The Art of Essay Writing

A Multifaceted & Multi-Pronged Perspective

"I really love that the idea of essay is an investigation. That's all anyone's life is."

David Shields

"An essay is a thing which one does himself;
and the point of essay is not the subject, ...
but the charm of personality."

Arthur Benson

The word 'essay' literally means an attempt or, to try to do something; and essay writing thereby means an interesting, educating and thought provoking attempt of writing. Essay writing is a multifaceted, multi-pronged and herculean effort to make a perfect use of thoughts and language, giving cohesive expression of your inner and outer self, in catchy and captivating words, which should go straight to the head and heart of the reader.

As the noted essayist, Arthur Benson wrote, "An essay is a thing which one does himself; and the point of essay is not the subject, ... but the charm of personality."

So, essay writing is essentially and apparently meant to check one's comprehension, thinking pattern, level of learning and expression. It is also a reflection of one's personality. There is a widely prevalent myth about essay writing that it is only a test of language. However, in practice, this is not so. Language is undoubtedly the medium of expression, carrier of ideas and costume of thoughts but essay writing is intrinsically and primarily the actualizations of one's true self in one's own words through a particular subject. Essay writing is a free flow of ideas that involves considerable skill, proficiency and experience.

The art of essay writing demands great skill to buttress your thoughts and reinforce your ideas. This skill needs to be developed deliberately and diligently. The management and articulation of ideas and language in cogent, coherent and convincing style are emblematic of good essay writing skills.

The primary purpose of essay writing is to check the ability to perceive, conceive, internalize, analyze and reproduce the ideas logically, rationally and reasonably. It is determined to take note of alertness of the mind, keenness to observe, inquisitiveness to know and learn and as a result to grow incessantly. So to all intents and purposes, essay writing is a means to assess the level of comprehension, which in the ultimate reckoning means to evaluate overall personality and maturity of the writer.

Essay writing demands from you a well built and properly laid thought process, which is essentially structured and properly layered. It also demands an impression of organically and evenly developed personality, able to cope up with any situation, counter any pressure and steadfastly perform, without bias, prejudice and angst.

As essay writing is the test of one's expression through a perfect convergence of thoughts and language. One must be competent to express views on a subject clearly, coherently and convincingly. The expression in the essay should be simple but impressive, not simplistic. The abstruse and ambiguous expression is never paying. Redundancy and verbosity, superfluity and superficiality should be avoided altogether. The potent warning by the essayist R.B. Sheridan can be followed as a guide in this regard: "Never say more than is necessary."

Without being a good reader, one can never be a good writer. So reading, reading and reading is the only salvation for good writing. One of the greatest essayists of all times Stephen King wrote: "If you don't have the time to read, you don't have the time (or the tools) to write. Simple as that." So it is of imperative necessity to develop the habit of regular reading from diverse sources which will boost your learning and broaden your thinking. This will automatically start manifesting in your writing and consequently your writing will start giving a powerful, stunning and forceful impression.

> Without being a good reader, one can never be a good writer. So reading, reading and reading is the only salvation for good writing. One of the greatest essayists of all times Stephen King wrote: "If you don't have the time to read, you don't have the time (or the tools) to write. Simple as that."

Dr A P J Abdul Kalam said: *Learning gives creativity; creativity leads to thinking; thinking provides knowledge and knowledge makes you great.*

So was said by Aldous Huxley: "*Words can be like X-Rays. If you use them properly, they will go through anything. You read and you're pierced.*"

So essay writing is an X-Ray of your personality, thinking pattern, your level of learning, information and knowledge. To make an effective impact through essays, one must therefore have a strong armoury of thoughts and a rich repository of vocabulary.

Words play the role of a clinching fist in essay writing. They must be in consonance and coherence with grammar, sentence structure and free flow of ideas. The value and beauty of words have been explained by writers from time to time:

> "A word after a word after a word is power."
>
> **Margaret Atwood**
>
> "Words are a lens to focus on one's mind."
>
> **Ayn Rand**
>
> "Words are the body of thoughts."
>
> **Carlyle**
>
> "Thought is impossible without words."
>
> **Emerson**

We think with words. It follows almost like a law of mathematics that the more words you know, the more clearly and powerfully you will think and the more ideas you will invite into your mind. You may have a million dollar idea, but it will be worthless if you cannot convert it into words and convince others of its value. The right words and their right use at a right time is the best means of expression and that is the power and glory of words.

The requirements of good essay writing can broadly be summed up as:

1. A good command over language with a rich repository of vocabulary and armoury of thoughts.
2. Conceptual clarity of grammar is a pre requisite of good writing.
3. Grammatical and spelling mistakes are to be avoided at all costs.
4. The use of adjectives wherever required to embellish the sentences is desirable but your essay should not be a claptrap of unwanted adjectives.

5. The wrong use of punctuation marks can mar the chances of good score because it can spoil the whole essence of an essay.
6. To be adroit maneuverer of weaving ideas and words, you must, over the passage of time, blend your natural talents and spontaneity with diligently developed writing skills.
7. Coherence and cogency are the biggest strengths of a good essay.
8. Candour and forthrightness in an essay is always rewarded.
9. Bumptiousness in your writing is very damaging.

From the ongoing discussions, it becomes clear that regular reading from diverse sources has no substitute for assimilation of ideas and thoughts. To develop a rich repository of vocabulary it is worth to read the internationally acclaimed *"Word Power Made Easy"* by Norman Lewis and keep enriching your knowledge from various other sources.

You may also improve your vocabulary and sharpen your intellect with ideas from some popular books listed below:

- *India After Independence* by Bipan Chandra
- *India After Gandhi* by Ram Chandra Guha
- *Social Problems in India* by Ram Ahuja
- *The Constitution and Citizenship Values* by Subhash Kashyap
- *Social Change in India* by M N Srinivas.

Some noted books for personality development are given below:

- *Light From Many Lamps* by Eichler Watson
- *The Guiding Light* by A P J Abdul Kalam
- *The Warrior of Light* by Paulo Coelho
- *Mega Living* by Robin Sharma
- *The Wisdom of Ages* by Wayne Dyer
- *The Road to Character* by David Brooks

The reading of biographies and autobiographies also leave a long lasting impression on your personality. Once you systematically work hard on these verticals of essay writing, you will notice a considerable enhancement in your writing skills.

A TALISMAN ON ESSAY WRITING FOR COMPETITIVE EXAMINATIONS

The Do's & Don'ts

- One must be very careful about the choice of topic for essay writing.
- The topic must be of your choice, close to your heart and must meet or approximate your area of interest.
- Before putting your ideas into black and white, you must have an anatomical framework of essay in your mind with broad bifurcation into opening, body and conclusion. Without it, you will rummage and end up making a mess of your own ideas.
- Try to start with a quote.
- The opening should be poignant, perspicacious and piercing.
- Then start linking ideas and filling the gaps.
- The words should be incisive and penetrating to make the ideas precipitate properly.
- Instead of making repetition of same words, the invariables/synonyms should be used to impart ornamental touches to your writing.
- The sentences should be crisp and not too long. Too long sentences should be avoided because there are chances of grammatical and structural mistakes. Never ever name or blame any party or government.
- The use of abrasive language should be avoided.
- Try to remain balanced, natural and spontaneous.
- Don't take your focus away from the topic. Stick to your topic and buttress your thoughts with examples and illustrations and reinforce your ideas with quotes and sayings of authorities on the concerned discipline.
- Don't be judgemental.
- Don't thrust your writing with utopian optimism and abysmal pessimism.
- Economy of words is always rewarding.
- The conclusion should always give a hope of bright and sustainable future.
- Always bear in mind that essay writing is a reflection of your comprehension, expression and level of learning, information and knowledge.
- In the words of Henry Miller, "Writing is its own reward."

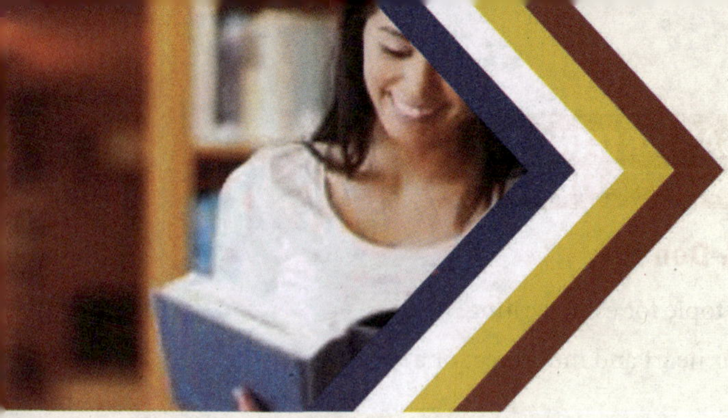

Contents

UPSC (MAIN) EXAM – 2025
ENGLISH
(Compulsory)

Time Allowed: 3 hours **Maximum Marks: 300**

Question Paper: Specific Instructions

Please read each of the following instructions carefully before attempting questions.

- *All questions are to be attempted.*
- *The number of marks carried by questions is indicated against it.*
- *Answers must be written in* **ENGLISH** *only.*
- *Word limit in questions, wherever specified, should be adhered to and if answered in much longer or shorter than the prescribed length, marks will be deducted.*
- *Any page or portion of the page left blank in the Question-cum-Answer Booklet must be clearly struck off.*

Q1. Write an essay in about 600 words on any *one* of the following topics : (100 Marks)

(a) The raw material of cinema is life

(b) No man is an island

(c) Eating habits and lifestyle in Contemporary India

(d) Folklore as a knowledge system

Ans. **No man is an island**

The phrase, '*No man is an island* 'emphasizes the interconnectedness of all humankind. People are interconnected and interdependent. People need each other. They love and hate, attract and repel, agree or disagree, but they cannot survive in isolation. Every human being is a part of greater whole that is humanity itself. No human being is isolated and separated from the rest of humanity, like an island entirely of its own.

No man is entirely self-sufficient. Human beings are social creatures who depend upon each other for survival, growth, and fulfillment. We are interconnected and interdependent. and any tragedy affecting one person or one part of the world ultimately impacts the entire humanity. The COVID-19 pandemic vividly demonstrated this reality. Although it originated in China, it spread across continents and affected people in every corner of the globe, proving that the entire humanity shares a common destiny.

Nowadays digitalization has further substantiated and vindicated the truthfulness of this statement. The world has become a global village where information travels instantaneously. News of a natural disaster, political upheaval, or economic crisis in remote part of the world can reach billions of people within moments. **The entire globe is literally a touch screen away.**

However, while technological advancements have connected people physically and digitally, but they have often disconnected them emotionally. Gadgets are replacing genuine human interactions. The difference between real world and virtual world is becoming blurred . Many youngsters are gradually mistaking virtual world engagements for authentic human relationships. While connectivity and correspondence on social media platforms continue to grow and multiply, real world relationships are shrinking day by day.

The social medial platform creators and handlers are playing with human psychology. The innate tendencies toward narcissism and self-glorification are amplified through constant pursuits of likes, shares, and followers. Human emotions are being commodified, while human values such as empathy and sympathy. love, compassion, pity, forgiveness and kindness are being relegated in the name of practicality, and success. Selfishness and self-centeredness are promoted and celebrated as indicators of achievement. In the garb of self-aggrandizement, and maximization of self-interests, the spirits of sharing and caring are eroding quickly.

Family members, friends, acquaintances, teachers, preachers, mentors, and colleagues play indispensable role in our lives. Various social, economic, political , religious , and professional institutions have organically evolved over a period of time to fulfill the needs and necessities of humans. In personal and professional life, no one can succeed and thrive in isolation. Every achievement is the outcome of shared values, efforts, and contributions of near and dear ones and cooperation received from numerous people throughout one's life.

The notion of a completely self-made individual or a solitary genius is largely a romanticized fallacy. The whole story of human progress is the outcome of exchange of ideas and actualization of those ideas into reality with efforts of various people in various capacities. The recent victory over corona virus vindicates this statement. Doctors, scientists, discoverers, health workers, policymakers and researchers put collective efforts to overcome the greatest challenge of recent times. Even the collective efforts and patience of ordinary citizens all over the world cannot be underrated and underestimated. **Their shared efforts and sacrifices underline the fact that no man is an island.**

Similarly, ongoing wars in various parts of the world continue to affect the lives of millions of people. These wars and conflicts create human crises, displacement, economic instability, scarcity of resources that extend far beyond national boundaries. Such events serve as powerful reminders that the fate of one nation or community is closely tied to the fate of others.

It is also a terrible need of the hour to make the young generations understand the pernicious effects of identifying their lives with gadgets and their overindulgence on social media platforms. They must be encouraged to cultivate the values of understanding, sympathy, compassion, and a genuine sense of human connection. Developing meaningful relationships and recognizing our shared humanity are crucial for personal well-being and social harmony.

Ultimately, the message of **'No man is an island** 'remains as relevant today as ever. Human beings are bound together by countless visible and invisible ties. Our joys and sorrows, successes and failures, challenges and triumphs are shared in one way or the other. Recognizing our interconnectedness is essential not only for individual growth but also for the progress and survival of humanity itself.

Q2. Read carefully the passage given below and write your answers to the questions that follow in clear, correct and concise language. (15 × 5= 75 Marks)

In proportion as a book is more loosely constructed, the paragraphs tend to become more diffuse. You often have to search through all the paragraphs of a chapter to find the sentences you can construct into a statement of a single argument. Some books make you search in vain, and some do not even encourage the search.

A good book usually summarizes itself as its arguments develop. If the author summarizes his arguments for you at the end of a chapter, or at the end of an elaborate section, you should be able to look back over the preceding pages and find the materials he has brought together in the summary. In *The Origin of Species*, Darwin summarizes his whole argument for the reader in a last chapter, entitled "Recapitulation and Conclusion." The reader who has worked through the book deserves that help. The one who has not cannot use it.

Incidentally, if you have inspected the book well before beginning to read it analytically, you will know whether the summary passages exist and if they do, where they are. You can then make the best possible use of them when interpreting the book.

Another sign of a bad or loosely constructed book is the omission of steps in an argument. Sometimes they can be omitted without damage or inconvenience, because the propositions left out can be generally supplied from the common knowledge of readers. But sometimes their omission is misleading, and may even be intended to mislead. One of the most familiar tricks of the orator or propagandist is to leave certain things unsaid, things that are highly relevant to the argument, but that might be challenged if they were made explicit. While we do not expect such devices in an honest author whose aim is to instruct us, it is nevertheless a sound maxim of careful reading to make every step in an argument explicit.

Whatever kind of book it is, your obligation as a reader remains the same. If the book contains arguments, you must know what they are, and be able to put them into a nutshell. Any good argument can be put into a nutshell. There are, of course, arguments built upon arguments. In the course of an elaborate analysis, one thing may be proved in order to prove another, and this may be used in turn to make a still further point. The unity of reasoning, however, can always be built up from the conclusions. The book you are reading, you are once more reminded, must be read through its arguments.

This is all very well to say, you may object, but unless one knows the structure of arguments *as a logician does*, how can one be expected to find them in a *book, or worse, to construct them* when the author does not state them compactly in a single paragraph?

The answer is that it must be obvious that you do not have to know about arguments "as a logician does." There are relatively few logicians in the world, for better or for worse. Most of the books that convey knowledge and can instruct us contain arguments. They are intended for the general reader, not for specialists in logic.

No great logical competence is needed to read these books. To repeat what we said before, the nature of the human mind is such that if it works at all during the process of reading, if it comes to terms with the author and reaches his propositions, it will see his arguments as well.

There are, however, a few things we can say that may be helpful to you in carrying out this rule of reading. *In the first place*, remember that every argument must involve a number of statements.

Of these, some give the reasons why you should accept a conclusion the author is proposing. If you find the conclusion first, then look for the reasons. If you find the reasons first, see where they lead.

In the second place, discriminate between the kind of argument that points to one or more particular facts as evidence for some generalization and the kind that offers a series of general statements to prove some further generalizations. The former kind of reasoning is usually referred to as inductive, the latter as deductive; but the names are not what is important. What is important is the ability to discriminate between the two.

In the literature of science, this distinction is observed whenever the difference is emphasized between the proof of a proposition by reasoning and its establishment by experiment. Galileo, in his *Two New Sciences*, speaks of mathematical demonstration. And in a concluding chapter of his book *On the Motion of the Heart*, the great physiologist William Harvey writes: "It ventricles flows through the lungs and heart and is pumped to the whole body." Sometimes it is possible to support a proposition both by reasoning from other general truths and by offering experimental evidence. Sometimes only one method of argument is available.

In the third place, observe what things the author says he must assume, what he says can be proved or otherwise evidenced, and what need not be proved because it is self-evident. He may honestly try to tell you what all his assumptions are, or he may be just as honestly leave you to find out for yourself. Obviously, not everything can be proved, just as not everything can be defined. If every proposition had to be proved, there would be no end to the process of proof. Such things as axioms and assumptions or postulates are needed for the proof of other propositions. If these other propositions are proved, they can, of course, be used as premises in further proofs.

Every line of argument, in other words, must start somewhere. Basically, there are two ways or places in which it can start: with assumptions agreed on between writer and reader, or with what are called self-evident propositions, which neither the writer nor reader can deny. In the first case, the assumptions can be anything, so long as agreement exists. The second case requires some further comment here.

In recent times, it has become commonplace to refer to self-evident propositions as "tautologies"; the feeling behind the term is sometimes one of contempt for the trivial, or a suspicion of legerdemain. Rabbits are being pulled out of a hat. You put the truth in by defining your words, and then pull it out as if you were surprised to find it there. That, however, is not always the case.

For example, there is a considerable difference between a proposition such as "a father of a father is a grandfather," and a proposition such as "the whole is greater than its parts." The former statement is a tautology; the proposition is contained in the definition of the words; it only thinly conceals the verbal stipulation, "Let us call the parent of a parent a 'grandparent.'" But that is far from being the case with the second proposition.

(a) What are the observations of the essayist on books in the passage? (15 Marks)

(b) Enumerate the points of comparison between a writer and a logician, as proposed in the passage. (15 Marks)

(c) What are the helpful rules of reading discussed in the essay? (15 Marks)

(d) What does the essayist mean by the phrase '*self-evident propositions*'? (15 Marks)

(e) According to the essay, what are '*tautologies*'? (15 Marks)

Ans. (a) The essayist says loosely written books have long, confusing paragraphs. Such books may omit important steps or mislead readers. Good books summarize arguments clearly in chapters or at the end. Darwin's *Origin of Species* is an example. The reader's job is to find and state arguments briefly, because real reading means following arguments.

(b) The essayist says readers do not need to be expert logicians to understand arguments. Writers of knowledge-based books write for general readers, not specialists. A logician studies logic deeply, but an ordinary reader only needs to follow the author's main ideas. If the mind works actively, it will naturally see the arguments.

(c) The essayist gives three main rules. First, find the conclusion of an argument and then look for its reasons, or the opposite. Second, learn to see the difference between inductive reasoning (from facts to generalization) and deductive reasoning (from general to general). Third, notice assumptions, proofs, and self-evident truths that form the base of reasoning.

(d) Self-evident propositions are truths that everyone accepts without proof. They are the starting points of arguments, like axioms in mathematics. Writers and readers both agree they cannot be denied. For example, "the whole is greater than its parts" is self-evident. Such statements form the foundation for proving other ideas and conclusions.

(e) Tautologies are statements that repeat a definition without adding new meaning. The truth is already hidden in the words used. For example, "the father of a father is a grandfather" only repeats the definition. It looks like reasoning, but it is not deep. True self-evident propositions are more meaningful than tautologies.

Q3. Make a precis of the following passage in about one-third of its length. Do not give or suggest a title to it. The precis should be written in your own words.(75 Marks)

Every individual soul is an undeveloped entity, which though not wholly emancipated from the animal instincts, is yet capable of transmuting them. By a willing acceptance of the commanding claims of spirit and a discipline of our nature into conformity with its law, we achieve growth. A redirection of interest and re-education of the unconscious mind alone can transform us from carnal-mindedness into spiritual-mindedness. It means restraint and discipline. There is real temptation, genuine struggle involved in every transcendence of the natural man. But this transcendence is the condition of the fulfilment of personality. Though the effort is costly, the reward is great. This transcendence is a phenomenon common to all progress. From the pursuit of its prey by the amoeba to the spiritual struggles of the striving soul, we have a continuously graded series of purposive efforts. We choose the goal everywhere and adapt the means. Only at the human level we can do so consciously and deliberately.

Man is neither the slave of circumstances nor the blind sport of the gods. The impulse to perfection working in the universe has become self-conscious in him. Progress happened in the subhuman world; it is willed in the human. Conscious purpose takes the place of unconscious variations. Man alone has the irrest consequent on the conflict between what he is and what he can be. He is distinguished from other creatures by his seeking after a rule of life, a principle of progress.

It is by transforming ourselves that we shall be able to transform the world. The soul of all improvement, it has been rightly said, is the improvement of the soul. We need not leave the building of the new civilization to luck — it is a matter for cunning also. There is a good deal to be done yet. The world is unfinished in several respects. It lies with us to retard or hasten the progress. The lesson of evolution is clear. Life does not work according to any set programme, reaching satisfying climaxes in the progress. It wanders, hesitates, sometimes breaks off abruptly, and then returns upon itself. The processes of nature are by no means economical. The history of the past tells us that, if we choose wrongly, we shall sooner or later be eliminated. Each of us can participate in the process of creating a better world, by understanding the purpose of the universe and identifying ourselves with it. Every individual is a unique entity possessing specific features and capable of contributing a distinctive good to the world. Self-finding is the essence of all perfection. By seeing life steadily and whole, we find our place in it. Each human individual is an association of qualities and functions whose focus can be variously situated and according as this centre is higher or lower, the person's character is superficial or deep. Whatever be the empirical foundations, the choice of the centre redeems them. It is by means of reflection and meditation that we seek a centre which can unify our nature, realize our specific place in the universe, and acquire the strength to play our parts, however humble and however arduous they may be. Hence the necessity for quiet contemplation and solitude.

Moral life is one of significance and social value. Mere instinctive reaction or impulsive activity is not moral conduct which must embody an idea or be significant. Crude materials of human nature must be shaped by spiritual ends. It is the form given to the material that matters. All expressions of human life are significant and every one of them is judged by its meaning and purpose. We cannot have any one convention of its type or pattern. Each man sees the world from a different angle from his fellow. Whatever ideal we choose, we must recognize its nature and believe in its possibility, devise a plan of action, and with suffering and self-sacrifice endeavor to realize it. Besides, the line of conduct to the progress of ardour strive to social preservation and harmony, which contribute to progress evolution aims at. Any line of conduct which is destructive of the human race or promotes discord cannot be regarded as moral. Moral life requires us to respect the dignity of every individual. It is the enrichment of life that comes from the recognition of others and adaptation to them.

Uniqueness is a quality which all of us share. The goal of the world process is a harmonious unity in which each individual finds his specific realization.

The law of moral progress may best be expressed as one of acceptance and adventure. When we take up the individual unit, we find that there are so many passions and impulses as the raw material of human nature. Any given endowment and ethical code, which calls upon us to repudiate this given endowment and destroy it, is not a satisfactory one. The given has to be accepted and on the basis of it we have to build higher. Man is never satisfied with mere acceptance or adjustment. There is an urge in his breast that makes him go forward and upward. The ultimate aim of life is not simply to maintain but to elevate the place. *(863 words)*

Ans 3. Precis

Every soul, though burdened with animal instincts, is capable of transcendence through discipline, meditation, and acceptance of the spirit's law. Growth requires real struggle, yet the reward is fulfilment of personality. From the amoeba's search for food to the striving human spirit, life reflects a graded series of purposive efforts, but man alone chooses goals consciously. He is neither the slave of fate nor the sport of chance; the universal impulse to perfection becomes self-conscious in him. Unlike animals, he can progress, resolve the conflict between what he is and what he can be, and seek principles of conduct. By transforming ourselves, we can transform the world, for the improvement of the soul is the foundation of civilization. The world remains unfinished, and progress depends on human choice; history shows that wrong decisions lead to decline. Evolution is not linear but full of trials, hesitations, and reversals, yet it points to the survival of the wise and disciplined. Each individual is unique, with qualities that can contribute to distinct good. Self-finding is the essence of perfection, and reflection and solitude help man discover his centre, unify his nature, and play his role. Moral life requires purposeful conduct, not mere instinct, and demands respect for the dignity of all. Actions destructive of humanity or fostering discord cannot be moral, for morality enriches life through harmony and mutual adaptation. True progress rests on acceptance of our given nature and adventurous striving to rise above it. The ultimate aim of life is not survival but elevation.

(a) Rewrite the following sentences after making the necessary corrections. Do not make unnecessary changes in the original sentence. (1×10= 10 Marks)

i. Meera have a phone that cannot fit into the pocket of her jacket.

ii. Despite the heavy rains yesterday, the children was able to reach the school on time.

iii. May I have another form !

iv. I catch them taking flowers from my garden yesterday.

v. The location of the film alternates from Mumbai and Chennai.

vi. We cannot put of taking a decision any longer.

vii. He is a honourable man.

viii. Sameer had food poisoning and had to had his stomach pumped.

ix. The local council is doing everything to help solved the water problem.

x. What have you did to the laptop ?

Ans.

i. Meera (has) a phone that cannot fit into the pocket of her jacket.

ii. Despite the heavy rain yesterday, the children(were) able to reach the school on time.

iii. May I have another form ?

iv. I (caught) them taking flowers from my garden yesterday.

v. The location of film alternates between Mumbai and Chennai.

vi. We cannot put (off) taking a decision anymore.

vii. He is (an) honourable man.

viii. Sameer had food poisoning and had to (have) his stomach pumped.

ix. The local council is doing every possible to help (solve) the problem.

x. What have you (done) to the laptop?

(b) Supply the missing words: (1 × 5= 5 Marks)

i. He was the best player ________ the pitch in the first half of the match.

ii. She broke the window to climb ________ it.

iii. We got ________ the train just in time.

iv. They cycled ________ India from Kashmir to Kanyakumari.

v. I stopped ________ the shop on the way home.

Ans.

i. *He was the best player (on) the pitch in the first half of the match*

ii. *She broke the window to climb (through) it.*

iii. *We got (on) the train just in time.*

iv. *They cycled (across) India from Kashmir to Kanyakumari.*

v. *I stopped (at) the shop on the way home.*

(c) Use the correct form of the verb given in the brackets : (1 × 5= 5 Marks)

i. The storm __________ a lot of damage to the standing crops. (do)

ii. She __________ an hour ago. (leave)

iii. The crowd __________ growing restless as the delay prolonged. (is)

iv. He __________ that the grass needed to be cut. (say)

v. As I walked through the gates the dog __________ running towards me. (come)

Ans.

i. *The storm (did) a lot of damage to the standing crops.*

ii. *She (left) an hour ago.*

iii. *The crowd (was) growing restless as the delay prolonged.*

iv. *He said that the grass needed to be cut.*

v. *As I walked through the gates the dog (came) running to me.*

(d) Write the antonyms of the following : (1 × 5= 5 Marks)

i. Feeble

ii. Scarce

iii. Query

iv. Captivity

v. Despair

Ans.

i. *Feeble- Strong*

ii. *Scarce – abundant*

iii. *Query – belief /conviction*

iv. *Captivity – freedom*

v. *Despair - Joy/Hope*

Q5. (a) Rewrite the following sentences as directed without changing the meaning : (1×10= 10 Marks)

i. Ram cannot swim, __________ ? (Add a question tag)

ii. Defend the status quo. Rethink the status quo. (Combine the sentences using 'either-or')

iii. Scarcely had the police gone, than a thief entered the house. (Remove 'than' and put 'when')

iv. My heart is much full of words. (Rewrite the sentence using 'too')

v. One of the Professors recommended us to do this at the University. (Change into Passive Voice)

vi. He may be innocent. I do not know. (Combine the sentences using 'whether')

vii. It was the girl's idea to protest. (Change from singular to plural form)

viii. She said, 'I have passed the examination.' (Change into Indirect Speech)

ix. It all happened quickly. We hardly noticed it. (Combine the sentences using 'so')

x. I cannot see. It is very dark. (Combine the sentences using 'for')

Ans.

i. Ram cannot swim, can he?

ii. Either defend the status quo or rethink the status quo.

iii. Scarcely had the police gone, when a thief entered the house.

iv. My heart is too full of words.

v. We were recommended by one of the professors to do this at the university

vi. I do not know whether he may be innocent.

vii. It was the girls' idea to protest.

viii. She said that she had passed the examination.

ix. It all happened so quickly that we hardly noticed it.

x. I cannot see for it is very dark .

(b) Use the following words to make sentences that bring out the meaning clearly. Do not change the form of the words. (No marks will be given for vague and ambiguous sentences) (1 × 5= 5 Marks)

i. Cease

ii. Surreal

iii. Grim

iv. Puppet

v. Image

Ans.

(i) Cease *- The child would not cease his constant whining.*

(ii) Surreal *- Sharing the dais with the Prime Minister was a dreamlike and surreal experience for Rajesh.*

(iii) ***Grim*** *– The flood situation in Punjab is very grim because of unprecedented rainfall.*

(iv) ***Puppet*** *- Media has nowadays become a puppet in the hands of politicians.*

(v) ***Image*** *- Some of the politicians are really image conscious.*

(c) Choose the appropriate word to fill in the blanks : (1 × 5= 5 Marks)

i. He looked very ________ about his success in the examination. (compliment/complacent)

ii. Car crashes are ________ in factories. (simulated/stimulated)

iii. One must not allow the fear of failure to ________. (inhabit/inhibit)

iv. She has written a book on the ________ effects of slavery. (pernicious/pretentious)

v. He is known for his ________ play. (foul/fowl)

Ans.

i. *Complacent*

ii. *Simulated*

iii. *Inhibit*

iv. *Pernicious*

v. *Foul*

(d) Use the following idioms/phrases in sentences of your own to bring out their meaning clearly: (1 × 5= 5 Marks)

i. A piece of cake

ii. Out of the blue

iii. Draconian law

iv. On a razor's edge

v. The rat race

Ans.

(i) A piece of cake ---- Clearing the interview was a piece of cake for the talented candidate.

(ii) Out of the blue – His sudden promotion came as out of the blue and everyone in the office was surprised.

(iii) Draconian law – Such a draconian law would not be tolerated in any democratic countery.

(iv) On a razor's edge – The survival of the Congress Party is on the razor's edge in the wake of Bihar elections.

(v) The rat race --- Preparing for civil services examinations has literally become a rat race for many undeserving candidates having no knowledge about the vastness and depth of syllabi.

UPSC (MAIN) EXAM – 2024
ENGLISH
(Compulsory)

Time Allowed: 3 hours | | ***Maximum Marks: 300***

Question Paper: Specific Instructions

Please read each of the following instructions carefully before attempting questions.

- *All questions are to be attempted.*
- *The number of marks carried by questions is indicated against it.*
- *Answers must be written in* **ENGLISH** *only.*
- *Word limit in questions, wherever specified, should be adhered to and if answered in much longer or shorter than the prescribed length, marks will be deducted.*
- *Any page or portion of the page left blank in the Question-cum-Answer Booklet must be clearly struck off.*

Q.1. Write an essay in about 600 words on any one of the following topics : (100 Marks)

(a) Paper books are more attractive than their electronic formats.

(b) Ethics in sports.

(c) War as a policy instrument for nations today.

(d) There is no place like home.

Ans. 'East or west – home is the best.'

'East or west -home is the best', is a proverb, conveying that home is the best place to be, no matter where you are in the world. It is like the well-known phrase **'There is no place like home.'** This expression reflects the sentiment that one's own home is a special and unique place unmatched by any other location.

The phrase gained popularity through its association with the famous line spoken by Dorothy in the classic film, 'The wizard of oz.' Dorothy repeats the phrase. **'There is no place like home,'** expressing her desire to return to her familiar and comforting environment after her adventure in the magical land of Oz. The phrase has since then become a cultural touchstone to convey a sense of safety, security, comfort and emotional connection people have with their homes.

Beyond the literal meaning of physical dwelling, 'There is no place like home,' evokes a deeper emotional, personal, and psychological connections. It also substantiates the idea that a home is not just a physical place, but a place where one feels a sense of belongingness, togetherness, sharing, caring, understanding, and familiarity. It vindicates a sense of one's own unique living space, personal nature and emotional bonds associated with it.

There is a Punjabi saying by Chajju Bhatia (a Sarraf /goldsmith by profession) of Lahore, Pakistan, who had become a Sufi bhagat(devotee), '**Jo Sukh Chajju de Chaubare, oh Balkh na Bukhara.**' The Chaubara or one storied room was used as a place of worship by Chajju which came to be known as 'Chajju da Chaubara.' His words attached unparalleled importance to one's home and made it an incomparable and matchless entity in anyone's life. He gave more importance to his one -storied home than the biggest trading centers of medieval times in central Asia – BALKH & BUKHARA. The home is one of the most sought-after trinities in life: 'Roti, Kapda aur Makan.'

Home is not merely a physical dwelling made of bricks and mortar, rather a place of peace and tranquility amidst chaos and confusion. It symbolizes feelings, emotions, sentiments and shared memories of those living under one roof. It is the fulcrum of one's life and family.

Home is the place of parental grooming, caring and nurturing with one's birth. Anyone can have a house, but blessed are they who have homes. It is the place to which your heart always years to go. It is one's sovereign kingdom or queendom. Everyone, irrespective of position or designation, longs to go home as and when they get a chance. Life begins with home and revolves around it throughout life.

It is the place where one gets acquainted with one's relations, feels the warmth and indispensability of relations. It is the most sacred institution of life where one is taught about one's ancestry, family traditions, cultural ethos, and is injected with a value system. It is the first school of life where one is immersed into and trained to acquire and assimilate basic moral teachings of honesty, sincerity, integrity, hard work, and truthfulness from their elders and siblings.

It is a centre of family gatherings, functions, celebrations, and sharing moments of joy and sorrow. it is the place where one loves to spend quality time with one's family and family friends. '**A house is made of walls and beams; a home is built with love and dreams**,' a beautiful quote by an anonymous author sums up the value of home and elucidates about the need of love and dreams needed to make a home. A home is the ultimate destination in everyone's life to feel happy, comfortable, and to share good and bad times.

The present-day corporate culture and crony capitalism have dwindled the significance and beauty of the home in the west. Broken homes became their mainstream culture. Our young generations (GEN -Z -a fad term) are also badly attracted to that Yankee and rococo culture of fun and frolic. The role of family, home, relations started losing their importance in our culture too. The infatuation with notions of freedom, and privacy started eclipsing sentiments of sharing, caring, and forbearance. This money centric approach literally made youngsters insensitive, emotionless, mechanical, and self-centered instruments and relations for them became just a matter of calculation of utility and non-utility, and home became just a destination for weekend breaks or unavoidable sabbaticals. The philosophy of, 'Use and Throw,' seems to them (GEN-Z) an extremely convenient tool of exploitation of near and dear ones' and hence the value of home, family, and relations is diminishing drastically having catastrophic repercussions on the future course and nature of society in india.

But the pandemic of covid -19 proved a blessing in disguise for our country. Millions of youngsters became unemployed. The pandemic proved a harsh reminder to make the youngsters to realize the value of family and home. All, without exception, big or small, employed or unemployed headed to their homes to realize, '**There is no place like a home**.'

Moreover, the present-day society has been undergoing the darkest phase of chronic trust deficit. In the present times of absence of loyalty, faith, and trust, or at the most shuttling and shifting loyalties, home is the only oasis where one can be at ease and with oneself and living with peace and solace in perfect symphony and harmony of head and heart.

Women are the true home makers and the pillars of a household. Just as a healthy mind resides in the healthy body, the strength and longevity of a home rely on the physical, mental, moral, and spiritual well-being of the women residing within it. As the saying goes, in a home where women are respected, gods dwell.

So, it is a truism that east or west, home is the best and there is no place like a home.

Q.2. Read carefully the passage given below and write your answers to the questions that follow in clear, correct and concise language : (15 × 5 = 75 Marks)

British rule in India was a relationship of economic and political domination between an imperial power and its colony. It was based on conquest, consolidated after several wars and followed economic policies designed to serve British interests. Both the parties knew it was unequal, exploitative and based on force. As such it raised moral questions and needed justification. Their self-respect, sense of morality and morale required the British to convince themselves they were right to rule over India. In order to ensure its orderly and continued existence and secure the co-operation and support of the Indians without whom they simply could not run the country, they also needed to convince their subjects that British rule was in the 'real' interest. It was, of course, possible for them to justify it to themselves in one way and to their subjects in another. However, they knew that such a strategy was open to the charge of inconsistency, even hypocrisy, and inherently precarious.

In order to achieve the dual objective of justifying their rule to themselves and their subjects in a single and consistent language, the British needed to show that they had something to give to the Indians which the latter badly needed, were unable to acquire unaided and was so precious as to compensate for whatever economic and political price they were required to pay. The logic of justification required a perfect match between British gifts and Indian needs. The British sought and the Indian deficiency. Following the fashion of the time the British wrapped their gifts in the language of civilisation, which had latterly replaced Christianity as the unifying principle in Europe, taken over its universalist and proselytising mission and built up an ambiguous and uneasy relationship with it. Although modern civilisation was a co-operative European product, the British role in its creation and dissemination was considerable. They were the first to industrialise themselves, more or less to recast their religion, ways of life and thought and major political, economic and other institutions in the light of the dominant liberal culture and to roam all over the world as its possessed by its inherently restless and universal spirit. They claimed to 'represent' or 'embody' it, to a greater degree than any other country and saw themselves as its transcendentally or historically accredited 'vehicle'.

Since their civilisation had in their view attained the highest possible level of human existence and cultivated capacities which all men qua men ought to develop, they had no doubt that it was universally desirable. All societies had a common destiny and destination, namely to become civilised in the British way and were to achieve this destiny by the same route. Hence the more 'advanced' among them, that is, those whose journey had brought them closer to the universal destination, provided the models for and had the moral duty to guide those who had not yet started, became stuck, were proceeding in a wrong direction or at an extremely slow pace. The British could not show that they represented the highest level of civilisation without so defining it that it broadly corresponded to their own ways of life and thought. Like all ideological systems they abstracted, reified and absolutised the distinctive features of their ways of life and thought and presented them as a universal norm for evaluating all societies, including their own. Their facts became values for others, an illicit logical move lying at the heart of every ideology. Other societies were therefore always deficient whereas the British was necessarily more or less perfect.

The British argued that they had brought to India the unique and most precious gift of civilisation. Since this civilisation was deemed to be universally desirable, India obviously needed it. All they had to do was show that India lacked it and was unable to acquire it unaided. Unlike some of the other British colonies India had a well-developed literati tradition, a long history of civic life and considerable philosophical, artistic, scientific and other achievements. Since these were supposed to be some of the indices of civilisation, obviously it could not be contemptuously dismissed as uncivilised. Some British writers and leaders did so dismiss it; most, however, acknowledged its great achievements, but contended that they were all in the past and did not redeem its contemporary degeneration. Its social structure and practices were oppressive, unjust and sometimes inhuman; its religions were incomprehensible, replete with meaningless rituals, polytheist, lacking a single authoritative text, and not really religions in the 'proper sense of the term; its modes of thought were 'mystical and mythological' and largely irrational; and its people were emotional, excitable, undisciplined, unambitious, lacking in self-control, unreliable and very like women and children. The British view of India did, of course, change over time, largely as a result of their increased knowledge of its past and the changes in their conceptions of themselves and the yardsticks they employed. Throughout their rule, however, they continued to think of it as neither wholly uncivilised nor fully civilised but 'semi-civilised' or 'only half-civilised', and of the Indians as a moderately talented people who needed to be disciplined, guided and trained in the ways of civilisation.

(a) Enumerate the agenda of the British rule in India. (15 Marks)

(b) Comment on the role of the British in spreading the idea of modern civilization. (15 Marks)

(c) Explain the statement ".... their civilization, in their view attained the highest possible level of human existence ....." (15 Marks)

(d) What made the British think that they gave India a precious gift of civilization? (15 Marks)

(e) According to the passage, the British changed their views about India over a period of time. Why? (15 Marks)

Ans.

(a) The agenda of Britishers was economic and political domination by imperial power over its colony. It was based on conquest and consolidation followed by economic policies to serve the British interests. To fulfill their agenda, they needed orderly and continued existence with the support and co-operation of Indians and to achieve this objective, they tried to convince Indians that Britishers have something to give to Indians which they terribly needed but were unable to acquire without aid of Britishers and that is training in civilizational values and ethos.

(b) Although modern civilization was a co-operative European product, the British role in its creation and dissemination was considerable. They were one of the first to industrialize themselves, to recast their religion, ways of life and thought and major political, economic and other institutions in the light of the dominant liberal culture and to roam all over the world as if possessed by its inherently restless and universal spirit. They claimed to 'represent' or 'embody' it to a greater degree than any other country' and saw themselves as its transcendentally or historically accredited 'vehicle'.

(c) Since their civilization had in their view attained the highest possible level of human existence and cultivated capacities which all men qua men ought to develop, they had no doubt that it was universally desirable. All societies had a common destiny and destination, namely, to become civilized in the British way and were to achieve this destiny by the same route. Hence the more 'advanced' among them, that is, those whose journey had brought them closer to the universal destination, provided the models for and had the moral duty to guide those who had not yet started, became stuck, were proceeding in a wrong direction or at an extremely slow pace.

(d) The British argued that they had brought to India the unique and most precious gift of civilization. Since this civilization was deemed to be universally desirable, India obviously needed it. All they had to do was to show that India lacked it and was unable to acquire it unaided. Throughout their rule, however, they continued to think of it as neither wholly uncivilized nor fully civilized but 'semi-civilized' or 'only half- civilized', and of the Indians as a moderately talented people who needed to be disciplined, guided and trained in the ways of civilization.

(e) The British view of India did, of course, change over time, largely because of their increased knowledge of its past and the changes in their conceptions of themselves and the yardsticks they employed. Some British writers and leaders acknowledged India's great achievements. Unlike some of the other British colonies, India had a well-developed literati tradition, a long history of civic life and considerable philosophical, artistic, scientific and other achievements. Since these were supposed to be some of the indices of civilization, obviously it could not be contemptuously dismissed as uncivilized. So, over a period, the British changed their views about India.

Q.3. Make a précis of the following passage in about one-third of its length. Do not give or suggest a title to it. The précis should be written in your own words :(75 Marks)

The mad rat race among nations over the globe for development jeopardised the health of man itself. Progress in agriculture and industry is taken a general criterion of development of any country. This craze resulted into unlimited exploitation of every bit of natural resource. The splendid plentifulness of nature is a heritage that should be conserved for future generations and not be spoiled.

Such activities of man had adverse effect on all forms of living organisms in the biosphere. The earth planet alongwith the atmosphere (air, land, water) that sustain life is called the biosphere. Biosphere extends into about 7 km of the earth surface itself, downward into the ocean to depths about 10.67 km and vertically into the air, to about 10 km, where life is found to exist.

Unlimited exploitation of nature by man disturbed the delicate ecological balance between living and non-living component of the biosphere. The unfavorable conditions created by man himself threatened the survival not only of man himself but also other living organisms. The number of the species likely to become rare, threatened, endangered or near extinction in the Red Data Book of the IUCN is increasing with time. It is very common to find warnings at public places, reading as "Air unfit for breathing", "Water unfit for drinking", "Do not eat fish caught here" and so on.

India today is one of the first ten industrialised countries of the world. Today we have a good industrial infrastructure in core industries like metals, chemicals, fertilisers, petroleum, food etc. What has come out of these ? Pesticides, detergents, plastics, solvents, fuels, paints, dyes, food additives etc. are some examples. Due to progress in atomic energy, there has also been an increase in radioactivity in the biosphere. Besides these, there are a number of industrial effluents and emissions particularly poisonous gases in the atmosphere. Mining activities also added to this problem particularly as solid waste.

Thus, pollution is a necessary evil of all development. Due to lack of development of a culture of pollution control, there has resulted a heavy backlog of gaseous, liquid and solid pollution in our country. It is to be cleaned. Thus pollution control in our country is a recent environmental concern. Not only in India, but in developed Western World also, pollution is a scare-word. Pollution is a man-made problem, mainly of effluent countries. The developed countries have been in a mad race to exploit every bit of natural resource to convert them into goods for their comfort, and to export them to needy developing world. In doing so, the industrialised countries dump lot of materials in their environment which becomes polluted. In one way pollution has been in fact "exported" to developing countries.

What is pollution? Pollution is an undesirable change in the physical, chemical or biological characteristics of air, water and soil that may harmfully affect the life or create a potential health hazard of any living organism. Pollution is thus direct or indirect change in any component of the biosphere that is harmful to the living component(s), and in particular undesirable for man, affecting adversely the industrial progress, cultural and natural assets or general environment.

What are pollutants? Any substance which causes pollution is called a pollutant. A pollutant may thus include any chemical or geochemical (dust, sediment, grit etc.) substance, biotic component or its product, or physical factor (heat) that is released intentionally by man into the environment in such a concentration that may have adverse harmful or unpleasant effects. A pollutant has also been defined as "any solid, liquid or gaseous substance present in such concentration as may be or tend to be injurious to the environment". Pollutants are the residues of things we make, use and throw away. There are many sources of such pollutants. The lakes and rivers are polluted by wastes from chemical and other factories, and the air by gases of automobile exhausts, industries, thermal power plants etc.

There has grown up a serious concern all over the world about the rivers turning murky, fish rotting on sea shores, trees withering, cities choking with foul air, toxic chemicals being cycled into food stuffs and disease epidemics appearing so frequently. **(697 words approximately)**

Ans.

The global race for development has led to the overexploitation of natural resources, endangering human health and the environment. Industrial and agricultural progress often seen as benchmarks of development have severely disrupted the ecological balance of the biosphere. This unchecked growth, focused on agriculture and industry, has disturbed the ecological balance, affecting all forms of life in the biosphere. The depletion of resources has led to the extinction of many species, and pollution warnings are now common. India, among the top ten industrialized nations, faces severe pollution from industries producing harmful substances like pesticides, plastics, and radioactive materials. Pollution, a byproduct of development, is a global concern. Developed nations have exported pollution to developing countries through their resource exploitation. Pollution involves undesirable changes in air, water, and soil, caused by harmful substances like chemicals, gases, and industrial waste. This growing problem affects not just the environment but also human health and safety, demanding immediate global attention. Pollutants, ranging from chemicals to industrial waste, contaminate rivers, air, and food sources, leading to widespread environmental degradation. As a result, pollution control has become a critical concern worldwide, especially in developed nations that have contributed heavily to this crisis by exporting pollutants to developing countries. The unchecked industrial growth and pollution now threaten the survival of many species, as highlighted in the IUCN's Red Data Book.

Q.4. (a) Rewrite the following sentences after making necessary corrections. Do not make unnecessary changes in the original sentence. (1×10= 10 Marks)

(i) Little learning is dangerous thing.

(ii) You are requested to kindly grant me leave.

(iii) Could you please advised me what I should do.

(iv) I envied he his success.

(v) If people feel good of coming to work, they will work better.

(vi) How terribly sad ?

(vii) Spanish is more widely used outside of Europe. (Add a question tag)

(viii) He played the piano one night in the village hall.

(ix) Many a men has succumbed to this temptation.

(x) If she gets the right grades, she'd go to university.

Ans.

(i) A little learning is a dangerous thing

(ii) You are kindly requested to grant me leave.

(iii) Could you please advise me what should I do?

(iv) I envied his success.

(v) If people feel good about coming to work, they will work better.

(vi) How terribly sad!

(vii) Spanish is more widely used outside of Europe. Isn't it?

(viii) One night he played the piano in the village hall.

(ix) Many men have succumbed to this temptation.

(x) If she gets the right grades, she will go to the university.

(b) Supply the missing words : (1 × 5= 5 Marks)

(i) Don't walk __________ the grass.

(ii) I lived in Uttarakhand __________ five years.

(iii) He stood tall __________ all his friends in the college.

(iv) The cat jumped __________ the well to escape from the dog.

(v) She walked __________ the forest to reach her village.

Ans.

(i) on

(ii) from

(iii) among

(iv) into

(v) slowly

(c) Use the correct form of the verb given in brackets : (1 × 5= 5 Marks)

(i) Two plus two __________ four. (make)

(ii) We need rain, the garden __________ so dry. (be)

(iii) She __________ with a baby girl last week. (bless, passive voice)

(iv) I just __________ even talking to him. (bear)

(v) __________ you just shut up for a minute! (can)

Ans.

(i) Makes

(ii) Is

(iii) Was blessed

(iv) Can't bear

(v) Can't

(d) Write the antonyms of the following : (1 × 5= 5 Marks)

(i) Optimist — __________

(ii) Gall — __________ *

(iii) Zest — __________

(iv) Profit — __________

(v) Quick — __________

Ans.

(i) Pessimist

(ii) Modesty/Humility

(iii) Apathy/Indifference

(iv) Loss

(v) Slow

Q.5. (a) Rewrite the following sentences as directed without changing the meaning : (1×10= 10 Marks)

(i) The mangoes are too cheap to be good. (Remove 'too')

(ii) The French surrendered Quebec to the English in 1759. (Change the Voice)

(iii) Mumbai is richer than most other cities in India. (Use superlative degree)

(iv) What though we happen to be late? (Change to Assertive)

(v) He betrayed his country, and this was to his eternal disgrace. *(Change to simple sentence)*

(vi) I spent two days in Cox's Bazar. It is one of the most attractive spots in Bangladesh. *(Combine by using a phrase in apposition)*

(vii) The soldiers arrived. The mob dispersed. *(Combine by using a Nominative Absolute Construction)*

(viii) Newton discovered that the force of gravitation made apples fall. *(Sequence of Tenses)*

(ix) Rama said to Arjuna, "Go away". *(Use indirect speech)*

(x) Everyone should do his duty. *(Concord)*

Ans.

(i) The mangoes are so cheap that they cannot be good.

(ii) Quebec was surrendered by the French to the English in 1769.

(iii) Mumbai is the richest city in India

(iv) It doesn't matter if we happen to be late.

(v) To his eternal disgrace, he betrayed his country.

(vi) I spent two days in Cox's Bazaar, one of the most attractive spots in Bangladesh.

(vii) When soldiers arrived, mob dispersed.

(viii) Newton discovered that the force of gravitation makes apples fall.

(ix) Rama ordered Arjuna to go away.

(x) Everyone should do one's duty.

(b) Use the following words to make sentences that bring out the meaning clearly. Do not change the form of the words. (1 × 5= 5 Marks)

(i) Speculate

(ii) Inquisitive

(iii) Forbearance

(iv) Nocturnal

(v) Ineffectually

Ans.

(i) Speculate- The police were speculating about the modus operandi of the criminal.

(ii) Inquisitive – Kids have very inquisitive minds

(iii) Forbearance – Forbearance and perseverance are essential traits of a strong personality.

(iv) Nocturnal – Nocturnal animals stay awake at night.

(v) Ineffectually – Parents nowadays ineffectually try to convince children to stay away from gadgets.

(c) Choose the appropriate word to fill in the blanks : (1 × 5= 5 Marks)

(i) The terrorists made it known that tourists would be ____________. *(target/targeted)*

(ii) I'll see you ____________ six. *(round/around)*

(iii) How much would it cost to re-lay the lawns? It'll cost ____________. *(thousand/thousands)*

(iv) She was forced to have her baby ____________. *(adopted/adapted)*

(v) My responsibilities were to organise the campaign, co-ordinate the regional branches, ____________ for volunteers, and raise funds. *(canvas/canvass)*

Ans.

(i) Targeted

(ii) Around

(iii) Thousands

(iv) Adopted

(v) Canvass

(d) Use the following idioms/phrases in sentences of your own to bring out their meaning clearly. (1 × 5 = 5 Marks)

(i) knock off

(ii) bite off more than one can chew

(iii) fair and square

(iv) by the skin of your teeth

(v) easier said than done

Ans.

(i) Knock off : The dealer agreed to knock off Rs. 100 from the original price.

(ii) Bite of more than one can chew: He bought the old hotel but soon realized that he had bitten off more than he can chew.

(iii) Fair and square : We won the match fair and square.

(iv) By the skin of your teeth : I escaped a terrible accident by the skin of my teeth.

(v) Easier said than done : Losing 20 kg weight in a month is easier said than done.

UPSC (MAIN) EXAM – 2023

ENGLISH

(Compulsory)

Time Allowed: 3 hours **Maximum Marks: 300**

Question Paper: Specific Instructions

Please read each of the following instructions carefully before attempting questions.

- *All questions are to be attempted.*
- *The number of marks carried by questions is indicated against it.*
- *Answers must be written in* **ENGLISH** *only.*
- *Word limit in questions, wherever specified, should be adhered to and if answered in much longer or shorter than the prescribed length, marks will be deducted.*
- *Any page or portion of the page left blank in the Question-cum-Answer Booklet must be clearly struck off.*

Q 1. Write an essay in about 600 words on any one of the following topics:(100 Marks)

(a) OTT and the future of Multiplexes

(b) Global warming in an unequal world

(c) Social media and the marketing of the self

(d) Happiness is a state of mind

Ans: Happiness is A State of Mind

Happiness is a state of mind. Happiness is journey, not a destination. Abraham Lincoln aptly observed **'Most folk are about as happy as they make up their minds to be.'** Throughout history, people have sought to understand and explain the meaning and art of happiness. Millions of words have been written on the subject. Innumerable poets and priests, philosophers and psychologists, teachers and preachers have attempted to discover a simple formula for what Sir Philip Gibbs called, **'the eternal quest of mankind'**- a happy ant contended life.

Happiness is what all people want, regardless of the many ways they may seek it. To be happy is the goal of life. Human ambitions, hopes, plans, and endeavors are in one way or the other, directed towards attainment of happiness. **'Happiness is the meaning and purpose of life, the whole aim and end of life,' declared Aristotle.**

But what is happiness? This enduring question has intrigued humans since inception of life on the planet earth. It sounds like different meaning to different people from different walks of life at different stages of life. Different people seek happiness in different ways. For an unsuccessful person, happiness lies in success, for a sick man, recovery of health is happiness, for a businessman happiness comes from profit, for a seeker of knowledge happiness comes through learning and wisdom. Thus, success, achievements, love, family, friends, health, and knowledge are potential sources of happiness.

There is one point, however, on which philosophers in every age agree: true happiness arises from within. It stems from a way of thinking about life. Among the millions of words written on happiness, this is the oldest and most enduring truth. if the principles of contentment are not present within us no amount of material success, pleasures or possessions, can make us truly happy.

Therefore, happiness is fundamentally a state of mind that originates from within. Neither wealth, status, power, nor worldly achievements can bring enduring and lasting happiness. Genuine happiness springs from a calm, contented, balanced state of mind.

The quest for happiness is always in vain unless you find it within yourself, within your own hearts and minds. The Roman philosopher Marus Aurileus wisely wrote in his Meditations **'Very little is needed to make a happy life, it is all within yourself, in your way of thinking.'**

James Allen, author of **As a man thinketh,** wrote, **'They themselves are the makers of themselves.'**

'Mind is the master-weaver, both inner garments of character and outer garments of circumstances. According to Allen human beings – by virtue of thoughts, which they nurture can either descend into hell of ignorance, pain , and agony or rise to the heavens of happiness, wisdom, and enlightenment.'

James Allen further propounded,

'Man is the maker of himself. Man is made or unmade by himself; in the armory of thoughts, he forges the weapons by which he destroys himself; or he also fashions the tools with which he builds for himself heavenly mansions of joy, strength, peace, and happiness. By the right choice and true application of thought, he ascends to divine perfection. By the abuse and wrong application of thought, he descends below the level of beast. Between these extremes are all grades of character, and man is their maker and master.'

These profound words highlight a timeless truth: our thoughts shape our character, our circumstances, our state of mind and ultimately our happiness. Happiness is not something that can be purchased, inherited, fetched or grabbed from someone or somehow from outside. It is cultivated from within through positive thinking, progressive attitude, contentment, gratitude and self-control.

Therefore, it is rightly said that happiness is a state of mind.

Q 2. Read carefully the passage given below and write your answers to the questions that follow in clear, correct and concise language: (15 × 5 = 75 Marks)

It must be emphasised that rights have corresponding duties as well as obligations. The two are correlated. Rights and duties of citizens are two sides of the same coin. The relationship between them is two fold. Firstly, society functions on the principles of reciprocity. My rights involve a duty, on the part of others to respect my rights and also a duty on my part to respect the similar rights of others. Society works on the principle of, "he who takes gives and he who gives takes". Indeed, my right is a part and parcel of the good of other members of society and, therefore, the degree of my enjoyment of a particular right has to be conceived in terms of the similar claims of other citizens. My right is integrally related to the rights of my fellow human beings. The one cannot exist without the other. A society in which people care less for their own duties and more for their rights, sooner or later, disintegrates. In their frantic effort for the vindication of their own rights at the expense of fellow human beings, society will be reduced to the status of a jungle in which ultimately the law of might will prevail. In order that everyone enjoys his or her rights it is necessary that we recognise our obligations towards others. We cannot say that we shall be free while others will be bound with their obligations. Such a position is quite untenable and inhuman.

Secondly, the logic of rights and duties also implies that if we have certain claims against the state, it is also our responsibility to contribute something towards its enrichment by doing a socially useful work. The state creates those conditions in which we can realise ourselves. In return for this, it is our duty to take advantage of these conditions and give our best to it. The best way in which we can contribute to the social stock is by following duties towards our nation, in recognising our social responsibilities and unscrupulously respecting the similar rights of others. One does not contribute only by being a son of a prime minister or a poet but by being oneself. I may not succeed in my life, but if I have given sufficient indications of sincere efforts to make such contribution, as I am capable of, my job is done. It is a duty of every one of us that we must develop our personality so as to be able to contribute our best to society. A citizen should make available valuable judgment on the various issues confronting it. One must pay one's taxes to the state and must refrain from interfering with the similar rights of other members of society. So long as the state helps in fostering a climate conducive to happiness of the individuals, the citizens must also help it in maintaining law and order and must honestly perform their public duties. They should leave no stone unturned for strengthening their own country and if need arises must be prepared to defend it at any cost. These obligations by being reciprocal in character do not impose restrictions on the rights of individuals; rather, they give them fuller and greater reality. To think that my rights can be separated from my duties is to be guilty of gross selfishness. It is only by performing a useful function in society that we contribute towards its enrichment. A state in which citizens care more about their rights, and less about their duties remains in a precarious situation. It would lead first to anarchy and then to its disintegration. In order to preserve my right it is necessary that I must convince my fellow human beings that in granting such a right they would be enabling me to participate in the good of society. I must show, that so far as the society does not secure me this right, it derogates me from the status of a human being and my capacity to make my contribution to social welfare. It is only in the apprehension of this equation between individual's functions and social well-being by the members of society that a true theory of rights can be constructed and society can be built on stable foundations.

(a) What is the correlation between rights and duties? **(15 Marks)**

(b) Enumerate the duties of the state mentioned in the passage. **(15 Marks)**

(c) What are the responsibilities of the citizens towards the nation? **(15 Marks)**

(d) Elaborate the principle on which society works. **(15 Marks)**

(e) Write the meaning of the idiom 'leave no stone unturned'. **(15 Marks)**

Ans. (a) Rights and duties are co-related. Rights have corresponding duties and obligations. One's rights are integrally related to the rights of his fellow human beings. One cannot exist without others. Rights and duties are two sides of the same coin. The relationship between them is twofold.

Firstly, society functions on the principles of reciprocity.

Secondly, if we have certain claims against the state, it is also our responsibility to contribute something towards its enrichment by doing socially useful work.

(b) The duties of the state are to create the conditions in which citizens can actualize themselves and it is also the duty of the state to foster a climate conducive to the maximization of happiness of individuals.

(c) It is the responsibility of the citizens to leave no stone unturned to strengthen the country and if the need arises they must be prepared to defend it at any cost.

A citizen must make valuable judgment on various issues of national concern.

Citizens must pay taxes and must refrain from interfering with the rights of other citizens.

Citizens must help in maintaining law and order and must perform their duties honestly.

It is also the duty of citizens to take advantage of the conditions created by the state and give their best to the state by contributing to social work by being themselves.

(d) Society functions on the principles of reciprocity which means everyone enjoys his/her rights without disturbing the rights of fellow human beings.

The principle of reciprocity postulates that one cannot exist without other. One's rights have corresponding duties.

This principle highlights that a society in which people care less for their duties and more for their rights disintegrates sooner or later.

The principle of reciprocity reminds everyone to enjoy his or her rights and recognize obligations towards others.

(e) To leave no stone unturned means to do one's best as per one's abilities to give the best.

Q 3. Make a précis of the following passage in about one-third of its length. Do not give a title to it. The précis should be written in your own words: (75 Marks)

Like all the sins except pride, anger is perversion, caused by pride, of something our nature which in itself is innocent, necessary to our own existence and good. Thus, while everyone is proud in the same way; each of us is angry or lustful or envious in his own way.

Natural, or innocent, anger is the necessary reaction of a creature when its survival is threatened by the attack of another creature and it cannot save itself (or its offspring) by flight. Such anger, accompanied by physiological changes, like increased secretion of adrenalin, inhibits fear so that the attacked culture is able to resist the threat to its extinction. In the case of young creatures that are not capable of looking after themselves, anger is a necessary emotion when their needs are neglected: a hungry baby does right to scream. Natural anger is a reflex reaction, not a voluntary one; it is a response to a real situation of threat and danger, and as soon as the threat is removed, the anger subsides. No animal lets the sun go down upon its wrath.

Anger, even when it is sinful, has one virtue; it overcomes sloth. Anybody, like a schoolmaster, a stage director or an orchestral conductor, whose business it is to teach others to do something, knows that, on occasions, the quickest – perhaps the only – way to get those under him to do their best is to make them angry.

Anger as a sin is either futile (the situation in which one finds oneself cannot or should not be changed, but must be accepted) or unnecessary (the situation could be mastered as well or better without it). Man is potentially capable of the sin of anger because he is endowed with memory – the experience of an event persists – and with the faculty of symbolization (to him, no object or event is simply itself). He becomes actually guilty of anger because he is first of all guilty of the sin of pride, of which anger is one of many possible manifestations.

Because every human being sees the world from a unique perspective, he can, and does, choose to regard himself as its centre. The sin of anger is one of our reactions to any threat, not to our existence, but to our fancy that our existence is more important than the existence of anybody or anything else. None of us wishes to be omnipotent, because the desires of each are limited. We are glad that other things and people exist with their own ways of behaving – life would be very dull if they didn't – so long as they do not thwart our own. Similarly, we do not want others to conform with our wishes because they must – life would be very lonely if they did – but because they choose to; we want 'devoted' slaves.

The middle class culture in which I grew up strongly discouraged overt physical expression of anger, it was far more permissive, for example, towards gluttony, lust and avarice. In consequence, I cannot now remember 'losing' my temper so that I was beside myself and hardly knew what I was doing. Since childhood, at least, I have never physically assaulted anyone, thrown things or chewed the carpet. (I do, now and again, slam doors.) Nor have I often seen other people do these things. In considering anger, therefore, most of my facts are derived from introspection and may not be valid for others, or from literature, in which truth has to be subordinated to dramatic effect.

In my own case – I must leave the psychological explanation to professionals – my anger is more easily aroused by things and impersonal events than by other people. I don't, I believe, expect others to do what I wish and am seldom angry when they don't. I do not mind losing at cards if the other players are more skilful than I, but, if I cannot help losing because I have been dealt a poor hand, I get furious. If traffic lights fail to change obligingly to red when I wish to cross the road, I am angry; if I enter a restaurant and it is crowded, I am angry. My anger, that is to say, is most easily aroused by a situation which is (a) not to my liking, (b) one I know I cannot change and (c) one for which I can hold no human individual responsible.

This last condition is the most decisive. I like others to be on time and hate to be kept waiting, but if someone deliberately keeps me waiting because, say, he is annoyed with me or wishes to impress me with his importance, I am far less angry than I am if I know him to be unpunctual by nature. In the first case, I feel I must be partly responsible – if I had behaved otherwise in the past, he would not have kept me waiting; and I feel hopeful – perhaps I can act in the future in such a way that our relationship will change and he will be punctual next time. In the second case, I know that it is in his nature to be late for others, irrespective of t relationship, so that, in order to be on time, he would have to become another person. ***(885 words)***

***Ans.* 3 Precis**

Anger, unlike pride, represents a twisted distortion of a natural, innocent aspect of our being. It stems from pride, corrupting a part of our nature that is otherwise benign and essential to our survival and well-being. Each person experiences anger, lust, or envy in their own unique manner, contrasting with the universal experience of pride. Natural anger serves as a vital response when our existence or that of our offspring is endangered by an external threat. This instinctual reaction, accompanied by physiological changes, aids in overcoming fear and enables resistance against extinction. In situations where the young are incapable of self-care, anger emerges as a necessary emotion, signalling neglect of basic needs. Even when sinful, anger possesses a virtue – it rouses individuals from slothfulness. Those tasked with instructing others often find that invoking anger can spur heightened performance. However, anger proves either futile, when circumstances cannot be altered, or unnecessary, when mastery could be achieved without it. The human capacity for anger arises from a combination of memory and the faculty of symbolisation, rooted in the sin of pride. Anger manifests as a response to threats not to our existence but to the illusion of our superiority over others. This perspective stems from the belief that our existence holds greater significance than others – a notion born of pride. Cultural norms may shape the expression of anger, with some societies discouraging overt displays while tolerating other vices. In personal experience, anger may be triggered more readily by impersonal events than by interpersonal conflicts. The intensity of anger often correlates with the inability to alter undesirable situations for which no individual can be held accountable. Ultimately, anger emerges as a complex interplay of personal disposition, societal influences, and situational dynamics.

(1/3rd of original text, from 885 words to 288 words)

Q 4. (a) Rewrite the following sentences after making necessary corrections. Do not make unnecessary changes in the original sentence: (1×10= 10 Marks)

(i) The book comprises of twelve chapters.

(ii) He scarcely comes to see me now.

(iii) If I will have time, I shall visit the art exhibition.

(iv) He bought the book before he met me.

(v) I found that he is guilty.

(vi) She is senior than me in service.

(vii) Shakespeare is Kalidasa of English literature.

(viii) Home is place where we earn our grace.

(ix) While I was travelling in a train, piece of luggage fell on my head.

(x) One of the students were absent for a week.

Ans. 4 (a)

(i) The book comprises twelve chapters.

(ii) He hardly comes to see me now.

(iii) If I have time, I shall visit the art exhibition.

(iv) He had bought the book before he met me.

(v) I found him guilty.

(vi) She is senior to me in service.

(vii) Shakespeare is the Kalidasa of English literature.

(viii) Home is the place where we earn our grace.

(ix) While I was travelling in a train, a piece of luggage fell upon my head.

(x) One of the students was absent for a week.

(b) Supply the missing words: **(1 × 5 = 5 Marks)**

(i) The regulations apply _______ all the employees.

(ii) Why are you afraid _______ my sister?

(iii) The decision depends _______ the statement of the witness.

(iv) The train will depart _______ platform number five.

(v) You should think _______ the matter again.

Ans. 4 (b)

(i) to

(ii) of

(iii) on

(iv) from

(v) over

(c) Use the correct form of the verbs given in brackets: **(1 × 5= 5 Marks)**

(i) My father _______ (be) eighty years old next Monday.

(ii) The workmen _______ (repair) the road near our house.

(iii) We _______ (wait) for you since yesterday.

(iv) She _______ (read) the newspaper, when I saw her.

(v) If water freezes, it _______ (turn) to ice.

Ans. 4 (c)

(i) will be

(ii) repaired

(iii) have been waiting

(iv) was reading

(v) will turn

(d) Write the antonyms of the following: **(1 × 5= 5 Marks)**

(i) Emigration

(ii) Negative

(iii) Prudence

(iv) Infernal

(v) Mandatory

Ans. 4 (d)

(i) Immigration

(ii) Positive

(iii) Imprudence

(iv) Heavenly

(v) Optional

Q 5. (a) Rewrite the following sentences as directed without changing the meaning: (1×10= 10 Marks)

(i) Few students knew the answer ________? (Add a tag question)

(ii) The problem is very complex. It cannot be solved easily. (Combine the sentences using 'too' – 'to')

(iii) He lost his purse. He lost his bicycle. (Combine the sentences using 'not only' – 'but also')

(iv) The teacher said, "something is better than nothing." (Change into indirect speech)

(v) Somebody stole my laptop. (Change into passive voice)

(vi) He ran very fast. He did not want to miss the last train. (Rewrite the sentence using 'so as')

(vii) Physics is the most interesting of all subjects I study. (Rewrite the sentence using comparative degree)

(viii) My friend does not drink. He does not smoke. (Combine the sentences using 'neither – nor')

(ix) Work hard. You will not succeed in life. (Rewrite the sentence using 'unless')

(x) I have some duties. I must perform them. (Rewrite the sentence using an infinitive)

Ans. 5 (a)

(i) Few students knew the answer, did they?

(ii) The problem is too complex to be solved easily.

(iii) He not only lost his purse, but also his bicycle.

(iv) The teacher said that something is better than nothing.

(v) My laptop was stolen by somebody.

(vi) He ran very fast so as not to miss the train.

(vii) Physics is a more interesting subject than all other subjects I study.

(viii) My friend neither drinks nor smokes.

(ix) Unless you work hard, you will not succeed in life.

(x) I have some duties to perform.

(b) Use the following words to make sentences that bring out the meaning clearly. Do not change the form of the words. (No marks will be given for vague and ambiguous sentences): (1 × 5= 5 Marks)

(i) Quarantine

(ii) Parody

(iii) Expedite

(iv) Gullible

(v) Veracity

Ans. 5 (b)

(i) Quarantine: During Covid-19, the infected people used to be quarantined.

(ii) Parody: R K Laxman, a cartoonist, was famous for his parodies.

(iii) Expedite: We should expedite work on the new edition of this popular book.

(iv) Gullible: Gullible people are easily led astray.

(v) Veracity: The fate of this case depends on the veracity of the statement of the witnesses.

(c) Choose the appropriate word to fill in the blanks: (1 × 5= 5 Marks)

(i) The _______ government did not last long. (coalition/collision)

(ii) The sun is _______ from the earth than the moon. (further / farther)

(iii) We reached an _______ agreement. (amicable / amiable)

(iv) His behaviour is so _______ that no one likes him. (childish/childlike)

(v) Coarse _______ are much in demand now for reasons of health. (serials / cereals)

Ans. 5 (c)

(i) Coalition

(ii) Farther

(iii) Amicable

(iv) Childish

(v) Cereals

(d) Use the following idioms/phrases in sentences of your own to bring out their meaning clearly: (1 × 5= 5 Marks)

(i) put out

(ii) to come to terms

(iii) in the blues

(iv) to go against the grain

(v) land of milk and honey

Ans. 5 (d)

(i) Put out: The fire in the building was put out in the nick of time.

(ii) To come to terms: She has come to terms with the loss of her son.

(iii) In the blues: He went in the blues for several weeks after losing his job.

(iv) To go against the grain: Though Asmita wanted to be a singer, she went against the grain and became a civil servant.

(v) Land of milk and honey: USA and Canada are considered lands of milk and honey for people from developing countries.

UPSC (MAIN) EXAM – 2022
ENGLISH
(Compulsory)

Time Allowed: 3 hours **Maximum Marks: 300**

Question Paper: Specific Instructions

Please read each of the following instructions carefully before attempting questions.

- *All questions are to be attempted.*
- *The number of marks carried by questions is indicated against it.*
- *Answers must be written in* **ENGLISH** *only.*
- *Word limit in questions, wherever specified, should be adhered to and if answered in much longer or shorter than the prescribed length, marks will be deducted.*
- *Any page or portion of the page left blank in the Question-cum-Answer Booklet must be clearly struck off.*

Q 1. Write an essay in about 600 words on any one of the following topics: (100 Marks)

(a) Mathematics: A mirror of modern civilization.

(b) New frontiers of science need to be explored in the current times.

(e) Education is a means of shaping character and of social change

(d) The role of literature in a common man's life

Ans: (d) The role of literature in a common man's life

Literature is one of the most interesting and significant expressions of humanity : P T Barnum

That literature reflects the society is a fact that has been widely acknowledged. Literature indeed reflects all the good and ills of the society. In its corrective function, literature mirrors the ills of the society with a view to making the society realize its mistakes and make amends. It also projects the virtues or good values in the society for people to emulate. Literature, as an imitation of human action, often presents a picture of what people think, say, and do in the society. In literature, we find stories designed to portray human life and action through some characters, who by their words, action and reaction, convey certain messages for the purpose of education, information and entertainment.

Literature and society mirror each other and impact each other. Literature inscribes the times and circumstances in a permanent form. It puts in black and white the senses and sensibilities, emotions and turmoil of its characters. Literature shapes and builds human nature, behaviour, habits, traits, customs, and traditions, agonies and ecstasies. Nicholas Kristof explains the value of literature in these words, 'Literature seems to offer lessons in human nature that help us decode the world around us and be better friends.'

Literature provides insights into the minds of other human beings, into the minds of authors and into the minds of characters. This is how Jhumpa Lahiri explains the impact of literature on society, '*Literature is such a profound and deep way to look into someone else's life, his mind, his hopes and thoughts. Books have opened so many doors for me, taking me to places where my normal life and its finite limits could never have.*'

In the era of television and internet, when reading habits are rapidly declining, it is great literature that can resurrect the habit of reading among children and youth of the present generation. More than a century old literary works, "*As a man thinketh,*" by James Allen and "*The Prophet*" by Khalil Gibran transformed the lives of millions and still have the same relevance in the present times especially when our youngsters are prone to the internet and the digital world. Literary classics are suitable for people of all ages and times, and transcend the barriers and boundaries of nations and nationalities. "*The Light from Many Lamps,*" by Lillian Eichler Watson, one of the best selling motivational books, impacted the life of our former President and the `Missile Man of India' Dr. A. P. J. Abdul Kalam. Dr Kalam has acknowledged in his autobiographical sketches that the above book was one of the best books read and re(read) by him innumerable times during his life. Back home, the literary works of Gandhi, Nehru, Tagore and others have impacted the lives of millions of people and will continue impacting them. The experiences shared by literary figures become the binding and driving force and will continue to guide the coming generations.

Literature provides a window into the past, allowing readers to see how their ancestors and others dealt with day-to-day life. Readers can see where their own people came from, and how the country they live in became what it is today. Literature can also let its readers look back at the mistakes made by their predecessors, and hopefully avoid those same mistakes. Modern literature also gives readers a view into present-day politics and an important view into the lives of the people around us. Fictional literature, on the other hand can give its readers special insight into the minds of writers to see how they envision the future. ***(589 words)***

Q 2. Read carefully the passage given below and write your answers to the questions that follow in clear, correct and concise language: (15 × 5 = 75 Marks)

Not so long ago a book on human origins would have devoted a substantial number of pages to descriptions of the fossil evidence for primate evolution. This was in part because it was assumed that at each stage of primate evolution one of the fossil primates would have been recognizable as the direct ancestor of modern humans. However, we now know that for various reasons many of these taxa are highly unlikely to be ancestral to living higher primates. Instead, this account will concentrate on what we know of the evolution and relationships of the great apes. It will review how long Western scientists have known about the great apes, and it will show how ideas about their relationships to each other, and to modern humans have changed. It will also explore which of the living apes is most closely related to modern humans.

Among the tales of exotic animals brought home by explorers and traders were descriptions of what we now know as the great apes, that is, chimpanzees. and gorillas, from Africa, and orangutans from Asia. Aristotle referred to "apes as well as to 'monkeys' and 'baboons" in his Historia animalia (literally the "History of Animals'), but his 'apes' were the same as the "apes' dissected by the early anatomists, which were short-tailed macaque monkeys from North Africa.

One of the first people to undertake a systematic review of the differences between modern humans and the chimpanzee and gorilla was Thomas Henry Huxley. In an essay entitled "On the relations of Man to the Lower Animals' that formed the central section of his 1863 book called Evidence as to Man's Place in Nature, he concluded the anatomical differences between modern humans and the chimpanzee and gorilla were less marked than the differences between the two African apes and the orangutan.

Darwin used this evidence in his *The Descent of Man* published in 1871 to suggest that, because the African apes were morphologically closer to modern humans than to the only great ape known from Asia, the ancestors of modern humans were more likely to be found in Africa than elsewhere. This deduction played a critical role in pointing most researchers towards Africa as a likely place to find human ancestors. As we shall see in the next chapter, those who considered the orangutan our closest relative looked to South-East Asia as the most likely place to find modem human ancestors.

Developments in biochemistry and immunology during the first half of the 20th century allowed the search for evidence about the nature of the relationships between modern humans and the apes to be shifted from traditional morphology to the morphology of molecules. The earliest attempts to use proteins to determine primate relationships were made just after the turn of the century, hut the first results of a new generation of analyses were reported in the early 1960s. The famous US biochemist Linus Pauling coined the name 'molecular anthropology for this area of research. Two reports, both published in 1963, provided crucial evidence. Emile Zuckerman, another pioneer molecular anthropologist, described how he used enzymes to break up the protein haemoglobin from blood red cells into its peptide components, and that when he separated them using a small electric current, the patterns made by the peptides from a modern human, a chimpanzee, and a gorilla were indistinguishable. The second contribution was by Morris Goodman, who has spent his life working on molecular anthropology, who used techniques borrowed from immunology to study samples of a serum (serum is what is left after blood has clotted) protein called albumin taken from modern humans, apes, and monkeys. He came to the Conclusion that the albumins of modern humans and chimpanzees were so alike in their structure that you cannot tell them apart.

Proteins are made up of a string of amino acids. In many instances one amino acid may be substituted for another without changing the function of the protein. In the 1960s and 1970s Vince Sarich and Allan Wilson, two Berkeley biochemists interested in primate and human evolution, exploited these minor variations in protein structure in order to determine the evolutionary history of the molecules, and therefore, presumably, the evolutionary history of the taxa being sampled. They, too, concluded that modern humans and the African apes were very closely related.

(a) What does the author say about earlier assumptions regarding evolution? (15 Marks)

(b) According to the author, how are modern humans and apes related?

(c) What later developments took place in the twentieth century in investigating the relationship of apes and humans?

(d) What were the attempts made to use proteins to determine primate relationships?

(e) In what way does the latest research prove the relationship between apes and humans?

Ans. (a) The author says that it was assumed that at each stage of primate evolution, one of the fossil primates would have been recognizable as the direct ancestor of modern humans. However, we now know that for various reasons that many of these taxa are highly unlikely to be ancestral to living higher primates. Instead, this account will concentrate on what we know of the evolution and relationships of the great apes. The author also reviews and explores western scientists' ideas about relationship of apes and humans.

(b) Aristotle's history of animals is also an attempt at tracing the relationship between apes and humans. The first person to make the systematic study on this subject was Thomas Henry Huxley. He concluded that the anatomical differences between modern humans and chimpanzee and gorilla are less marked than the differences between two African apes and orangutan. Darwin used this evidence in his The Descent of Man published in 1871 to suggest that because the African apes were morphologically closer to modern humans than to the only great ape known from Asia, the ancestors of modern humans were more likely to be found in Africa than elsewhere. This deduction played a critical role in pointing most researchers towards Africa as a likely place to find human ancestors.

(c) During the first half of the 20th century, developments in biochemistry and immunology facilitated investigation into the nature of the relationships between modern humans and the apes, and shifted the focus of study from traditional morphology to the morphology of molecules. The earliest attempts to use proteins to determine primate relationships were made just after the turn of the century, but the first results of a new generation of analyses were reported in the early 1960s. The famous US biochemist Linus Pauling coined the name 'molecular anthropology' for this area of research. Two reports, both published in 1963, provided crucial evidence about relationship between humans and apes.

(d) Emile Zuckerman, another pioneer molecular anthropologist, described how he used enzymes to break up the protein haemoglobin from blood red cells into its peptide components, and that when he separated them using a small electric current, the patterns made by the peptides from a modern human, a chimpanzee, and a gorilla were indistinguishable. The second contribution was by Morris Goodman, who has spent his life working on molecular anthropology, who used techniques borrowed from immunology to study samples of a serum (serum is what is left after blood has clotted) protein called albumin taken from modern humans, apes, and monkeys. He concluded that the albumins of modern humans and chimpanzees were so alike in their structure that you cannot tell them apart.

(e) In the 1960s and 1970s, Vince Sirach and Allan Wilson, two Berkeley biochemists interested in primate and human evolution, exploited these minor variations in protein structure in order to determine the evolutionary history of the molecules, and therefore, presumably, the evolutionary history of the taxa being sampled. They, too, concluded that modern humans and the African apes were very closely related.

Q 3. Make a précis of the following passage in about one-third of its length. Do not give a title to it. The précis should be written in your own language: (75 Marks)

Everyone must have had at least one personal experience with a computer error by this time. Bank balances are suddenly reported to have jumped into the millions, appeals for charitable contributions are mailed over and over to people with crazy-sounding names at your address, department stores send the wrong bills, utility companies write that they're turning everything off, that sort of thing. If you manage to get in touch with someone and complain, you then get instantaneously typed, guilty letters from the same computer, saying, 'Our computer was in error, and an adjustment is being made in your account."

These are supposed to be the sheerest and blindest accidents. Mistakes are not believed to be part of the normal behaviour of a good machine. If things go wrong, it must be a personal, human error, the result of fingering, tampering, a button getting stuck, someone hitting the wrong key. The computer, at its normal best, is infallible.

I wonder whether this can be true. After all, the whole point of computers is that they represent an extension of the human brain, vastly improved upon but nonetheless human, super-human maybe. A good computer can think clearly and quickly enough to beat you at chess, and some of them have even been programmed to write obscure verse. They can do anything we can do, and more besides.

It is not yet known whether a computer has its own consciousness, and it would be hard to find out about this. When you walk into one of those great halls now built for the huge machines, and stand listening, it is easy to imagine that the faint, distant noises are the sound of thinking, and the turning of the spools gives them the look of wild creatures rolling their eyes in the effort to concentrate, choking with information. But real thinking, and dreaming, are other matters.

On the other hand, the evidence of something like an unconscious, equivalent to ours, are all around, in every mail. As extensions of the human brain, they have been constructed with the same property of error, spontaneous, uncontrolled, and rich in possibilities.

Mistakes are at the very base of human thought, embedded there, feeding the structure like root nodules. If we were not provided with the knack of being wrong, we could never get anything useful done. We think our way along by choosing between right and wrong alternatives, and the wrong choices have to be made as frequently as the right ones. We get along in life this way. We are built to make mistakes, coded for error.

We learn, as we say, by 'trial and error. Why do we always say that? Why not trial and rightness', or 'trial and triumph'? The old phrase puts it that way because that is, in real life, the way it is done.

A good laboratory, like a good bank or a corporation or government, has to run like a computer. Almost everything is done flawlessly, by the book, and all the numbers add up to the predicted sums. The days go by. And then, if it is a lucky day, and a lucky laboratory, somebody makes a mistake: the wrong buffer, something in one of the blanks, a decimal misplaced in reading counts, the warm room off by a degree and a half, a mouse out of his box, or just a misreading of the day's protocol. Whatever, when the results come in, something is obviously screwed up, and then the action can begin.

The misreading is not the important error; it opens the way. The next step is the crucial one. If the investigator can bring himself to say, 'But even so, look at that t then the new finding, whatever it is, is ready for snatching. What is needed, for progress to be made, is the move based on the error.

Whenever new kinds of thinking are about to be accomplished or new varieties of music, there has to be an argument beforehand. With two sides debating in the same mind, haranguing, there is an amiable understanding that one is right and the other wrong. Sooner or later the thing is settled, but there can be no action at all iif there are not the two sides, and the argument. The hope is in the faculty of wrongness, the tendency toward error. The capacity to leap across mountains of information to land lightly on the wrong side represents the highest of human endowments. ***(750 words)***

Ans. **Precis**

We all have experienced computer errors, which are not very uncommon. Errors in bank balances, wrong bills by department stores, wrong emails etc. have occasionally affected all of us one time or another. When we complain, an instant and usual reply is "computer error", accompanied by an assurance for rectification. Computers being a fail-safe machine, errors occur owing to the lapses on the part of human beings. A computer- that can think clearly- is programmed by humans and acts as an extension of the human brain. It's a matter of wonder whether the computer has consciousness. The computer may give a semblance of thinking when it produces a faint, distant noise while being functional. However, thinking and dreaming are altogether different matters. Computers, as extension of human intelligence, may be attributed to be equipped with the unconscious memory, corresponding to that of human beings. Fallibility is embedded in human mechanisms and had it not been so, we could not have produced the invaluable. Humankind has progressed by trial and error. A good bank or a corporation, or a government supposed to be working well, and modelled on an error-free computer, has a propensity to be erroneous. These erroneous tendencies are rectified and made functional again after remedial human interventions. Dialectic- an oppositional thinking- is a must for making improvement in human affairs. There can be no advancement in human well-being and intelligence, unless we give credit to the human susceptibility of being wrong and to be corrigible. Accepting the phenomenon of darkness/ignorance is the biggest driving force to make a move towards light and enlightenment. ***(258 words)***

Q 4. (a) Rewrite the following sentences after making necessary corrections. Do not make unnecessary changes in the original sentence: (1×10= 10 Marks)

(i) Every man, woman and child were rescued.

(ii) No sooner I am out, than the students make a noise.

(iii) Walk carefully lest you may not fall.

(iv) The patient died before the doctor arrived.

(v) Time and tide waits for none.

(vi) Into what kind of mess have you got me into ?

(vii) I learned the answer would come sooner than I expected.

(viii) Hardly he had stepped out than it began to rain.

(ix) Either of the five dancers will dance tonight.

(x) My client was neither aware nor party to the plot.

Ans. *(i) Every man, woman and child was rescued.*

(ii) No sooner am I out, than the students make a noise.

(iii) Walk carefully, lest you should fall.

(iv) The patient had died before the doctor arrived.

(v) Time and tide wait for none.

(vi) What kind of mess have you got me into?

(vii) I knew the answer would come sooner than I expected.

(viii) Hardly had he stepped out when it began to rain.

(ix) One of the five dancers will dance tonight.

(x) My client was neither aware nor a party to the plot.

(b) Supply the missing words: (1*5= 5 Marks)

(i) She started the work __ a few days.

(ii) There is no exception__ this rule.

(iii) We are accountable to God__ our actions.

(iv) The police is entrusted__ the enforcement of law and order.

(v) The girl was hit with a stone__her brother.

Ans. *(i) within*

(ii) to

(iii) for

(iv) with

(v) by

(c) Use the correct forms of the verbs given in brackets: (1*5= 5 Marks)

(i) After she__ (take) her lunch, she went to the theatre.

(ii) The doctor __ (examine) the patients every evening.

(iii) They__ (build) that bridge since 2003.

(iv) He __ (play) cards, when I saw him.

(v) If she works hard, she __ (get) a first class.

Ans. *(i)* *had taken*

(ii) *examines*

(iii) *have been building*

(iv) *was playing*

(v) *will get*

(d) Write the antonyms of the following:

(i) Ecstasy

(ii) Advocate

(iii) Anaemic

(iv) Allow

(v) Hyperbole

Ans. *(i)* *Ecstasy – depression*

(ii) *Advocate – reject/oppose*

(iii) *Anaemic – energetic /strong*

(iv) *Allow – disallow*

(v) *Hyperbole - understatement*

Q 5. (a) Rewrite the following sentences as directed without changing the meaning: (1 × 10 = 10 Marks)

(i) He is a learned man. He cannot make that mistake. (Combine the sentence by using "too" –"to")

(ii) Brutus was not without love for Caesar__ ? (Add a question tag)

(iii) As soon as he went there, the uproar commenced. (Remove as soon as' and put no sooner than")

(iv) Either the father or the son has not taken it. (Use 'neither - nor")

(v) You tell me the truth. I shall not punish you. (Rewrite the sentence beginning 'unless'.)

(vi) The Prince said, "It gives me great pleasure to be here this evening". (Change into Indirect Speech)

(vii) The minister was spoken to by them. (Change into active voice)

(viii) Not only Rama but also Gopal did it. (Remove 'not only – but also" and put 'as well as')

(ix) The farmer worked so hard, that he might not starve. (Remove 'so' and 'that' and put 'lest")

(x) Hardly had I arrived at the gate, when my servant brought the horse. (Remove 'hardly and put 'scarcely')

Ans. *(i) He is too learned a man to make that mistake*

(ii) Brutus was not without love for Caesar, was he?

(iii) No sooner did he go there, than the uproar commenced.

(iv) Neither the father nor the son has taken it.

(v) Unless you tell me the truth, I shall punish you.

(vi) The prince said that it gave him great pleasure to be there that evening.

(vii) They spoke to the minister.

(viii) Rama as well as Gopal did it.

(ix) The farmer worked that hard, lest he should starve.

(x) Scarcely had I arrived at the gate, that my servant brought the horse.

(b) Use the following words to make sentences that bring out their meaning clearly. Do not change the form of the words. (No marks will be given for vague and ambiguous sentences): (1 × 5 = 5 Marks)

(i) Misogynist

(ii) Unprecedented

(iii) Orchard

(iv) Morale

(v) Volunteer

Ans. *(i) Misogynist – She was angry with the Church because of its misogynist teachings on women and their position in society.*

(ii) Unprecedented- The corona pandemic caused unprecedented loss of lives all over the world.

(iii) Orchards – The Shimla belt in Himachal Pradesh is very famous for its apple orchards.

(iv) Morale – The morale of workers in the party is at its lowest ebb in the present circumstances.

(v) Volunteers – Many volunteers did great social services during the time of the covid pandemic.

(c) Choose the appropriate word to fill in the blanks: (1 × 5= 5 Marks)

(i) Modem youth is fond of __ life. (ostentatious/ostensible)

(ii) The poetry of Keats has a __ beauty. (sensational/sensuous)

(iii) King Ashoka did not approve of the __ sport of hunting. (barbarous/barbaric)

(iv) Everyone despised him for his __ behaviour. (obnoxious/noxious)

(v) The __ party was attacked by militants. (petrol / patrol)

Ans. *(i) Ostentatious*

(ii) sensuous

(iii) Barbaric

(iv) Obnoxious

(v) Patrol

(d) Use the following idioms/phrases in sentences of your own to bring out their meaning clearly: (1 × 5 = 5 Marks)

(i) back seat driver

(ii) call it a day

(iii) wet behind the ears

(iv) set off

(v) run out of

Ans. *(i)* ***Back seat driver :*** *Bharat tries to sound like an authority on the subject but he's actually a backseat driver.*

(ii) ***Call it a day :*** *When Rajesh found it difficult to continue with his marriage, he decided to call it a day and sought divorce.*

(iii) ***Wet behind the ears :*** *Don't rely on his advice about shares and stocks; he's still wet behind the ears.*

(iv) ***Set off :*** *Panic on the stock market set off a wave of selling from investors.*

(v) ***Run out of :*** *Many people ran out of money during the time of the Covid pandemic.*

UPSC (MAIN) EXAM – 2021

ENGLISH

(Compulsory)

Time Allowed: 3 hours ***Maximum Marks: 300***

Question Paper: Specific Instructions

Please read each of the following instructions carefully before attempting questions.

- *All questions are to be attempted.*
- *The number of marks carried by questions is indicated against it.*
- *Answers must be written in* **ENGLISH** *only.*
- *Word limit in questions, wherever specified, should be adhered to and if answered in much longer or shorter than the prescribed length, marks will be deducted.*
- *Any page or portion of the page left blank in the Question-cum-Answer Booklet must be clearly struck off.*

Q 1. Write an essay in about 600 words on any one of the following topics: (100 Marks)

(a) Social Media: A Challenge to Societal Harmony

(b) The Role of NGOs in Social Change

(c) Education as a Means to Serve Humanity

(d) The Crying Need for Embracing Minimalism

Ans. **Education As A Means to Serve Humanity**

Be Yourself, Love Yourself;

And Lift Yourself- All By Yourself.

The ongoing war against Covid-19 and its newer variants clearly vindicate the importance of disseminating awareness and education in the service of humanity. All over the globe, when the entire human community was shaken to its roots and the survival of our civilization itself was under threat, it is with help of education, creating awareness and scientific knowledge that the vaccines researched and developed by scientists could be put into use to save humanity from this deadly pandemic.

This deadly pandemic of the 21st century highlights the importance of education as a means of service to humanity. If the ultimate goal of education in any society is not the service to humanity, such a society cannot survive for long. When the goal of education is the service to humanity, it elevates mankind, leads to spiritual development of human beings, orientates them to nurture feelings for fellow human beings, inculcates a value system that helps sustain oneself and others.

Humanity is not about maintaining goody-goody relationships but it is about building bonds of mutual understanding, goodwill, and cooperation and all inclusive growth and sustainable development with the help of a sustainable value system respecting and helping each other. Education plays the most important role in all these human endeavors.

Education is the sum total of civilized values, behaviour, and human character. It is the systematic way to learn, acquire knowledge and awareness, imbibe values and utilize these for overall progress and prosperity in life and rendering service to the society and humanity. Education is one of the most important ingredients that differentiate humans from other creatures. Education enables us to lead a stable, secure, successful, meaningful and sustainable life. Education capacitates us to help ourselves and others. It helps to develop critical thinking, a free and independent thought process devoid of superstition, fanaticism, and any bias or prejudice.

Character is the essence of human existence. It differentiates one man from the other. Education is the most important tool of character building. History is replete with umpteen number of iconic characters endowed with value education e.g. Dr. Abdul Kalam, Mahatma Gandhi, Dr. B. R. Ambedkar, Abraham Lincoln, Benjamin Franklin and many others. These names mentioned here reinforce the importance of education in character building.

Education gives us a sense of right and wrong which makes us tolerant and respectful to each other, develop a sense of social justice and stand for its distribution, invest in human dignity so as to grow fraternity. It broadens our understanding and facilitates developing a fair sense of judgment and plays a great role in creating responsible citizens who can discharge their responsibilities towards society.

Education creates opportunities and possibilities, and empowers us to make use of these opportunities for human progress and prosperity. Human beings have done wonders, made discoveries, done research and explored the universe, conquered fatal diseases, created facilities and luxuries and what not with the help of education to make human life worthy, meaningful and majestic.

However, one cannot deny the fact that misuse of education, especially scientific education, has led to wars, development of arms and atomic weapons causing irreparable losses of life and property. It is a blot on the of face entire humanity. The misuse of nuclear weapons is a potent threat looming large over the entire humanity.

Education is thus a double edged sword. But all said and done, it is a continuous and lifelong process of learning and applying the knowledge gained for progress, prosperity, success and glory of humanity. ***(592 words)***

Q 2. Read the passage given below carefully and write your answers to the questions that follow in clear, correct and concise language. (75 marks)

Life on planet earth has been possible for millions of years largely because of certain basic services associated with the biosphere. Important among these are: Climate and radiation regulation; Microbial transformations and decomposition; Biological diversity; and Opportunities for sustainable advances in biological productivity.

We now find ourselves in a state where these essential services are in jeopardy, largely as a result of human induced damage to the basic life support systems of land, water, flora, fauna and the atmosphere. Symptoms of an impending and general breakdown of the life support and ecological systems are already here. Some of these are mounting population growth; vanishing source of drinking water; vanishing forests, plants and animal biodiversity; intensifying drought and floods; loss of grazing lands; growing degradation of fertile land and desertification; deterioration of the quality of air and water; accumulation of toxic and non-biodegradable wastes in the biosphere; explosive growth of rural and urban unemployment and mushrooming of urban slums. It is the poor and the marginalized urban and rural people who are suffering most from such environmental breakdown.

The threats to climate change and radiation regulation are receiving the most prominent public attention largely because of all-pervasive nature of their potential harmful impact. "Our Common Future" the report of the World Commission of Environment and Development by the United Nations is indicative that ecologically the fates of people whether rich or poor everywhere are intertwined. Recent reports on the state of the world paint a frightening picture of the rapid depletion of the world's natural resources coupled with rising social and economic problems. They reflect the widespread frustration about the inability of current approaches to solve the interlinked problems of environment and development and call for major changes in the way people think, use the finite resources of earth and programme their development. Developing countries like ours are faced with the urgent need for accelerating economic growth in a manner that the poor become the main beneficiaries and not the rich. We should also avoid proceeding on those developmental paths where environmental costs are high and the developmental activities cannot be sustained for long. The new paradigm of development should promote economic activities and life-styles based on the concept of "man with nature" and not "man against nature".

Today, we are passing through an era of global change whether it is in politics or economics. Inequity in the resource distribution and consumption between the developed and the developing nations of world has become most apparent. The earth is undergoing drastic climatic changes. The last few years have been the warmest ones ever recorded. The heat trap works differently in different latitudes and altitudes having a tremendous effect on major crops like wheat. The protective ozone layer is being slowly damaged giving rise to medical problems for human beings and affecting several plants and their yield, animals and their behavior.

Though the causes of pollution of our soils, lakes and vegetation are different, the effect is the same. Mercilessly everyday pristine wild habitats are being destroyed. Nearly half of our country is tilled for agriculture and only 11 per cent of the land area has to bear the brunt of growing population, housing, roads and factories and its "carrying capacity" is under severe stress.

The dreaded nuclear autumn or nuclear winter is a potential threat to the environment which might result in large scale habitat destruction, species extinction, air pollution, toxic chemicals, acid rain, ozone depletion etc. A nuclear non proliferation movement with abolition of nuclear weapons, has to be spearheaded enthusiastically.

Experts have predicted that serious food shortages could occur during this decade. Such a prognosis is based on three major factors – Soil erosion; Unsustainable utilization of groundwater; and Deforestation. They are together reducing the global potential for food production by nearly 14 million tonnes each year. New technologies, including biotechnology, are unlikely to help in achieving a quantum jump in productivity improvement at least during this decade. Due to the continuing damage to the ecological foundations of stable and sustainable agriculture, land degradation and water depletion ecological access to food may become the most important food security challenge of the 21st century.

(a) According to the passage what are the factors responsible for the evolution of life on earth?

(b) What does the author mean by environmental breakdown? What are its impacts?

(c) What suggestions does the author offer to balance environment, development and inequity in consumption?

(d) How is life on earth being affected by climate change as per the passage?

(e) How is environmental breakdown related to probable food shortage?

Ans. (a) Life on planet earth has been possible for millions of years largely because of: climate and radiation regulation; microbial transformations and decomposition; biological diversity; and opportunities for sustainable advances in biological productivity.

(b) By the environmental breakdown, the author means a human induced damage to the basic life support systems of land, water, flora, fauna and the atmosphere. The symptoms and impact of an impending and general breakdown of the life support and ecological systems are: mounting population growth; vanishing source of drinking water; vanishing forests, plants and animal biodiversity; intensifying drought and floods; loss of grazing lands; growing degradation of fertile land and desertification; deterioration of the quality of air and water; accumulation of toxic and non-biodegradable wastes in the biosphere; explosive growth of rural and urban unemployment and mushrooming of urban slums. It is the poor and the marginalized urban and rural people who are suffering most from such environmental breakdown.

(c) The author offers to balance environment, development and inequity in consumption, by accelerating economic growth in a manner that the poor become the main beneficiaries and not the rich. The new paradigm of development should promote economic activities and life-styles based on the concept of "man with nature" and not "man against nature".

(d) The earth is undergoing drastic climatic changes. The last few years have been the warmest ones ever recorded. The heat trap works differently in different latitudes and altitudes having a tremendous effect on major crops like wheat. The protective ozone layer is being slowly damaged giving rise to medical problems for human beings and affecting several plants and their yield, animals and their behavior.

(e) The environmental breakdown is related to probable food shortage because of three major factors – soil erosion; unsustainable utilization of groundwater; and deforestation. They are together reducing the global potential for food production by nearly 14 million tonnes each year. New technologies, including biotechnology, are unlikely to help in achieving a quantum jump in productivity improvement at least during this decade. Due to the continuing damage to the ecological foundations of stable and sustainable agriculture, land degradation and water depletion, ecological access to food may become the most important food security challenge of the 21st century.

Q 3. Make a précis of the following passage in about one-third of its length. Do not give a title to it. The précis should be written in your own language. (75 marks)

Recent decades have witnessed an upsurge of literature on Indians settled abroad. Mainly three types of writings can be distinguished: historical, diplomatic and anthropological. The historical works provide an account of the phases of emigration of Indians and their early life situations in foreign lands. The diplomatic works read like country reports on the status and problems of Indians beyond seas. The anthropological works are in the nature of ethnographic accounts with their accent on cultural continuity and change.

Varieties of writings apart, the existing literature shares three notable features in common. One, much of it is in the form of country-specific profiles. Cross-country comparisons are few and far between. Two, most of it is descriptive, with analytical ideas and imaginative hypotheses in short supply. Three, for most part, it tends to project the problem in colonial perspective.

There are broadly two ways in which the problem of Indians abroad has been looked at: the colonial and the nationalist. The colonial way maintains that Indians went abroad driven by their domestic economic compulsions, or greed or avarice; that they were 'heathens', lazy, cunning and quarrelsome; that they tended to cling tenaciously to their culture in order to make up for the loss on economic front or to cope with their status loss on the social front; that they were so carried away by their desire to grab wealth and power that they had no compunction at throwing the natives out of employment and power in the latter's own lands; and, that their difficulties in foreign countries were largely of their own making. All this is clearly indicative of the way colonialists and their ideologues look at the problem and would have us look at it.

As against this, the nationalist way contends that in most cases Indians did not go abroad on their own, but were indeed taken, taken under various arrangements as instruments of colonial domination; that they were not led by their own predatory instincts, instead they were lured and duped by colonial designs; that they did not plunder the country they went to, instead they served its development needs and worked hard to better the lot of its residents; that they were not lazy but industrious, not cunning but thrifty, not indolent but enterprising; that they had been tolerated only as long as they were prepared to play second fiddle to the natives, but once they began to assert their rights they were pushed out; and, that their difficulties in foreign lands were not of their own making, but of the making of neo-colonial powers which keep playing political games in the Third World countries.

In the study of Indians abroad it is the functionalist orientation that predominates. This is evident from the fact that the existing literature is preoccupied with the question of the cultural identity and integration, to the relative neglect of the question of class and power. It is a pity that no systematic attempt has been made to look at the problem in terms of other perspectives.

Indians are not the only people who have ventured out of their homeland in such vast numbers. Their number looks small when compared to overseas Chinese and overseas British. Their relatively lesser numbers notwithstanding, Indians form large enough numbers outside India and significant enough groups in several countries to merit serious research attention as well as civil concern.

Spread over most parts of the world, Indians are found more in some regions than in others. They are concentrated in South, Southeast and Southwest Asia, in South Africa and East Africa, in Western Europe, North America and the Caribbean. Taking 1,500 as the minimum figure, overseas Indians are found in as many as 53 countries. They form a majority in at least three foreign countries: Mauritius (74 percent), Fiji (49 percent) and Guyana (53 percent). They are close to majority in Trinidad and Tobago where they are 40 percent as against 43 percent of the blacks.

In respect of their regional derivations and settlements there are noticeable some broad interesting patterns. There is a preponderance of South Indians, particularly Tamils, in South and Southeast Asia and South Africa, of East Indians in West Indies, of Punjabis and Gujaratis in Africa, Europe and North America. This is not to underestimate the presence of Indians of other regional origins in these parts of the world, but just to indicate that there are some perceptible regional linkages between the regions of origin and of settlement.

***Ans.* Precis**

Three main types of writings can be distinguished on Indians settled abroad: historical, diplomatic and anthropological. The historical account provides phases of emigration, diplomatic works outline problems of Indians beyond seas, and anthropological dwells into cultural continuity and change. The two broad ways to look at the problem are– colonial and nationalist.

The colonial approach tries to highlight that Indians went abroad driven by their domestic economic compulsions, or greed or avarice or desire to grab wealth and power. But unlike colonialist approach, the nationalist views emigration as outcome of colonial domination; not led by their predatory instincts but were lured and duped by colonial designs. They didn't loot or plunder any country; rather served its needs and contributed to its development. The Indians settled abroad were not lazy and cunning but very industrious and enterprising. Their problems were not their own making but were created by neo- colonial powers.

No systematic attempt has been made to their problems in the proper perspective. Indians form in large numbers and significant groups in several countries who merit serious concern and research. The preponderance of south Indians, in south and southeast Asia and South Africa, of east Indians in west indies and of Punjabis and Gujaratis in Africa, Europe and north America, indicate some perceptible regional linkages between regions of origin and of settlements. ***(235 words)***

Q 4. (a) Rewrite the following sentences after making necessary corrections. Do not make unnecessary changes in the original sentence. (10 marks)

(i) My sister prefers dogs than cats.

(ii) I don't approve to your smoking in public.

(iii) One of my student has got the prestigious Commonwealth Scholarship this year.

(iv) The fresher the fruit, the best it tastes.

(v) He questioned my motif behind meeting the director.

(vi) The director went and bidded goodbye to the composer.

(vii) His acceptance of your fancy story indicates his credible nature.

(viii) Are you invited for the office party?

(ix) When I will reach home, I will let you know the details of the event.

(x) The University comprises of several Departments.

Ans. *(i) My sister prefers dogs to cats.*

(ii) I don't approve of your smoking in public.

(iii) One of my students has got the prestigious Commonwealth Scholarship this year.

(iv) The fresher the fruit, the better it tastes.

(v) He questioned my motive behind meeting the director.

(vi) The director went and bid goodbye to the composer.

(vii) His acceptance of your fancy story indicates his credulous nature.

(viii) Are you invited to the office party?

(ix) When I reach home, I will let you know the details of the event.

(x) The University comprise of several Departments.

(b) Supply the missing words. (5 marks)

(i) The homestay provides its guests ________ all the facilities.

(ii) At last, I got rid ________ my old scooter.

(iii) All my expenses were paid ________ by the office.

(iv) A waiter is a person who waits ________ customers at a restaurant.

(v) The company entered ________ an agreement with the supplier.

Ans. *(i) The homestay provides its guests with all the facilities.*

(ii) At last, I got rid of my old scooter.

(iii) All my expenses were paid for by the office.

(iv) A waiter is a person who waits on customers at a restaurant.

(v) The company entered into an agreement with the supplier.

(c) Use the correct forms of the verbs given in brackets. (5 marks)

(i) My goodness, someone ________ away my phone and left his in its place by mistake. (Take)

(ii) If you ________ in time, I'll leave without you. (Reach)

(iii) I ________ the rules of grammar these days. (Learn)

(iv) I used to have a pair of binoculars, but I ________ it yesterday because I needed money. (Pawn)

(v) The decision ________ before I joined the meeting. (Make)

Ans. *(i) My goodness, someone took away my phone and left his in its place by mistake.*

(ii) If you don't reach in time, I'll leave without you.

(iii) I am learning the rules of grammar these days.

(iv) I used to have a pair of binoculars, but I had pawned it yesterday because I needed money.

(v) The decision was made before I joined the meeting.

(d) Write the antonyms of the following: (5 marks)

(i) Guilty

(ii) Impoverish

(iii) Approve

(iv) Eligible

(v) Scarce

Ans. *(i) Innocent*

(ii) Enrich

(iii) Disapprove

(iv) Ineligible

(v) Surplus

Q 5. (a) Rewrite the following sentences as directed without changing the meaning. **(10 marks)**

(i) Has anyone ever hypnotized you? (Change into passive voice)

(ii) The judge said to the witness, "Were you present at the scene of crime?" (Change into indirect speech)

(iii) He does not love his daughter. He does not love his wife either. (Join the sentences into one by using 'neither – nor')

(iv) Much though I wanted, I could not reach her. (Rewrite the sentence using 'however')

(v) As soon as the concert ended, it began to rain. (Replace 'as soon as' with 'hardly', making other suitable changes)

(vi) As the bus to the airport was late, we could not catch the plane. (Begin the sentence with – 'Had the bus .... not')

(vii) He was so nervous that he could not perform well in the interview. (Use 'too – to' combination)

(viii) I have never kept a pet as I don't enjoy their company. (Rewrite the sentence beginning with 'since')

(ix) They will enjoy the programme, ___________? (Add a question tag)

(x) If you are going out take an umbrella as it is cloudy today. (Rewrite the sentence beginning with 'It being –')

Ans. *(i) Have you ever been hypnotized?*

(ii) The judge asked the witness if he had been present at the scene of the crime.

(iii) He neither loves his daughter nor his wife.

(iv) However much I wanted her, I could not reach her.

(v) Hardly had the concert ended, it began to rain.

(vi) Had the bus to the airport not been late, we could have caught the plane.

(vii) He was too nervous to perform well in the interview.

(viii) Since I don't enjoy the company of a pet, I have never kept a pet.

(ix) They will enjoy the programme, will they not?

(x) It being a cloudy day, take an umbrella if you go out.

(b) Use the following words to make sentences that bring out their meaning clearly. Do not change the form of the words. (No marks will be given for vague and ambiguous sentences). **(5 marks)**

(i) Philanthropist

(ii) Temperamental

(iii) Sarcastically

(iv) Devise

(v) Preclude

Ans. *(i) Mother Teresa needs no introduction; she was a philanthropist all through her life.*

(ii) Mr. Saxena is a very temperamental person.

(iii) Hemant spoke sarcastically to his wife when she was in the kitchen.

(iv) The need to devise new ways of imparting education was very obvious during the pandemic.

(v) This law will preclude the existence of higher rights.

(c) Choose the appropriate word to fill in the blanks. (5 marks)

(i) The man had a guilty __________ so he turned himself in. (conscience / conscious)

(ii) I used my __________ to help my neighbour. (discretion / discrimination)

(iii) The train has been ______ for an hour (Stationary / stationery)

(iv) A __________ of shoppers crowded the market after the lockdown was lifted. (hoard / horde)

(v) My experiences in the alien place were __________ due to issues of food and language. (climactic / climatic)

Ans. *(i) The man had a guilty conscience so he turned himself in.*

(ii) I used my discretion to help my neighbour.

(iii) The train has been stationary for an hour.

(iv) A horde of shoppers crowded the market after the lockdown was lifted.

(v) My experiences in the alien place were climactic due to issues of food and language.

(d) Use the following idioms / phrases in sentences of your own to bring out their meaning clearly. (5 marks)

(i) Length and breadth

(ii) Rank and file

(iii) A thorn in the flesh

(iv) Move heaven and earth

(v) Step into someone's shoes

Ans. *(i) The songs of Lata Mangeshkar are popular throughout the length and breadth of the country.*

(ii) The entire rank and file of Punjab Congress was up against its president.

(iii) My younger brother was a thorn in the flesh when we were enjoying my birthday party.

(iv) He moved heaven and earth to get his pension credited to his account.

(v) When the children step into the shoes of their parents, they feel the concerns of their parents.

UPSC (MAIN) EXAM – 2020

ENGLISH

(Compulsory)

Time Allowed: 3 hours **Maximum Marks: 300**

Question Paper: Specific Instructions

Please read each of the following instructions carefully before attempting questions.

- *All questions are to be attempted.*
- *The number of marks carried by questions is indicated against it.*
- *Answers must be written in* **ENGLISH** *only.*
- *Word limit in questions, wherever specified, should be adhered to and if answered in much longer or shorter than the prescribed length, marks will be deducted.*
- *Any page or portion of the page left blank in the Question-cum-Answer Booklet must be clearly struck off.*

Q 1. Write an essay in about 600 words on any one of the following topics: 100

(a) Indian Judicial System Needs Overhauling.

(b) Not Rural or Urban, India Needs Rurban Growth.

(c) Relevance of Hindi as the National Language.

(d) COVID-19 Pandemic and the Indian Economy.

Ans. **Indian Judicial System Needs Overhauling.**

"Laws too gentle are seldom obeyed; too severe are seldom executed."

Benjamin Franklin

"Justice, justices and justicing is the need of the hour".

Justice Krishna Iyer

The constitutional scheme in a mature democracy is of distribution of powers between the three main wings of governance – the Legislature, the Executive and the Judiciary. To the judiciary is assigned the role of interpreting the Constitution and the laws and to ensure that each wing keeps itself within the limits delineated for it. The added responsibility for the judiciary is to keep itself in check by the practice of self-restraint. In this sense, the pre-eminent role of enforcement of the Rule of Law is the primary concern of the judiciary. The Rule of Law is a part of the basic feature which cannot be abrogated in exercise of the amending power of Parliament under article 368 of the Constitution. The functioning of the justice delivery system and the need for judicial reforms has to be viewed in this perspective.

It cannot be seriously doubted that for quite some time now, the best talent in the legal profession is not available for the appointment of judges. The problem is more acute in the subordinate judiciary where selection has to be made only from the residue after the brighter persons have chosen other professions and those in the Bar prefer not to leave it. The quality of justice administered ultimately depends on the quality of personnel manning the courts. As the significance of the justice delivery system is paramount in a democracy, it is essential to ensure that its personnel are at least as qualified and competent as that of any other branch. Urgent steps are therefore needed to ensure appointments from the best available talent and enforcement of accountability by methods in keeping with the dignity of the office.

The imperative reforms to be introduced without delay to overhaul Indian judicial system are:

(*i*) to fill up all the existing vacancies of judges;

(*ii*) increase the number of judges and other judicial officers at various levels;

(*iii*) provide higher salaries, better perks and status and raise the retirement age for judicial officers at all levels;

(*iv*) ensure to the judiciary greater independence including financial autonomy;

(*v*) Intensive training and orientation programmes should be organized for the members of the judiciary at all levels at the time of their entry. There should be refresher courses for upgradation of training and orientation programmes at regular intervals during the service for judicial officers from the lowest to the highest courts;

(*vi*) The recommendations made by the National Judicial Pay Commission for Subordinate Judiciary could be considered for application equally to High Courts and the Supreme Court;

(*vii*) Open declaration of assets and liabilities to be made yearly by all judges – lowest to the highest, from the Munsifs to the Chief Justice of India;

(*viii*) Right to speedy, time bound affordable justice equally available to all citizens to be enshrined as an enforceable fundamental right under the Constitution;

(*ix*) Improving the quality of legal education and training, attracting better talent to the Bar and the Bench;

(*x*) Need to simplify procedures and court practices, amending CrPC, IPC, Evidence law etc; providing full security and protection to witnesses;

(*xi*) Greater recourse to parallel and alternative dispute resolution (ADR) mechanisms like Lok Adalat, Nyaya Panchayats at village, block and district levels; the initiative of fast track courts and consumer courts is welcome;

(*xii*) Retirement age for all the judges of the High Courts and the Supreme Court may be raised to 70 years but they should be strictly barred from any office of profit or employment thereafter, not even Governorship or paid Chairmanship of any Committee or Commission;

(*xiii*) Need to restrict the number of appeals; frequent adjournments not be allowed; firm time limits for final disposal of cases; allowing submission of written arguments; time limits for delivery of judgement after conclusion of hearing;

(*xiv*) Judgements to be short, precise and to the point, only one agreed judgement in each case, no separate or dissenting judgements which only confuse the people;

(*xv*) The colonial and feudal hangover of the luxury of long summer and other vacations must come to an end. Judges may be required to work for at least 220 or 230 days in a year with longer daily working hours. In cases of shortage of court rooms, courts may sit in shifts particularly where arrears accumulate. For clearing the existing arrears, a time bound programme may be devised and announced;

(*xvi*) Also, where the advocate is convinced that his client has really no case, he should be advised not to waste money and time – his own and the courts'. He can advise his client to seek out of court compromise or settlement;

(*xvii*) Advocates may be categorized as A, B, C, and D and their fees regulated by law and cash payments to be strictly avoided.

Urgent judicial reforms are a high priority today. But they should not be seen in isolation. Judicial reforms themselves can succeed only when accompanied by other essential reforms in Legislature and Executive. As the quality of legislation and administration improves and there is greater probity in public life, many cases related to the Constitution and day to day administration would never reach the Courts. This will enable them to focus on normal civil and criminal cases like murder, violence etc. for which the courts have been set up in the first place. Citizens would then see a qualitative difference in the way that justice is being dispensed.

Q 2. Read the passage give below carefully and write your answers to the questions that follow in clear, correct and concise language: 15 × 5 = 75

When Tolstoy led a party composed of his family and visitors to harvest a field for a widow, he was doing two things. In part, he was saying that everyone ought to do his share of what he called "bread labour", and earn his keep by the sweat of his brow. At the same time, he was affirming that each of us should help our less fortunate neighbours. Mahatma Gandhi agreed whole-heartedly with both these principles, but he linked them more closely than Tolstoy with what he saw as the decadence of industrial life that takes people away from the home and village crafts, which are varied and rewarding, to the soul-destroying monotony of machines. Even before either of these great men had given their philosophy to the world, an American author named Thoreau, had built himself a hut in the woods to prove that he could support himself by the simples manual work; and in Britain, Ruskin had led his students out from Oxford to build a raised footpath across the water meadows to a village to demonstrate the dignity of labour. The path remains of this day, almost one hundred and fifty years later, lined with tall poplars, as a memorial to a fine ideal.

One could trace the history of such ideas still further back, to the writings of Jean-Jacques Rousseau, who preached the dignity and equality of man and the educational value of Nature and manual work, from the Swiss city of Geneva in the eighteenth century. It was however, a Swiss called Pierre Ceresole, a contemporary of Gandhiji, who took these basic principles and used them to promote international reconciliation.

Pierre was no ordinary Swiss, for it is rare for ordinary people to have the courage to dream and attempt to put them into practice. Pierre's father's family originated in Italy, his mother's family came from France, he had a German grandmother and had relations in England. He used to point out the stupidity of frontiers.

Pierre described how, at the age of seventeen, he was walking in the woods and experienced "something which seemed to me like a solemn dedication to truth … in which the first necessity was to recognize one's own faults. In a blinding fashion there came to me the Vision of Truth amid Nature's mysteries and solitude." He had the habit of keeping a pencil and a notebook with him for entering his stray thoughts, and from these notebooks, of which there are more than a hundred, it is seen that he fretted over the many failures of the Western way of life and yet was generous about the people he met. Despite being an engineer, Pierre, in order to work his way, took a job on a poultry farm and later in an oil-field. While he was in Honolulu, Hawaii, he earned his living by teaching French, but this resulted in his being paid more than he needed for his keep; he gave all his savings away to charity.

From Hawalli he moved on to Japan, experiencing there an entirely new way of life which helped him to see more clearly the virtues and follies of European culture. Returning home at the outbreak of the war, in 1914, he gave all the money inherited from his father to the State, saying, "I believe that the teachings of Christ are superior to good business sense." Later he wrote, "Two thousand years ago there came a radiant light, full of peace and loving kindness – and we immediately crucified it."

Pierre had been impressed with the sacrifice and heroism in war and wanted something equally positive mobilized in the cause of peace. He organised the first international work-camp at a war-devastated village in France. The idea was that people of different nationalities, including those whose countries had recently been enemies of one another, should be joined side by side in honest work to rebuild not only the concrete things but also the feelings of brotherhood that are shattered by war. The number of volunteers and the number of camps began to grow rapidly, and what had been the Swiss Service Civil became the Service Civil International (SCI). Pierre died in 1945 after World War II.

Pierre Ceresole had the satisfaction of doing what he believed to be right. Each year a growing number of volunteers go to work-camps and there is scarcely a country that has not heard of them. Anyone can become a work-camper, and for many this is the place to start – planting young trees and crossing the frontiers.

(a) What were the principles of Tolstoy with which Mahatma Gandhi agreed?

(b) How are Thoreau and Ruskin linked to Gandhi and Tolstoy in the passage?

(c) What was Pierre's philosophy of life?

(d) What is SCI and how did it come into existence?

(e) How is Pierre's work different from the work of those mentioned in the passage?

Ans. (*a*) Tolstoy gave two principles with which Mahatma Gandhi agreed. One was that everyone ought to do his share of what he called "bread labour", and earn his keep by the sweat of his brow. The other was that each of us should help our less·fortunate neighbours.

(*b*) Thoreau and Ruskin were linked to Gandhi and Tolstoy in their simple ways of thinking and living. Thoreau proved that he could support himself by simple manual work and Ruskin demonstrated the dignity of labour.

(*c*) Pierre believed in the vision of truth and nature's mysteries and solitude. He fretted over the failure of western ways of life. He earned his living by teaching and gave away his savings to charity.

(*d*) SCI is Service Civil International. It came into existence with the efforts of Pierre. Pierre had been impressed with the sacrifice and heroism in war and wanted something equally positive mobilized in the cause of peace. He organised the first international work-camp at a war-devastated village in France. The idea was that people of different nationalities, including those whose countries had recently been enemies of one another, should be joined side by side in honest work to rebuild not only the concrete things but also the feelings of brotherhood that are shattered by war. The number of volunteers and the number of camps began to grow rapidly, and what had been the Swiss Service Civil became the Service Civil International (SCI).

(*e*) Pierre's work is different from those mentioned in the passage in a way that he translated his beliefs into action and put his theories in the practice. He used the principles and preaching of his contemporaries and predecessors to promote international reconciliation. He organized an international work camp to bring together people of different nationalities devastated by war to rebuild the feelings of brotherhood shattered by war. So, he was a man of action.

Q 3. Make a précis of the following passage in about one-third of its length. Do not give a title to it. The précis should be written in your own language: 75

Ashoka set an extraordinary example by making himself available at all times for consultation, whether he was relaxing, say, in the palace gardens, or even while being massaged. By hearing and settling disputes he kept in touch with the details of administration. The disputes over water rights and grazing rights, and the problem of money-lending were all familiar to him. To complete the picture of how the emperor and his people lived, it is essential to consider the castes which were already forming in India's first great empire. In Ashok's empire there was first the priestly caste who lived as monks or holy men and performed the rites at the temples. They regarded themselves as superior to all others and their influence was so great that it was sometime a threat to the power of the emperor himself. Next in importance came the three largest castes, the herdsmen, cultivators and craftsmen; while the soldiers, officials and councilors, who were less important, were relatively few. Finally there were slaves and others outside the caste system altogether.

Thus the life of the emperor and his people can be made out from the legends and scraps of writing which have been preserved. It was the extraordinary empire that Ashoka crafted with new ideas which grew from his study of Buddha and his followers.

Gautam, the Buddha, had lived nearly three hundred years earlier. Little is known with certainty about him as he grew up, but innumerable legends have formed around his life. Some of these are common to many religious leaders in Asia, such as a capacity for walking on water or multiplying food. Buddhism taught Ashoka the importance of the right way to live. According to a legend, talking to a victorious kind, Buddha asked:

"What would you do if you were told a landslide was about to destroy you and your city?"

The king replied: "I would live righteously. There would be nothing else to do."

Gautam further asked: "Old age and death are rolling down upon you. What are you going to do?"

The king smiled and answered: "Live righteously."

Gautam Buddha taught that the aim of life was to escape from the petty hopes, fears and hatred which make people little-minded, and to become serene and happy by rising above them. Nothing was written down about him or his sayings until shortly before Ashoka's time, but then the tales began to accumulate as they were recounted in Buddhist monasteries where the monks gathered and lived. Gradually the Buddhist religion separated itself from Hinduism and spread to other countries – and Ashoka to an extent was responsible for this.

He was alert to new religious ideas and he must have met and talked to Buddhist followers. However, his conversion was not sudden, like St. Paul's on the road of Damascus, nor did he have an experience such as Gautam had when the right way to live became suddenly clear as he sat meditating one day under a Banyan tree. The great event in Ashoka's reign was the Kalinga War. The Kalinga War was to Ashoka what the Banyan tree was to Gautam Buddha.

Most men, when victorious, become so drunk with power that they will listen to good advice neither from statesmen nor prophets, but Ashoka was appalled at the contradiction between the cruelty he saw and the lessons of Buddhism he had learned. Ashoka's greatness can be measured by what he caused to be written on rocks after the victory. He got the inscriptions engraved so that any sons or great-grandsons that he might have would not think of gaining conquests but would live in peace and contentment. Ashoka denounced fame and glory and announce that to him the only glory was following Dhamma.

Towards the end of his reign, he kept contact with a large number of Asian countries, but instead of sending only the usual sort of envoys, he sent missionaries to explain Dhamma in the countries they visited. His influence as a wise ruler was therefore spread far more widely than if he had marched with his victorious armies. Later, Buddhism spread to Burma, Thailand and China, where a standard of humility for great ruler and a belief in serenity, goodness and a reverence for life, were accepted and have still not died out. It is doubtful whether there can ever be peace between countries unless this first lesson is learned: the power of rulers must be guided by kindness and wisdom. Although Emperor Ashoka appeared to be a failure, since his subjects gave up Buddhism and within fifty years his empire fell to pieces; he was a man whose influence, like that of Jesus' or Socrates', was extended by his death. (***792 words***)

Ans. PRECIS

Ashoka set an extraordinary example by making himself available at all times for consultation. He kept in touch with the details of administration, be it; the disputes over water rights and grazing rights, and the problem of money-lending. Gautama, the Buddha, who had lived nearly three hundred years earlier and Buddhism taught Ashoka the importance of the right way to live. Buddha taught that the aim of life was to escape from the petty hopes, fears and hatred which make people little-minded, and to become serene and happy by rising above them. Gradually the Buddhist religion separated itself from Hinduism and spread to other countries – and Ashoka to an extent was responsible for this. Ashoka sent Buddhist missionaries to Burma, Thailand and China to explain Dhamma and spread Buddhism. Ashoka was alert to new religious ideas; however, his conversion was not sudden, like St. Paul's on the road of Damascus. The great event in Ashoka's reign was the Kalinga War. The Kalinga War was to Ashoka what the Banyan tree was to Gautam Buddha. Most men, when victorious, become so drunk with power that they will listen to good advice neither from statesmen nor prophets, but Ashoka was appalled at the contradiction between the cruelty he saw and the lessons of Buddhism he had learned. Ashoka denounced fame and glory and announced that to him the only glory was following Dhamma. Although Emperor Ashoka appeared to be a failure, since his subjects gave up Buddhism and within fifty years his empire fell to pieces; he was a man whose influence, like that of Jesus' or Socrates', was extended by his death.(***272 words***)

Q 4. (a) Rewrite the following sentences after making necessary corrections. Do not make unnecessary changes in the original sentence: **1 × 10 = 10**

(i) Have you brought some mangoes?

(ii) The Ganga is the sacred river.

(iii) I and Chetan did all the work.

(iv) He said it himself.

(v) Blessed is he that has found a job.

(vi) He is much ill to do any work.

(vii) One of the boy was absent for a week.

(viii) Gopal came home lately.

(ix) She was sitting besides him.

(x) Our hoard is small and our hearts are large.

Ans. *(i) Have you brought any mangoes?*

(ii) The Ganga is a sacred river.

(iii) Chetan and I did all the work.

(iv) He said it to himself.

(v) Blessed is he who has found a job.

(vi) He is too ill to do any work.

(vii) One of the boys was absent for a week.

(viii) Gopal came home late.

(ix) She was sitting beside him.

(x) Our hoard is little and our hearts are large.

(b) Supply the missing words: **1 × 5 = 5**

(i) I am going away ________ the end of January.

(ii) Our flat is ________ the second floor of the building.

(iii) What time did they get ________ the hotel?

(iv) I've no idea who Tom Alter was. I've never heard ________ him.

(v) The problem is getting serious; we've to do something ________ it.

Ans. (i) I am going away <u>by/ towards</u> the end of January.

(ii) Our flat is <u>on</u> the second floor of the building.

(iii) What time did they get <u>into</u> the hotel?

(iv) I've no idea who Tom Alter was. I've never heard <u>about</u> him.

(v) The problem is getting serious; we've to do something <u>about</u> it.

(c) Use the correct forms of the verbs given in the brackets: **1 × 5 = 5**

(i) If you __________ a wallet in the street what would you do with it? (find)

(ii) We are late. The film __________ by the time we get to the cinema. (start)

(iii) What was wrong with you? Why __________ to the hospital? (go)

(iv) I am thinking __________ a house. (buy)

(v) She took a bottle from the bag she __________ all the way from home. (carry)

Ans. *(i) If you find a wallet in the street what would you do with it?*

(ii) We are late. The film will start by the time we get to the cinema.

(iii) What was wrong with you? Why did you go to the hospital? (go)

(iv) I am thinking to buy a house.

(v) She took a bottle from the bag she had carried all the way from home.

(d) Write the antonyms of the following: **1 × 5 = 5**

(i) **Boring** *Ans. Interesting*

(ii) **Accept** *Ans. Reject*

(iii) **Exit** *Ans. Enter*

(vi) **Misanthropic** ***Ans. Philanthropic***

(v) **Descent** *Ans. Ascent*

Q 5. (a) Rewrite the following sentences as directed without changing the meaning: **1 × 10 = 10**

(i) He said to him, "Is your name not Ahmad?" (Change into indirect speech)

(ii) Why did your brother write such a letter? (Change into passive voice)

(iii) No sooner did he enter the house than he took off his coat. (Use "as soon as")

(iv) Sohan doesn't smoke and he doesn't drink. (Use "neither ….. nor")

(v) We must eat or we cannot live. (Change into a simple sentence)

(vi) Your sister helped you to do the assignment, __________? (Add a question tag)

(vii) The doctor will see you today only if it is an emergency. (Use "unless")

(viii) You can borrow the book if you return it soon. (Use "provided that")

(ix) I can't explain the situation. It is too complicated. (Use "too ….. to"

(x) He owed his success to his father. (Change into a complex sentence)

Ans. *(i) He asked if his name was not Ahmad.*

(ii) *Why was such a letter written by your brother?*

(iii) *As soon as he entered the house, he took off his coat.*

(iv) *Sohan neither smokes nor drinks.*

(v) *We must eat to live.*

(vi) *Your sister helped you to do the assignment, did she not?*

(vii) *The doctor will not see you today unless it is an emergency.*

(viii) *You can borrow the book provided that you return it soon.*

(ix) *The situation is too complicated to be explained.*

(x) *He owed the reason of his success to his father.*

(b) Use the following words to make sentences that bring out their meaning clearly. Do not change the form of the words. (No marks will be given for vague and ambiguous sentences) : 1 × 5 = 5

(i) Altruist

(ii) Senility

(iii) Glib

(iv) Ostensible

(v) Tortuous

Ans. **(i)** Mother Teresa was an ***altruist*** and a philanthropist.

(ii) The old man was showing signs of ***senility.***

(iii) No one was convinced with his ***glib*** answers.

(iv) The ostensible reason Pankaj gave for his absence from the meeting was illness.

(v) The streets of the town are narrow, tortuous and inaccessible to four wheelers.

(c) Choose the appropriate word(s) to fill in the blanks: 1 × 5 = 5

(i) There are millions of stars in __________. (space/ the space)

(ii) Keats' poetry is full of __________ imagery. (sensual/ sensuous)

(iii) Leave aside the interest, she won't pay even the __________amount. (principle/ principal)

(iv) Research demands an __________ study of the subject. (intense/ intensive)

(v) This is not an __________ list at all but shows the kind of range that is available. (exhaustive/ exhausting)

Ans. **(i)** *There are millions of stars in* **space**.

(ii) *Keats' poetry is full of* **sensuous** *imagery.*

(iii) *Leave aside the interest, she won't pay even the* **principal** *amount.*

(iv) *Research demands an* **intensive** *study of the subject.*

(v) *This is not an* **exhaustive** *list at all but shows the kind of range that is available.*

(d) Use the following idioms/ phrases in sentences of your own to bring out their meaning clearly. Do not change the form of the words: 1 × 5 = 5

(i) Cold comfort

(ii) End in smoke

(iii) Feather one's nest

(iv) Incumbent upon

(v) Laugh in one's sleeve

Ans. ((i) A drop in the unemployment rate was ***cold comfort*** for those without a job.

(ii) Without funds, all his plans of starting a NGO ***ended in smoke.***

(iii) In the name of company's expansion, Mr. Sharma was ***feathering his own nest*** at the company's cost.

(iv) It is ***incumbent upon*** all the law abiding citizens to abide by the traffic rules.

(v) The mayor's opponents were ***laughing in their sleeves*** when a scam was attributed to him.

UPSC (MAIN) EXAM – 2019
ENGLISH
(Compulsory)

Time Allowed: 3 hours **Maximum Marks: 300**

Question Paper: Specific Instructions

Please read each of the following instructions carefully before attempting questions.

- *All questions are to be attempted.*
- *The number of marks carried by questions is indicated against it.*
- *Answers must be written in* **ENGLISH** *only.*
- *Word limit in questions, wherever specified, should be adhered to and if answered in much longer or shorter than the prescribed length, marks will be deducted.*
- *Any page or portion of the page left blank in the Question-cum-Answer Booklet must be clearly struck off.*

Candidates should attempt all questions.

The number of marks carried by each question is indicated at the end of the questions.

Answer must be written in English.

Q 1. Write an essay in about 600 words on any one of the following topics:

(a) ***Indian universities are Indian in their geographical locations only***

(b) Journalism has been rendered into sensationalism

(c) Information is not knowledge

(d) Even a layman can transform a society

ESSAY

Ans. ***<u>JOURNALISM HAS BEEN RENDERED INTO SENSATIONALISM</u>***

"Sensationalism is a type of editorial bias in mass media in which events and topics in news stories and piece are overhyped to present biased impressions on events, which may cause a manipulation to the truth of a story. Sensationalism may have reporting about generally insignificant matters and events that do not influence overall society and biased presentations of newsworthy topics in a trivial or tabloid manner contrary to the standards of professional journalism."

WIKIPEDIA

The credibility of Indian journalism is fast eroding, as the country's journalists have been criticized time and again for sensationalism. The way some media groups especially TV anchors and presenters manipulate the news and portray one-sided information has seen the country drop three places in the recent World Press Freedom Index. There have been instances such as Mumbai terror attack, film actor Sridevi's death, Aarushi murder case, etc where journalists virtually became prosecutor and judge by laying false accusations, creating a vicious atmosphere and generally sensationalizing events and issues. Rather than taking a cautious and principled stand on sensitive issues, they go all out in presenting an exaggerated and distorted picture resulting in social strife and law and order issues. This is what is known as "Yellow Journalism." The term came to be used in the mid-1890s to characterize the sensational journalism that used some yellow ink in the circulation war between Joseph Pulitzer's *New York World* and William Randolph Hearst's *New York Journal*. Today, sensationalism has become rampant and has taken the form of an epidemic in media circles. Compared to the visual media, the print media is comparatively subdued and responsible to some extent in its coverage. On the other hand, television in its frenzy to capture eyeballs, go to the extreme in sensationalism. The judiciary has taken note of this and in *Rajgopal v. State of Tamil Nadu* the Supreme Court has observed that a citizen has a fundamental right to safeguard the privacy of his own and his family. This law, though known to everyone is not followed in letter and spirit by the Indian media.

In the mad race for more viewership/ TRPs, television channels and related media resort to sensationalism and twisted, manufactured news. Although print media doesn't need to bother about TRPs, they have a phenomenon called paid news which is endemic and affects media across the board. It was earlier used only by business houses but the growing reach has ensured all sorts of clients are available to buy news from media houses.

The impact of media is really sometimes a double edged sword. Excessive coverage or hype or distortion of sensitive news has led to communal riots at times. The illiterates are more prone to provocations than the literates. Constant repetition of news, especially sensational news creates problems for the incumbent government and security agencies. Commercialization has created a stiff competition among various media houses. In order to outdo each other, the various media including print, audio and visual often crosses the boundaries of decency and indulges in cheap journalism, titillation and news and articles that are provocative and sensational. Media experts say this is one of the means of attracting readers and viewers to a particular newspaper or television channel. We can only hope that with the passage of time, media would become a more mature and responsible entity. Yet, it is to be admitted that for all its negatives, media in India has also a positive impact on our society. Their readiness to take issues of social importance like Swachch Bharat, women's health and hygiene, pollution and environmental issues have created a visible impact in society.

Q 2. Read carefully the passage given below and write your answers to the questions that follow in clear, correct and concise language: 15 × 5 = 75

History has a great variety of definitions and applications. In the broadest sense, it considers every action and every thought that man has had since his first appearance and records every significant advance or recession. It attempts to evaluate all the developments in science, in art, in literature, in philosophy, in architecture, in sociology, in politics, in war, in religion, and in law. It sketches as complete a picture as possible of everything that has influenced man directly or indirectly.

History, more than any other subject, has been enslaved and distorted for selfish purposes. Members of the clergy have used it to glorify and to promote the interests of the church, statesmen have utilized it to sway masses, and writers have distorted facts to substantiate their conclusions. War spirit has been kindled through undue emphasis upon facts, if not falsification of them. The historian is likely to exaggerate the history of his own country – sometimes unintentionally – because of his environment and sometimes in order to facilitate the sale of his book. In all countries, there are zealots in responsible positions who cannot bear to have their fatherhood criticized. Truth is frequently sacrificed at the altar of patriotism. Henry C. Lea, an outstanding American historian, declared that history should be "a serious attempt to ascertain the severest truth as to the past and set it forth without fear or favour." Michelet, a famous French historian, believed that "sacrilege and the mocking of false goods are the historian's first duty, his indispensable instrument for re-establishing the truth."

The slight progress that we have made in the direction indicated by Lea and Michelet is rather discouraging, but there is a trend toward a broader and more inclusive point of view in the writing and teaching of history. World history, correctly interpreted, puts the individual state in the proper perspective and lessens the dangers of excessive nationalism. History has become more than war and politics. To make the story complete, the historian of the new school makes use of the work of the ethnologist, the anthropologist, the geographer, and archaeologist, the geologist, the psychologist, the astronomer, the zoologist, the biologist, the chemist, the sociologist and the economist. He is concerned with man's cultural advances and his society, as well as with charters, constitutions, and wars.

There are dangers, as well as virtues, in the vast scope of the "new history". Overpopularization and underspecialization tend to cheapen history and to destroy some of its qualities as a basic and sober study. There are decided advantages in the comprehension of the broad scope of history, but, in addition, the student should be able to appreciate the depth of the subject. Years of research have been spent and volumes have been written on a single topic. Without these specialized works, surveys would be of no particular value. However, some of the historians of the "new history" have sacrificed important fundamental facts in order to make a chronicle of heroic persons and romantic occurrence. They have overstepped the point where history and fiction should meet. The historian should make his description of the past lifelike hence, he should include grim realities as well as romantic incidents.

One of the important aspects of the "new history" is the emphasize upon man's cultural developments, popularly termed civilization. Civilization is difficult to define and evaluate. Just where it began and where man's actions and thoughts became human is impossible to determine. Man, like animals, has senses but some are less acutely developed; man has emotions, most of which are present, but latent, in animals. Comfort seems to be the chief goal of the lower forms of animal life, but man pushes beyond that towards something that he has difficulty in defining. This intangible something maybe called civilization. Professor Lynn Thorndike believes that civilization "is the product of our higher qualities as exercised first by original and superior individuals and then accepted or followed by a sufficient number of human beings to make it a social fact." Buckle held that moral and intellectual progress is the basis of civilization. Emerson believed that civilization is a progress and Bertrand Russell, a modern philosopher , thinks that it is the progress and predominance of science. Perhaps we can agree that acknowledge of nature, progress in art, an ethical code, a government, and a degree of material prosperity are essential in any form of civilized society. Civilization became possible when chaos and insecurity were minimized. Curiosity and constructiveness were encouraged when fear was overcome and man turned his attention toward the understanding and embellishment of life.

(a) *Why does the author consider history an all-inclusive area of study?*

(b) *According to the author, how has history suffered distortions and why?*

(c) *How does the author describe the new school of historians?*

(d) What are the dangers associated with "new history"?

(e) Why is it difficult to define and evaluate civilization?

Ans. (a) The author considers history an all-inclusive area of study because it considers every action and every thought that man has had since his first appearance and records every significant advance or recession. It also attempts to evaluate all the developments in science, in art, in literature, in philosophy, in architecture, in sociology, in politics, in war, in religion, and in law. It attempts to sketch as complete a picture as possible of everything that has influenced man directly or indirectly.

(b) History has been enslaved and distorted for selfish purposes. Members of the clergy have used it to glorify and to promote the interests of the church, statesmen have utilized it to sway masses, and writers have distorted facts to substantiate their conclusions. War spirit has been kindled through undue emphasis upon facts, if not falsification of them. The historian is likely to exaggerate the history of his own country – sometimes unintentionally – because of his environment and sometimes in order to facilitate the sale of his book. In all countries, there are zealots in responsible positions who cannot bear to have their fatherhood criticized. Truth is frequently sacrificed at the altar of patriotism.

(c) The historian of the new school makes use of the work of the ethnologist, the anthropologist, the geographer, and archaeologist, the geologist, the psychologist, the astronomer, the zoologist, the biologist, the chemist, the sociologist and the economist. He is concerned with man's cultural advances and his society, as well as with charters, constitutions, and wars.

(d) There are dangers, as well as virtues, in the vast scope of the "new history". Overpopularization and underspecialization tend to cheapen history and to destroy some of its qualities as a basic and sober study.

(e) Civilization is difficult to determine and define. Just where it began and where man's actions and thoughts became human is impossible to determine. The comfort seems to be the chief goal of the lower forms of animal life, but man pushes beyond that towards something that he has difficulty in defining. This intangible something may be called civilization and this intangible makes civilization indefinable and indeterminable.

Q 3. Make a précis of the following passage in about one-third of its length. Do not give a title to it. The précis should be written in your own language. **75**

In Hind Swaraj (1909), a text which is often privileged as an authentic statement of his ideology, Gandhi offered a civilizational concept of Indian nation. The Indians constituted a nation or praja, he asserts, since the pre-Islamic days. The ancient Indian civilization – "unquestionably the best" – was the fountainhead of Indian nationality, as it had an immense assimilative power of absorbing foreigner of different creed who made this country their own. This civilization, which was "sound at the foundation" and which always tended "to elevate the moral being" had "nothing to learn" from the "godless" modern civilization that only "propagated immorality". Industrial capitalism, which was the essence of this modern civilization, was held responsible for all conflicts of interest, for it divorced economic activities from moral concerns and thus provided imperatives for imperial aggression. Indians themselves were responsible for their enslavement, as they embraced capitalism and its associated legal and political structures. "The English have not taken India; we have given it to them." And now the railways, lawyers and doctors, Gandhi believed were

impoverishing the country. His remedy for this national infliction was moral and utopian. Indians must eschew greed and lust for consumption and revert to village based self-sufficient economy of the ancient times. On the other hand, parliamentary democracy – the foundational principle of Western liberal – political system and therefore view the general will of the people, but of the political parties, which represented specific interests and constricted the moral autonomy of parliamentarians in the name of party discipline. So for him it was not enough to achieve independence and then perpetuate "English rule without the Englishmen"; it was also essential to evolve an Indian alternative to Western liberal political structures. His alternative was a concept of popular sovereignty where each individual controls or restrains her/ his own self and this was Gandhi's subtle distinctions between self-rule and mere home rule. "Such Swaraj", Gandhi asserted, "has to be experienced by each one for himself." If this was difficult to attain, Gandhi refused to consider it as just a "dream". "To believe that what has not occurred in history will not occur at all". Gandhi replied to his critic, "is to argue disbelief in the dignity of man." His technique to achieve it was satyagraha, which he defined as truth force or soul force. In more practical terms, it meant civil disobedience – but something more than that. It was based on the premise of superior moral power of the protestors capable of changing the heart of the oppressor through a display of moral strength. Non-violence or ahimsa was the cardinal principle of his message which was non-negotiable under all circumstances.

It is not perhaps strictly correct to say that Gandhi was rejecting modernity as a package. Anthony Parel notes in his introduction to Hind Swaraj that this text is presented in the genre of a dialogue between a reader and an editor, "a very modern figure", with Gandhi taking on this role. Throughout his career he made utmost use of the print media, editing Indian Opinion during his South African days, and then Young India and Harijan became the major communicators of his ideas. And he travelled extensively by railways while organizing his campaigns. Yet, by offering an ideological critique of the Western civilization in its modern phase, Gandhi was effectively contesting the moral legitimacy of the Raj that rested on a stated assumption of superiority of the West.

It will be, however, misleading to suggest that Gandhi was introducing Indians to an entirely new kind of politics. And so far as mass mobilization was concerned, the Home Rule Leagues of Tilak and Annie Besant prepared the ground for the success of Gandhi's initial satyagraha movements. Indeed, when in 1914, Tilak was released from prison and Annie Besant, the World President of the Theosophical Society, then stationed in Madras, joined the Congress, they wanted to steer Indian politics to an almost similar direction. But although Tilak was readmitted to Congress in 1915 due to Besant's intervention, they failed to reactivate the party out of its almost decade-long inertia.

Gandhi succeeded in uniting both the moderates and extremists on a common political platform. In the divided and contestable space of India politics, he could effectively claim for himself a centrist position, because he alienated neither and tactically combined the goal of the moderates with the means of the extremists. He adopted the moderates goal of swaraj, but was "delightfully vague" (to borrow Nehru's expression) about its definition, as any specific definition, he knew, would alienate one or the other group. So each group could interpret it in their own ways. His method of satyagraha looked very much like the passive resistance of the extremists; but his insistence on non-violence alleviated the fears of the moderates and other propertied classes, apprehensive or agitational politics. There was also a rift in the Muslim community around this time, between the Aligarh old guards and the younger generation of Muslim leaders. Gandhi aligned himself with the younger leaders by supporting the khilafat issue. He highlighted its anti-British aspects and underplayed its pan-Islamic tendencies, and thus for the first time united the Hindus and the Muslims in a combined battle against the British.

Ans. **PRECIS**

Mahatma Gandhi in his seminal book Hind Swaraj expounded the civilizational concept of the Indian nation. Ancient Indian civilization had the assimilative power of absorbing diverse foreign creeds capable of elevating the moral fabric of its people. Indian civilization, according to Gandhi was superior to modern western capitalistic industrial civilization which he considered bereft of godliness and marked by alienation between a person's economic activities and moral concerns.

According to Gandhi, by embracing capitalism and Western values blindly we have only nurtured greed, lust & mindless consumption. In the process, we have impoverished the nation and hence even in the post colonial times, the hegemony of English sustains. The alternative to western civilization, he proposes is the self-rule (Swaraj), which is based on the soul force and emphasizes the dignity of man. This self rule can be realized by Satyagraha (civil disobedience) and ahimsa (Non violence).

It is not correct to say that Gandhi rejected modernity completely. He was dependent on such modern technologies as print media for the publication and dissemination of his ideas and thoughts. Gandhiji rejected the western civilization and legitimacy of the Raj only on the basis of it's over exalted & over glorified superiority.

It would also be incorrect to say that Gandhi was new to politics. His Satyagraha would not have gained momentum in mobilising masses, had Annie Besant and Tilak not prepared the ground for that. Gandhi was successful in uniting and mobilising moderates and extremists, Hindus and Muslims, men and women of all hues in the fight against British. For doing so he heavily depended on his Satyagraha or "Passive Resistance". Non-violence or ahimsa was the cardinal principle of his message which was non-negotiable under all circumstances.

Q 4. (a) Rewrite the following sentences after making necessary corrections. Do not make unnecessary changes in the original sentence. 1 × 10 = 10

(i) *The manager was angry upon the employee.*

(ii) *One of the answer was wrong.*

(iii) *You should buy new furnitures for your house.*

(iv) *They pitched the tent besides the lake.*

(v) *The wood-cutter was falling the trees in the forest.*

(vi) *The hens had stopped lying eggs.*

(vii) *The mother sings until the child does not go to sleep.*

(viii) *There was no one to look at the children in the hostel.*

(ix) *The reply is awaited for.*

(x) *The chairman flew the flag.*

Ans. (i) The manager was angry with the employee.

(ii) One of the answers was wrong.

(iii) You should buy new furniture for your house.

(iv) They pitched the tent beside the lake.

(v) The wood-cutter was felling the trees in the forest.

(vi) The hens had stopped laying eggs.

(vii) The mother sings until the child goes to sleep.

(viii) There was no one to look after the children in the hostel.

(ix) The reply is awaited.

(x) The chairman unfurled the flag.

(b) Supply the missing words: **1 × 5 = 5**

(i) *Hard work is telling ___________ your health.*

(ii) *The book is hard to come ___________.*

(iii) *The lady is the heir ___________ a large estate.*

(iv) *I was disgusted ___________ his behaviour.*

(v) *He did not agree ___________ my proposal.*

Ans. (i) Hard work is telling **on** your health.

(ii) The book is hard to come **by**.

(iii) The lady is the heir **to** a large estate.

(iv) I was disgusted **with** his behaviour.

(v) He did not agree **to** my proposal.

(c) Use the correct forms of the verbs given in brackets: **1× 5 = 5**

(i) *The child (steal) the show last evening.*

(ii) *The man (read) the newspaper when I entered the room.*

(iii) *The teacher said that the sun (be) stationary.*

(iv) *You might (ask) her name.*

(v) *He (suffer) from fever for five days.*

Ans. (i) The child ***stole*** the show last evening.

(ii) The man ***was reading*** the newspaper when I entered the room.

(iii) The teacher said that the sun ***is*** stationary.

(iv) You might have ***asked*** her name.

(v) He ***suffered*** from fever for five days.

(d) Write the antonyms of the following: **1× 5 = 5**

(i) *Noble* ***Ans.*** Ignoble

(ii) *Loyal* ***Ans.*** Disloyal

(iii) *Straight* ***Ans.*** Crooked

(iv)	*Partial*	**Ans.**	Partial
(v)	*Sterile*	**Ans.**	Fertile

Q 5. (a) Rewrite the following sentences as directed, without changing the meaning: **1× 10 = 10**

(i) *The old man said, "I have been visiting this temple for many years." (Change into indirect speech).*

(ii) *Allow the pilgrims to pass. (Change into passive voice).*

(iii) *No sooner had she heard the news that she fainted. (Use 'as soon as').*

(iv) *He was not intelligent. He was not industrious. (Rewrite the sentence using 'neither … nor').*

(v) *When the dog is sleeping, let it be peacefully. (Turn into a simple sentence).*

(vi) *He only laughed. He did not do anything else. (Rewrite the sentence using 'but').*

(vii) *The evil practice will continue if the government does not adopt stringent measures. (Use 'unless').*

(viii) *He was allowed to go so that he might see his ailing mother. (Use 'in order that').*

(ix) *The burden was too heavy for the old man to carry. (Remove 'too').*

(x) *She was frightened by the man's glaring eyes. (Turn into a complex sentence).*

Ans. (i) The old man told that he had been visiting that for many years.

(ii) The pilgrims should be allowed to pass.

(iii) As soon as she heard the news, she fainted.

(iv) He was neither intelligent nor industrious.

(v) Let the dog sleep peacefully.

(vi) He only laughed but did not do anything else.

(vii) The evil practice will continue unless the government adopts stringent measures.

(viii) He was allowed to go in order that he might see his ailing mother.

(ix) The burden was so heavy that the old man couldn't carry it.

(x) She was frightened when she saw the man's glaring eyes.

(b) Use the following words to make sentences that bring out their meaning clearly. Do not change the form of the words. (No marks will be given for vague and ambiguous sentences). **1× 5 = 5**

(i) *Disdain*

(ii) *Contagious*

(iii) *Stagger*

(iv) *Insular*

(v) *Didactic*

Ans. (i) Disdain – She expressed ***disdain*** at the adulation the industry gives to beauty over talent .

(ii) Contagious – Chicken pox is a ***contagious*** disease.

(iii) Stagger – He was ***staggering*** because he was heavily drunk.

(iv) Insular – The ***insular*** man had lived on a deserted island for several years and so he was not communicative

(v) Didactic – His way of teaching is too ***didactic***.

(c) Choose the appropriate word to fill in the blanks: **1× 5 = 5**

(i) He remained __________ to his seat. (glowed/ glued)

(ii) You should wear __________ garments in summer. (lose/ loose)

(iii) He __________ before the boss. (coward/ cowered)

(iv) The player was crying __________. (foul/ fowl)

(v) The chief was __________ of the latest development. (apprised/ appraised)

Ans. (i) He remained **glued** to his seat.

(ii) You should wear **loose** garments in summer.

(iii) He **cowered** before the boss.

(iv) The player was crying **foul**.

(v) The chief was **apprised** of the latest development.

(d) Use the following idioms/ phrases in sentences of your own to bring out their meaning clearly. Do not change the form of the words: **1× 5 = 5**

(i) With a view to

(ii) Go berserk

(iii) Cut adrift

(iv) At sea

(v) Ins and outs

Ans. (i) With a view to – He put fencing all around the field with a view to protect it from stray animals.

(ii) Go berserk – Some of the spectators went berserk when India defeated Pakistan.

(iii) Cut adrift – English art became insular and in the process cut adrift from the European mainstream.

(iv) At sea – He was at sea when the guest started discussing quantum physics during dinner.

(v) Ins and Outs – His friend is keen to understand the ins and outs of politics.

UPSC (MAIN) EXAM – 2018
ENGLISH
(Compulsory)

Time allowed: 3 hours **Maximum Marks: 300**

Question Paper: Specific Instructions

Please read each of the following instructions carefully before attempting questions.

- *All questions are to be attempted.*
- *The number of marks carried by questions is indicated against it.*
- *Answers must be written in* **ENGLISH** *only.*
- *Word limit in questions, wherever specified, should be adhered to and if answered in much longer or shorter than the prescribed length, marks will be deducted.*
- *Any page or portion of the page left blank in the Question-cum-Answer Booklet must be clearly struck off.*

Candidates should attempt all questions.

The number of marks carried by each question is indicated at the end of the questions.

Answer must be written in English.

Q 1. Write an essay in about 600 words on any one the following topics:100

(a) ***Impact of Westernization on the Indian Family***

(b) Literature Mirrors Society

(c) Women in Indian Politics

(d) Rural Urban Divide in India

ESSAY

Ans. ***LITERATURE MIRRORS SOCIETY***

Literature is the garden of wisdom ***James Ellis***

The history of literature is history of mind ***W H Prescott***

Literature is one of the most interesting and significant expressions of humanity ***P T Baruman***

The recently released biopic *Manto* which chronicles the life and times of the famous Urdu author Saadat Hasan Manto vindicates the statement that literature mirrors society. All the literary creations of Manto referred to in the film – *Khol Do, Thanda Ghosht, Toba Tek Singh* and others are the potent portrayal of harsh realities and bleeding wounds of people of both the wounded nations of India and Pakistan. The literary creations of Manto bring home the observation of Alexander Solzhenitsyn, *"Literature becomes the living memory of a nation."*

Literature and society mirror each other and impact each other. Literature inscribes the times and circumstances in permanent form. It puts in black and white, the senses and sensibilities, emotions and turmoil of its characters. Literature shapes and builds human nature, behaviour, habits, traits, customs, and traditions, agonies and ecstasies. Nicholas Kristof explains the value of literature in these words, *"Literature seems to offer lessons in human nature that help us decode the world around us and be better friends."*

Gao Xingjian has beautifully explained the true value of literature in these words, *"it's in literature that true life can be found. It is under the mask of fiction that you can tell the truth."* Literature makes and creates reality out of fiction and fiction out of reality. It is the garden of life portraying life in its variegated colours of good and evil, bold and beautiful. This aspect of literature has been captured by Roberto Bolano in these words, *"Literature is a vast forest and masterpieces are the lakes, the towering trees or strange trees, the lovely, eloquent flowers, the hidden caves but a forest is also made up of ordinary trees, patches of grass, puddles, clinging vines, mushrooms and little wild flowers."*

If literature is the expression of the thoughts of the society, books are the specimens of conversations of an age, presented in the spirit of the era's flavor and spirit. Great literature brings forth stark and unpleasant truths and that is why Gao Xingjian said, *"Literature is subservient to nothing but truth."* It is also such a potent weapon to weave the past, present and future into one single thread and weave the different colours of life on the canvas .

C S Lewis says, *"Literature adds to reality, it simply doesn't describe it. It enriches the necessary competencies that daily life requires and provides; and in this respect, it irrigates the deserts that our lives have already become."*

Literature makes us feel the drama, romance, betrayal, humour and almost all other feelings that we go through life or see around us.

Literature is also thought provoking; it allows us to raise questions and give us deep understanding of issues, situations, conflicts, human nature, behaviour, eccentricities, and idiosyncrasies. It provides insights into the minds of other human beings, into the mind of authors and into the minds of characters. This is how Jhumpa Lahiri explains the impact of literature on society, *"Literature is such a profound and deep way to look into someone else's life, his mind, his hopes and thoughts. Books have opened so many doors for me, taking me to places where my normal life and its finite limits could never have."*

Literature also allows us to question our most prominent beliefs, values, morality, and the infinite when we read all time classics like *Siddhartha*, *Brothers Karamazov*, *Le Miserables* and many others.

If literature is a true reflection of a society, it does very well to influence the younger generations and guide them for tomorrow. Literature has helped in shaping civilizations and changing political systems.

Finally, in the era of television and internet, when reading habits are rapidly declining, it is great literature that can resurrect the habit of reading among children and youth of the present generation.

Q 2. Read carefully the passage given below and write your answers to the questions that follow in clear, correct and concise language: 15 × 5 = 75

It is often said that the Ghaznavid and Ghurid soldiers regarded death in a war against infidels a martyrdom in the cause of Islam. But it is more likely that the real draw was the attraction of plunder, the likes of which they had not seen in campaigns in more arid lands. For Indian commanders, apart from plunder, battles incorporated the niceties of a sport with its own rules of play. Immortalizing the heroism of kings in battle, the poets and bards empathized the rules of war and chivalry. To apply the chivalric code in minor campaigns may have relieved the tedium of war, but the campaigns against the Ghurids were of an entirely different nature and this may not have been realized initially. Notions of honour and devotion were often placed above expediency, and gradually the astrologically determined auspicious moment for attach took precedence over strategy and tactics. Inflated claims to valour, such as the hero who could defeat a thousand warriors simultaneously, began to enter the rhetoric of courtly literature.

The organization of Indian armies added to their weakness. Each army had as its permanent core the standing army, but many of the soldiers were local levies or soldiers supplied by Samantas where this was part of the latter's obligation to the suzerain. In addition, mercenaries were a visible section of the armies of these times. Such a collection of soldiers had not always been trained to fight as a consolidated army. It was possibly also the dispersed of the army that gave it a license to plunder indiscriminately. Villagers were harassed and looted by armies on the march, particularly if the campaign coincided with the harvesting of the crop, as it often did. For peasants and merchants, war was a nightmare that disrupted the routine of earning a livelihood. Laying waste vast tracts of inhabited and cultivated land, merely because it was part of the enemy's territory, was a proud boast attributed to Prithviraj Chauhan on defeating the Chandela ruler.

Historians have sometimes commented, perhaps more from hindsight, on why Indian rulers did not make a conjoint effort through the centuries to defend the North-Western passes. Time and again invaders came through these passes, yet little was done to prevent this, the defence of the region lying arbitrarily in the hands of the local rulers. It appears the construction of a series of fortification along the passes was not thought feasible. Perhaps the need for defence was not given priority, the area being viewed as a natural frontier. Alternatively, given the mountainous terrain, the only routes for pastoralists and caravan were through the passes and it was therefore thought better to leave them open. The local kings and chief who controlled the passes derived an income from this trade. There would have been familiarity too with those coming across the passes and therefore a slow recognition that sometimes friendliness had turned into hostility. The effectiveness of mountains as a frontier was also thwarted by the many occasions when the Punjab was conquered from across the borders or was involved in the politicos of Afghanistan and Central Asia. This closeness militated against a properly focused perspective on political developments across the borderlands and in Central Asia.

Invasions by outsiders are known in many parts of the world: the Huns attacking Rome, the Arabs invading Spain or the Spanish and Portuguese conquering Latin America. The potentialities of invasions were recognised only in Hindsight. These invasions were mounted by alien peoples who were little known, if at all, to the societies they invaded. But the Turks had been a contiguous people, familiar from trade in horses and other commodities and from the Turkish mercenaries employed in some Indian Armies. However, the historical scene in Central Asia and West Asia had now changed, with new political ambitions after the rise of Islam. For the rulers of Northern India, to recognize this would have required an understanding of a wider range of politics beyond the areas enclosed by the immediate frontiers. This does not appear to have been an Indian concern. Indians who travelled to different parts of Asia on a variety of assignments wrote little about what they observed, remaining silent on the politics of other lands. It was almost as if the exterior landscape was irrelevant. Political interests therefore tended to be parochial. This marks a striking contrast to the world of the Chinese and the Arabs, both made aware of distant places through the detailed accounts of travelers and traders. The Arabs had a fascination for the geography of other lands and the Chinese were wary of happenings in their neighbourhood in Central Asia.

Alberuni, in the opening chapter of this book, suggests other reasons for this lack of recording observations concerning the wider perception of the world, which one may or may not agree with: "The Hindus believe that there is no country but theirs, or nation like theirs, no king like theirs, no religion like theirs, no science like theirs ...... They are by nature niggardly in communicating what they know, and they take the greatest possible care to withhold it from men of another caste from among their own people, still more of course from any foreigner".

(a) *What was then nature of campaigns against Ghurids?*

Ans. *The campaigns against the Ghurids were of an entirely different nature. Notions of honour and devotion were often placed above expediency, and gradually the astrologically determined auspicious moment for attack took precedence over strategy and tactics. Indeed, claims to valour, such as the hero who could defeat a thousand warriors simultaneously, began to enter the rhetoric of courtly literature.*

(b) According to the passage "the Indian rulers did not find it necessary to fortify the North-Western Pass". Why?

Ans. *The Indian rulers didn't find it necessary to fortify the north western pass as they thought that fortifications along the passes are not feasible. Moreover, passes were considered as a natural frontier.*

(c) Explain the statement "The potentialities of invasions were recognised only in hindsight".

Ans. *The statement means that the repercussions and complications were realised by the invaded societies and rulers after they suffered invasion. They had no forethought of the consequences of war in advance.*

(d) Give your critical observations on Alberuni's comments on Hindus.

Ans. *Alberuni believed that the Hindus suffered from superiority complex with regard to their nation and rulers. There were no exchanges taking place between the intercaste people, and almost none with foreigners. These remarks/ observations about Hindus seem prejudiced and demeaning too.*

(e) Enumerate the major view points of the given passage.

Ans. *The key ideas/ view points of the given passage is about the invasions that this country and its people suffered from in the past. The passage also highlights the divisive tendencies and closed mindedness of Indian rulers who, in view of their petty interests compromised with the safety and security of the nation.*

Q 3. Make a precis of the following passage in about one-third of its length. Do not give a title to it. The precis should be written in your own words: 75

The Renaissance in India was not like the Renaissance in Europe. It was not a return to India of the past. It was essentially, a matter of spirit which produced striking changes in the realm of religion, society and culture along with a demand for natural regeneration. There arose a new self-consciousness among the people of India. The soul of India began to unfold itself and break the shackles of the past. It is maintained that the Renaissance in India stirred the Indian soul to its very depth and Modern India owes everything to the Renaissance which was followed by reformation movements all over India. It also paved the way to national regeneration. The spirit of Renaissance and the subsequent reform movements affected almost all the aspects of national life. There were new developments in religious, social and political life. There were new trends in the fields of education, literature, fine arts and science.

The view of Sir Jadunath Sarkar is that the Indian Renaissance was at first an intellectual awakening which profoundly affected our literature, education thought and art. In the next succeeding generation, it became a moral force and reformed the Indian society and religion. In the third generation it brought about the economic modernization of India and ultimately political emancipation.

In his book entitled, "The Renaissance in India", Sri Aurobindo had attempted an analysis of the Renaissance in India. He points out that the eighteenth and early nineteenth centuries in India were periods of political decline, defeat and anarchy which practically killed the creative spirit in religion and art. India began to imitate Europe and forgot her own achievements in the past. However, the life-breath of the nation moved as a subordinate undercurrent in the religious movements of Bengal and Punjab, in the political aspiration of Maharashtra and the literary activity of Bengal.

Sri Aurobindo points out that the Renaissance in India in the nineteenth century had three aspects. In the first place, it aimed at a recovery of the old spiritual gospel contained in the sacred books of the country. The researches of European Indologists helped the people in the West and India to understand and appreciate the achievements of the Indians in the past. Philosophers and thinkers like Schopenhauer, Emerson, Thoreau and Royce highly praised India's wisdom in the past. Indian saints and mystic leaders in India also helped the same process.

Secondly, this re-invigorated spirituality inspired fresh activity in the fields of philosophy, literature, art, etc. Thirdly, an attempt was made to deal in an original way with modern problems in the light of the new inspiration.

Sri Aurobindo did not compare the Indian Renaissance with the European Renaissance of the fifteenth century. He compared it with the Celtic Renaissance when Ireland wanted to go back to the older culture after a long period of British domination. In his analysis of the Indian Renaissance, Sri Aurobindo put great emphasis on the recovery of the spiritual tradition and heritage of the past. According to him, the establishment of new religious sects in India was a central event in the Indian Renaissance. The Brahmo Samaj, the Arya Samaj, Ramkrishna Paramhans and Vivekananda, the neo-Vaishanavism of Bengal and the Renaissance in Islam tried to go back to the past and recover the light of old wisdom. Sri Aurobindo referred to the cosmopolitanism, eclecticism, religious rationalism and logic of the Brahmo Samaj. Of all the leaders of the Renaissance in India, Dayananda appealed most to Sri Aurobindo. He considered him as a unique personality which created a Vigorous Aryan manhood in India. Aurobindo found a national instinct in the reliance of Dayananda on Vedic wisdom. To quote Aurobindo, Dayananda "brings back an old Aryan element into the national character". Aurobindo gave credit to the Theosophical Society for getting some recognition in the West for some of the psychic, occult and esoteric achievements of the old Hindus. According to Aurobindo, Ramakrishna Paramhans was "the man who had the greatest influence and has done the most to regenerate Bengal". Vivekananda proclaimed to the world that India was awake not only to exist but also to conquer. In India itself, Vivekananda was a leader who wanted "preservation by reconstruction". Aurobindo also referred to the achievement of J.C. Bose and Rabindranath Tagore in the field of Indian Renaissance. Aurobindo believed that the spiritual and intellectual advance of India was bound to come. To quote him, "The Renaissance in India is as inevitable as the rising of tomorrow's Sun and Renaissance of a great nation of three hundred millions with so peculiar a temperament, such unique traditions and ideas of life, so powerful an intelligence and so great a mass of potential energies cannot but be one of the most formidable phenomena of the modern world".

Ans. PRECIS

Unlike the Renaissance in Europe, Indian Renaissance was essentially an inward looking process of spirit which produced striking changes in the realm of religion, society and culture along with a demand for natural regeneration.

Due to the effect of various reformation movements, renaissance in India stirred a new self-consciousness among the Indian people and resulted in new trends in the field of education, literature, fine arts and science. Sir Jadhunthsarkar defined the Indian renaissance in terms of a spiritual awakening, a moral force, economic modernization and political emancipation. Sri Aurobindo articulated the Renaissance in India as a vibrant force profoundly impacting the lives of the people primarily in Bengal, Panjab and Maharashtra. To him, renaissance was a force that countered political decline, defeat, anarchy and blind imitation to Europe rampant in the 18th and early 19th centuries in India. Sri Aurobindo likened Indian renaissance with the Celtic revival of the old culture of Ireland that suffered British domination for a quite long. Sri Aurobindo also underscored the salience of the outstanding ideas and ideals of the Brahmo Samaj, Arya Samaj and the intervention of Ramakrishna Paramahamsa and Vivekananda in the making of Indian renaissance. Above all, Swami Dayanand's appeal to return to Vedic wisdom, bringing back of Aryan elements in the building of national character and Rabindranath Tagore's literary-spiritual-cultural contributions, were considered by Aurobindo as seminal forces in the fostering of Indian renaissance. Sri Aurobindo also believed that renaissance as the most formidable force that led to advances in spiritual and intellectual awakening in the modern India, was bound to occur.

Q 4. (a) Rewrite the following sentences after making necessary corrections. Do not make unnecessary changes in the original sentence: 1 × 10 = 10

(i) *He died with fever.*

Ans. He died of fever.

(ii) Ram acted with my proposal.

Ans. Ram acted on my proposal.

(iii) She quarreled against me over the property issue.

Ans. She quarreled with me over the property issue.

(iv) Be careful for your mother's health.

Ans. Be careful about your mother's health.

(v) A Sikh, tall than any of his comrades, rushed forward.

Ans. A Sikh, taller than any of his comrades, rushed forward.

(vi) ***They cheated each another.***

Ans. They cheated each other.

(vii) ***Old father looks to his children.***

Ans. An old father looks to his children.

(viii) Many a man have been ruined by speculation.

Ans. Many men have been ruined by speculation.

(ix) ***Let him and I go together.***

Ans. Let him and me go together.

(x) ***The priest was very kind for all of us.***

Ans. The priest was very kind to all of us.

(b) Supply the missing words: **1 × 5 = 5**

(i) *The boy cannot cope ________ the pressure in the school.*

Ans. The boy cannot cope ***with*** the pressure in the school.

(ii) *Do not take law ________ your own hands.*

Ans. Do not take law *into* your own hands.

(iii) *The criminal was whisked ________ to the court.*

Ans. The criminal was whisked *away* to the court.

(iv) *I want to push ________ as soon as I finish my work.*

Ans. I want to push ***it*** as soon as I finish my work.

(v) *The girl ________ into depression two years ago.*

Ans. The girl ***went*** into depression two years ago.

(c) Use the correct forms of the verbs in brackets: **1× 5 = 5**

(i) *Her path was ________ with flowers. (strew)*

Ans. Her path was ***strewn*** with flowers.

(ii) *He had ________ his speech before we arrived. (begin)*

Ans. He had **begun** his speech before we arrived.

(iii) *The book has ________ the test of time. (stand)*

Ans. The book has ***stood*** the test of time.

(iv) *Recently the price of petrol has ________ up. (go)*

Ans. Recently the price of petrol has ***gone*** up.

(v) *The old beggar was ________ by a mad dog. (bite)*

Ans. The old beggar was **bitten** by a mad dog.

(d) Write the antonyms of the following: **1× 5 = 5**

(i) *Sagacious* ***Ans.*** Duffer

(ii) *Attenuate* ***Ans.*** Aggravate

(iii)	*Bawdy*	**Ans.**	Decent
(iv)	*Dormant*	**Ans.**	Active
(v)	*Dunce*	**Ans.**	Sensible

Q 5. (a) Rewrite the following sentences as directed without changing the meaning: **1× 10 = 10**

(i) *Rabi said, "I'll eat rice for lunch today". (Change into an indirect speech)*

Ans. Rabi said that she would eat rice for lunch that day.

(ii) *The man was running the shop for long. (Change into passive voice)*

Ans. The shop was being run by the man for long.

(iii) *He was in Delhi. He did not meet his friend. (Rewrite by using 'though')*

Ans. Though he was in Delhi, yet he didn't meet his friend.

(iv) *I landed at the airport. It started raining. (Rewrite by using 'no sooner')*

Ans. No sooner did I land at the airport, than it started raining.

(v) *Thought we were under the British rule we had a rich cultural heritage. (Change into a simple sentence)*

Ans. We had a rich cultural heritage inspite of being under British rule.

(vi) *India can change only when education is reached to all. (Use 'unless')*

Ans. Unless education is reached to all, India can't change.

(vii) *People in a developing country are both rich and poor. (Rewrite by using 'either' and 'or')*

Ans. People in a developing country are either rich or poor.

(viii) *If you work hard you will achieve success. (Rewrite by using 'in order to')*

Ans. In order to achieve success, you have to work hard.

(ix) *Most of the corrupt politicians do not find themselves in jail. (Change into a complex sentence).*

Ans. Though most of the politicians are corrupt, yet they don't find themselves in Jail.

(x) *He is old. He cannot climb stairs. (Rewrite by using 'too')*

Ans. He is too old to climb stairs.

(b) Use the following words to make sentences that bring out their meaning clearly. Do not change the form of the words. **1× 5 = 5**

(i) *Mandatory*

Ans. It has been made mandatory for research scholars to get their research papers published in journals.

(ii) *Dilemma*

Ans. I was in a dilemma to finalize the publishers for my book.

(iii) *Petrified*

Ans. The petrified child clung to his mother.

(iv) *Obfuscate*

Ans. The politicians are apt to obfuscate the real issues.

(v) *Diligent*

Ans. He is bound to succeed because he is both diligent and disciplined.

(c) Choose the appropriate word to fill in the blanks: 1× 5 = 5

(i) *The terrorists ________ fear in the minds of the people. (install/ instill)*

Ans. The terrorists ***instill*** fear in the minds of the people.

(ii) *The boys ________ to the words of their teacher. (return/ retort)*

Ans. The boys ***retort*** to the words of their teacher. (return/ retort)

(iii) *Ever since the dictator's ________ has arrived people are suffering. (rain/ reign)*

Ans. Ever since the dictator's ***reign*** has arrived people are suffering.

(iv) *It is almost ________ to suggest that he does not lie. (ascertain/ ascetic)*

Ans. It is almost ***ascertain*** to suggest that he does not lie.

(v) *An individual's life is just a ________ to the grand history of mankind. (preclude/ prelude)*

Ans. An individual's life is just a ***prelude*** to the grand history of mankind.

(d) Use the following idioms/ phrases in sentences of your own to bring out their meaning clearly. Do not change the form of the words: 1× 5 = 5

(i) *Through thick and thin*

Ans. During good and bad times

He is a true friend indeed who stood by me ***through thick and thin.***

(ii) *Sitting on the fence*

Ans. To play safe

Sitting on the fence, he always ***plays safe*** never supporting any party openly.

(iii) *Threw cold water*

Ans. To discourage

His wife ***threw cold water*** on his business plans.

(iv) *Foot the bill*

Ans. To pay the bill

You just place order of recipes of your own choice and don't worry about bill, I will ***foot the bill.***

(v) *Chapter and verse*

Ans. To speak authoritatively

He always speaks authoritatively citing ***chapter and verse*** from settled case laws.

UPSC (MAIN) EXAM – 2017
ENGLISH
(Compulsory)

Time allowed: 3 hours **Maximum Marks: 300**

Question Paper: Specific Instructions

Please read each of the following instructions carefully before attempting questions.

- *All questions are to be attempted.*
- *The number of marks carried by questions is indicated against it.*
- *Answers must be written in* **ENGLISH** *only.*
- *Word limit in questions, wherever specified, should be adhered to and if answered in much longer or shorter than the prescribed length, marks will be deducted.*
- *Any page or portion of the page left blank in the Question-cum-Answer Booklet must be clearly struck off.*

Candidates should attempt all questions.

The number of marks carried by each question is indicated at the end of the questions.

Answer must be written in English.

Q1. Write an essay in about 600 words on any one of the following topics: 100

(a) Recent Economic Reforms in India

(b) Threats to Environment

(c) Uses and Abuses of Social Networking

(d) Caring for the Aged

ESSAY

Uses And Abuses of Social Networking

"By giving people the power to share, we're making the world more transparent."
Mark Zuckerberg

It is a hard fact and also a paradox that technology has connected the world, but is also in a sense disconnecting human beings like never before. This is more so in the case of the present phenomenon known as social networking. There is no doubt that social networking has become a formidable, indispensable and inseparable reality of our life. It offers a strange and sometimes weird synchronicity of the real world and the virtual world. The lines are getting increasingly blurred between these two realities and the messaging is getting distorted. While it is certainly true that social networking has improved the quality of discourse and social interaction, it also a poses a hidden danger when it is not handled with care.

Social networking is quite useful if used rightly and judiciously as it provides information at very little or zero cost. But endless hours of peering at sites and messages and getting addicted to it are also a serious social and health problem. The amount of time people spend on social media is increasing by leaps and bounds. Teens now spend up to nine hours a day on social platforms, while 30% of all time spent online is now allocated to social media interaction.

While this constant urge for social networking has certainly improved connectivity with distantly placed friends, relatives, etc, it has come at the cost of a precipitious drop in live, face-to-face interaction.

Life in 'likes' has become the lifeline of life. Status updates are now one of the most sought after social symbols. People are so prone to social networking that it is reaching levels of craziness just falling short of madness.

There are people, especially youngsters, who start their day with a bed tea or coffee while updating their facebook status, and go to bed saying goodbye to people from the virtual world instead of near and dear ones around them. They share even the minute details of their lives with no thought of the consequences. Their lives have become a never ending wait for likes and comments posted on their sites. People wish marriage anniversary to their spouses through sites sitting in separate rooms under the same roof. Are these healthy indicators of social networking? No. Certainly not! We need to reflect and introspect ourselves before it is too late.

On the positive side, social networking is playing a great role in creating awareness of social and environmental issues. A host of national and international issues concerning the environment are transmitted across the globe in a very effective manner. In times of natural calamities, these sites are able to mobilise community support in a scale that can never be accomplished by the traditional means of communication.

Global social networking audiences surpassed 2 billion users in 2016. The most popular social network worldwide is Facebook; with 1.86 billion monthly active users by the end of 2016. Other popular social networks include WeChat, Twitter, Instagram, Tumblr and Sina Weibo.

However, it is the youth and young children who are most vulnerable to the harmful side effects of this phenomenon. The undesirable engagement on social networking sites is pushing the present younger generation to a bottomless pit where they may find themselves alone, deserted, confused, misinformed and misunderstood. It is time that societies, governments, NGOs and other social organisations realise the magnitude of the problem and take suitable measures to create awareness on this. We must try to create awareness about the judicious use of social media and prevent the present youth from falling prey to its abuse.

To conclude, in the words of Alexis Ohanian (founder of Reddit) "It takes discipline not to let social media steal your time." **(628 words)**

Q.2. Read carefully the passage given below and write your answers to the questions that follow in clear, correct and concise language: 15 × 5 = 75

Man, since antiquity, has been an inveterate traveller. Only the motivations for travel have changed. In ancient times, the main motivations for travel were trade, pilgrimage and conquest. It is not often realised how extensive were the contacts among the peoples several thousand years ago.

For instance, there was considerable interchange of ideas and knowledge between India and West Asia and the Graeco-Roman civilization.

Travel became the means of acquiring culture in Europe. The tradition of the Grand Tour which started in the 17th century was more firmly established in the 18th and the 19th centuries by the emergence of an affluent mercantile class. After the Second World War, Europe lay in ruins. The Marshall Plan which was introduced by the United States for the revival of the economies of European countries made tourism as one of its planks. It provided large amount of money for the reconstruction of hotels and tourism infrastructure of Western Europe. What was more significant was that for the first time tourism was viewed as an engine for economic development. This made the Governments start assuming responsibility for the promotion of tourism.

Three technological inventions have fuelled the growth of travel on a large scale in successive periods. First, the steam engine which made travel by rail and steamship possible before 1914; then the internal combustion engine which popularise travel by automobile in the inter-War years and lastly, the jet propulsion engine which has led to the international tourist explosion of the post-War era.

The Government of India also took note of the new phenomenon of tourism and its economic implications. In 1947, the private sector consisted of a number of hotels and travel agencies in the main cities mainly owned and operated by foreign interests. As it happened in other industries after Independence, the control of many of these hotels passed into the hands of Indian entrepreneurs. At the same time, a number of new indigenously owned and operated travel agencies and hotels started being set up. In the last 50 years, the Indian travel industry has shown remarkable enterprise. Some of the leading Indian hotel groups and travel agencies have branched out overseas and their performance is highly regarded in the international tourism remarks.

The tourism revolution which started in full measure 50 years ago has not run its course. There are several reasons for taking a long-term optimistic view of tourism. First, the increase in leisure time in industrialised societies; paid holidays which were introduced as a social welfare measure have now become an accepted feature not only in industrialised countries but also in many developing countries. The length of paid holidays has increased. The working week, both in public and private sectors, has come down to 40 hours spread over 5 days. Evidently Governments will have to concern themselves with the quality of use of leisure. Tourism has become a preeminent form of recreation for the younger people. This is reflected in the increase in travel in the age group of 18 to 25 years. Second, the rise in literacy and educational standards. Third, better healthcare has made it possible for retired persons, above 60 years, to undertake travel for pleasure. Fourth, the increase in discretionary incomes in real terms in the last twenty years, partly due to income elasticity. Many research studies have established that increase in income level in real terms resulted in increase in propensity for travel. And lastly, taking a vacation, generally twice a year, has become a way of life in modern societies.

Questions

(a) What, according to the author, were the main motivations for travel in ancient times?

Ans. *In ancient times, the main motivations for travel were trade, pilgrimage and conquest.*

(b) What was the state of tourism in Europe and the United States?

Ans. *Travel was the means of acquiring culture in Europe. The tradition of the Grand Tour which started in the 17th century was more firmly established in the 18th and the 19th* *centuries by the emergence of an affluent mercantile class. After the Second World War, Europe lay in ruins. The Marshall Plan which was introduced by the United States for the revival of the economies of European countries made tourism as one of its planks. It provided large amount of money for the reconstruction of hotels and tourism infrastructure of Western Europe. What was more significant was that for the first time tourism was viewed as an engine for economic development. This made the Governments start assuming responsibility for the promotion of tourism.*

(c) What part did technology play in the growth of tourism?

Ans. *Three technological inventions have fuelled the growth of travel on a large scale in successive periods. First, the steam engine which made travel by rail and steamship possible before 1914; then the internal combustion engine which popularised travel by automobile in the inter-War years and lastly, the jet propulsion engine which has led to the international tourist explosion of the post-War era.*

(d) How does the author describe the state of tourism in the post-Independence India?

Ans. *In 1947, the private sector operated a number of hotels and travel agencies in the main cities. These were mainly owned and operated by foreigners. As it happened in other industries, after Independence the control of many of these hotels passed into the hands of Indian entrepreneurs. At the same time, a number of new indigenously owned and operated travel agencies and hotels started coming up. In the last 50 years, the Indian travel industry has shown remarkable enterprise. Some of the leading Indian hotel groups and travel agencies have branched out overseas and their performance is highly regarded in the international tourism rankings.*

(e) Why does the author think that there is a bright future for tourism in modern societies?

Ans. *The author thinks that tourism has a very bright future because of rapidly rising income levels. The author says income elasticity and tourism are directly proportional. Moreover, rising literacy and education level giving stimulus to standard of living and taking regular vacation and going out on tourist places is becoming a way of life in modern societies. Tourism is one of the fastest growing industries worldwide and governments are taking full responsibility for promotion of this industry and are becoming one of the biggest resources of revenue generation. Health facilities enabling the aged and retired people to enjoy once they are free from their personal and professional responsibility is also adding to the growth of tourist industry. So, there is no doubt that the tourism industry has a very bright future.*

Q3. Make a précis of the following passage in about one-third of its length. Do not give a title to it. The précis should be written in your own language: 75

The work of a lawyer or a politician must contain in a more delectable form a great deal of the same pleasure that is to be derived from playing bridge. Here, of course, there is not only the exercise of skill but the outwitting of a skilled opponent. Even where this competitive element is absent, however, the performance of difficult feats is agreeable. A man who can do stunts in an aeroplane finds the pleasure so great for the sake of it he is willing to risk his life. I imagine that an able surgeon, in spite of the painful circumstances in which his work is done, derives satisfaction from the exquisite precision of his operations. All skilled work can be pleasurable, provided the skill required is either variable or capable of indefinite improvement. If these conditions are absent, it will cease to be interesting when a man has acquired his maximum skill. A man who runs three-mile races will cease to find pleasure in this occupation when he passes the age at which he can beat his own previous record. Fortunately there is a very considerable amount of work in which new circumstances call for new skill and a man can go on improving, at any rate until he has reached middle age. In some kinds of skilled work, such as politics, for example, it seems that men are at their best between sixty and seventy, the reason being that in such occupations a wide experience of other men is essential. For this reason, successful politicians are apt to be happier at the age of seventy than any other men of equal age. Their only competitors in this respect are the men who are the heads of big businesses.

There is, however, another element possessed by the best work, which is even more important as a source of happiness than is the exercise of skill. This is the element of constructiveness. In some work, though by no means in most, something is built up which remains as a monument when the work is completed. We may distinguish construction from destruction by the following criterion. In construction, the initial stage of affairs is comparatively haphazard, while the final state of affairs embodies a purpose; in destruction, the reverse is the case: the initial state of affairs embodies a purpose, while the final state of affairs is haphazard, that is to say, all that is intended by the destroyers is to produce a state of affairs which does not embody a certain purpose. Destruction, is of course necessary very often as a preliminary to subsequent construction; in that case it is part of a whole which is constructive. But not infrequently a man will engage in activities of which the purpose is destructive without regard to any construction that may come after. Frequently he will conceal this from himself by the relief that he is only sweeping away in order to build afresh, but it is generally possible to unmask this pretence, when it is a pretence, by asking him what the subsequent construction is to be. On this subject it will be found that he will speak vaguely and without enthusiasm, whereas on the preliminary destruction he has spoken precisely and with zest. This applies to not a few revolutionaries and militarists and other apostles of violence. They are actuated, usually without their own knowledge, by hatred; the destruction of what they hate is their real purpose, and they are comparatively indifferent to the question of what is to come after it. Now I cannot deny that in the work of destruction as in the work of construction there may be joy. It is a fiercer joy, perhaps at moments more intense, but it is less profoundly satisfying, since the result is one in which little satisfaction is to be found. You kill your enemy, and when he is dead your occupation is gone, and the satisfaction that you derive from victory quickly fades. The work of construction, on the other hand, when completed, is delightful to contemplate, and moreover is never so fully completed that there is nothing further to do about it. The most satisfactory purposes are those that lead on indefinitely from one success to another without ever coming to a dead end; and in this respect it will be found that construction is a greater source of happiness than destruction. **(735 words)**

PRECIS

The work of a lawyer/ doctor or politician which is amenable to indefinite improvement is considered superior and more appealing than that of a stunt performer.

A capable surgeon, in spite of the painful circumstances in which his work is done, derives satisfaction from the exquisite precision of his operations. All skilled work can be pleasurable, provided the skill required is either variable or capable of indefinite improvement.

A racer even with maximum skills ceases to derive pleasure as he/ she passes the age. A successful politician, on the other hand, even at sixty/ seventy is at his/ her best, growing/ progressing with a wider and greater experience.

For this reason, successful politicians are apt to be happier at the age of seventy than any other men of equal age. Their only competitors in this respect are the men who are the heads of big businesses.

Despite initial obstacles, a constructive work embodies a purpose, stands as a monument when completed and is a source of profound satisfaction. On the contrary, an act of destruction, despite its initial purpose, ends in a state of dissatisfaction. At times, however, destruction is taken as a preliminary to subsequent construction. The violent work of few revolutionaries and militarists may be put in this category. These people are activated by hate and their sense of satisfaction and sense of victory is gone when their enemy gets eliminated. So, when contemplated, constructive work is always delightful and is a greater source of happiness than destruction. **(250 words)**

Q 4. (a) Rewrite the following sentences after making necessary corrections. Do not make unnecessary changes in the original sentence: 1 × 10 = 10

(i) The older the wine, better it tastes.

Ans. *The older the wine, the better it tastes.*

(ii) You cannot cross the bridge until you do not come to it.

Ans. *You cannot cross the bridge until you come to it.*

(iii) He asked me what was my profession.

Ans. *He asked me what my profession was.*

(iv) Give me a pencil to write.

Ans. *Give me a pencil to write with.*

(v) Netaji is one of the bravest patriot of the country.

Ans. *Netaji is one of the bravest patriots of the country.*

(vi) I met an one-eyed beggar in the street.

Ans. *I met a one-eyed beggar in the street.*

(vii) The traders dealing with garments are jittery about the impact of GST.

Ans. *The traders dealing with garments are feeling jittery about the impact of GST.*

(viii) His efficiency soon made him the boss's blue-eyes boy.

Ans. *His efficiency soon made him the boss's blue-eyed boy.*

(ix) She does not know cooking doesn't she?

Ans. *She does not know how to cook, does she?*

(x) No sooner the bell rang than the children rushed out of their classrooms.

Ans. *No sooner did the bell ring than the children rushed out of their classrooms.*

(b) Supply the missing words: **1 × 5 = 5**

(i) The quarrel was unnecessary as they were making a __________ out of a mole hill.

Ans. *The quarrel was unnecessary as they were making a* ***mountain*** *out of a mole hill.*

(ii) Let us ring __________ the New Year gaiety.

Ans. *Let us ring* ***in*** *the New Year gaiety.*

(iii) The custom of *Sati* was done away __________ during the British period.

Ans. *The custom of Sati was done away* ***with*** *during the British period.*

(iv) One should not always blow one's own __________.

Ans. *One should not always blow one's own* ***trumpet.***

(vi) I cried myself __________ to make him clear.

Ans. *I cried myself* ***aloud*** *to make him clear.*

(c) Use the correct forms of the verbs in brackets: **1 × 5 = 5**

(i) Bread and butter __________ his usual breakfast. (be)

Ans. *Bread and butter* ***is*** *his usual breakfast.*

(ii) Some of the protestors were __________ by bullets. (hit)

Ans. *Some of the protestors were* ***hit*** *by bullets.*

(iii) When I came out of the building I saw that it __________. (rain)

Ans. *When I came out of the building I saw that it* ***was raining.***

(iv) Floods __________ if it continues to rain. (occur)

Ans. *Floods* ***may occur*** *if it continues to rain.*

(v) I __________ for you since 10 o'clock. (wait)

Ans. *I* ***have been waiting*** *for you since 10 o'clock.*

(d) Write the antonyms of the following: **1 × 5 = 5**

(i)	Amateur	**Ans.**	*Amateur – Professional*
(ii)	Heavenly	**Ans.**	*Heavenly – Earthly*
(iii)	Perfect	**Ans.**	*Perfect – Imperfect*
(iv)	Variable	**Ans.**	*Variable – Stable*
(v)	Vertical	**Ans.**	*Vertical – Horizontal*

Q 5. (a) Rewrite each of the following sentences as directed without changing the meaning: **1 × 10 = 10**

(i) The truth of the matter is too obvious to require any proof. (Remove 'too')

Ans. *The truth of the matter is so obvious that it doesn't require any proof.*

(ii) Radhika says, "I have pain in my knee." (Change into indirect speech)

Ans. *Radhika says that she has pain in her knee.*

(iii) He is not hungry. He is not thirsty. (Combine the sentences using 'neither … nor')

Ans. *He is neither hungry nor thirsty.*

(iv) Give him a glass of water. (Change into passive voice)

Ans. *He should be given a glass of water.*

(v) The prisoner was set free by the court. (Change into active voice)

Ans. *The court set free the prisoner.*

(vi) He was ill. He came to school. (Rewrite as one sentence beginning with 'despite')

Ans. *Despite being ill, he came to school.*

(vii) When the sun rises, the birds leave their nests. (Change into a compound sentence)

Ans. *The sun rises and the birds leave their nests.*

(viii) Those who come late shall be punished. (Change into simple sentence)

Ans. *The late comers shall be punished.*

(ix) Both his parents died in a train accident, ___________? (Add a question tag)

Ans. *Both his parents died in a train accident, didn't they?*

(x) Gold is the costliest metal. (Use comparative degree)

Ans. *Gold is costlier than any other metal.*

(b) Use the following words to make sentences that bring out their meaning clearly. Do not change the forms of the words (No marks will be given for vague and ambiguous sentences): **1 × 5 = 5**

(i) Evidence

Ans. *The evidence provided by the eyewitness was decisive in the case.*

(ii) Condemnation

Ans. *Demonetisation earned lot of condemnation for the Prime Minister.*

(iii) Constitute

Ans. *A committee was constituted by the government to inquire into the incident.*

(iv) Territorial

Ans. *The second agreement was patriarchal and of a strictly territorial nature.*

(v) Unseemly

Ans. *It is quite unseemly for a judge to use his official influence for personal necessities.*

(c) Choose the appropriate word to fill in the blanks: **1 × 5 = 5**

(i) He ran like a __________ through the forest. (doe/ dough)

Ans. *He ran like a* ***doe*** *through the forest.*

(ii) The teacher encouraged the students to understand things and not learn by __________. (wrote/ rote)

Ans. *The teacher encouraged the students to understand things and not learn by* ***rote.***

(iii) Indians were determined to throw away the __________ of foreign rule. (yolk/ yoke)

Ans. *Indian were determined to throw away the* ***yoke*** *of foreign rule.*

(iv) After his morning prayers, the priest remained __________ for the rest of the day. (idle/ idol)

Ans. *After his morning prayers, the priest remained* ***idle*** *for the rest of the day.*

(v) The hunter killed the bird sitting on the __________. (bow/ bough)

Ans. *The hunter killed the bird sitting on the* ***bough.***

(d) Use the following idioms/ phrases in sentences of your own to bring out their meaning clearly. Do not change the form of the words: 1 × 5 = 5

(i) Wild goose chase

Ans. *Wild goose chase – It will be a wild goose chase for Ms Banerjee to be President of India.*

(ii) Crocodile tears

Ans. *Crocodile tears – He wept when he heard the news, but he was shedding only crocodile tears.*

(iii) Sea change

Ans. *Sea change – Books by A.P.J. Abdul Kalam are inspiring and can create a sea change in your attitude and outlook towards life.*

(iv) Fool's paradise

Ans. *Fool's paradise – You must be in a fool's paradise if you think that it will rain at the time of such hot summers.*

(v) On cloud nine

Ans. *After her immaculate performance at Founders Day of her school, Anaadi was on cloud nine.*

UPSC (MAIN) EXAM – 2016
ENGLISH
(Compulsory)

Time allowed: 3 hours **_Maximum Marks: 300_**

Question Paper: Specific Instructions

Please read each of the following instructions carefully before attempting questions.

- *All questions are to be attempted.*
- *The number of marks carried by questions is indicated against it.*
- *Answers must be written in* **ENGLISH** *only.*
- *Word limit in questions, wherever specified, should be adhered to and if answered in much longer or shorter than the prescribed length, marks will be deducted.*
- *Any page or portion of the page left blank in the Question-cum-Answer Booklet must be clearly struck off.*

Candidates should attempt all questions.

The number of marks carried by each question is indicated at the end of the questions.

Answer must be written in English.

Q 1. Write an essay in about 600 words on any one topic: (100)

(a) Majoritarianism conflicting with the constitutional spirit, an unhealthy trend in true democracy.

(b) The Indian girl child – still a victim of exploitation.

(c) Industrialisation should not affect but contribute to agricultural growth in India.

(d) Mass media has great responsibility in transforming the society.

ESSAY

Mass media has great responsibility in transforming the society.

Mass media, earlier simply called media, starting its journey from print, moved on to electronic media and then accelerated its journey at a meteoric pace with the onset of satellite and the IT revolution. It is now a component of social networking sites like Facebook, Twitter, WhatsApp and Instagram etc. Media, referred to as the fourth estate, is one of the most powerful institutions of a free and democratic society. Media, rather more aptly mass media, have undergone such exponential growth that nobody and no aspect of the society can go unnoticed by it. Mass media in its latest avatar have encompassed within its fold issues ranging from the most profound to the most inane. The reach of the media and its impact ranges from personal to political, social to economical, astronomical to astrological, past to present, present to future aspects of life on this planet. With its influence reaching gargantuan proportions, its role and responsibility has also increased manifold. The extent and intensity of the role of mass media in transforming society can be gauged from this fact that a household may not have a cooking gas connection but will have TV and a cable connection. A rickshaw puller, a domestic help and even beggars on the roads and streets with mobile and access to internet speaks volumes about the penetration of mass media in society.

Mass media are both the watchdogs of public behaviour of elected officials and custodians of popular goodwill as they seek to report on the developments in society. Hence, mass media are especially relevant to society because without the media, we would never know what is happening in the world around us. We would be without the moral compass and ethical conscience needed to hold society together. The important point here is that like all opinion makers, **mass media has both a duty and a responsibility towards society.** This is the reason it is considered a vital part of modern democracies.

The transition from print media to digital media (TV, internet and social media) have made mass media more powerful and influential as it gives them access to millions of viewers without geographical constraints unlike the case with the traditional print media. This hold over society is however a double edged sword. It can be used to brainwash and manipulate public sentiments while at the same time can be a powerful tool for transforming society. Therefore mass media has a great responsibility of being ethical and honest in its day to day functioning and approach. This is precisely for this reason that they should not succumb to the temptations of taking the easy way out, as they now are responsible for events on a global scale as opposed to happenings on a local or regional level.

The mass media are now in a position wherein they can make or mar the chances of celebrities, politicians, businesspersons, and sportspersons. Hence the responsibility which has been vested with them by society has to be exercised judiciously and not carelessly or with a hidden agenda. Mass media has come a long way since the time they used to report on city and council events. Now, they have a global platform and global responsibilities, which means that they should have a conscience as well.

The legendary media theorist, Marshall McLuhan, coined the term "The Global Village" to indicate the mass production and the mass consumption of media images and content across the world. The term denotes the coming together of the countries of the world in one gigantic web of media landscapes. To take an example, the popular US news channel, CNN, and the venerable British news channel, BBC, are available throughout the world. Similarly, in entertainment, we have the Star Group that is beamed throughout the world.

In knowledge and information category, we have *National Geographic* and *Discovery* that are available all over the world. What this means is that the ready availability of the same content throughout the world is binding the people in all countries to a common theme of oneness and shared media consumption. Hence, the term 'Global Village' is relevant to indicate this phenomenon.

In the 1990s with the wave of economic and political liberalisation of many countries in the world, the global broadcasters entered countries like India in a big way. Though China had and still has restrictions on the kind of content that can be viewed in that country, the opening up of the Indian media landscape to foreign channels represented a revolution in the way media is produced and consumed in our country. Many experts have pointed to the liberalisation of the Indian mindset because of the consumption of global media. Indeed, many Indians were exposed to the West for the first time and the imagery of a western lifestyle and consumer choices meant that the aspirational values of Indians went up. This was reflected in the burgeoning consumer culture that was the hallmark of the Indian consumer story since the late 1990s. What this means is that Indians are no longer the monochromatic television viewers who had to contend with just one channel, but instead were consuming media images from across the world.

Similarly, many African countries were exposed to satellite television around this period for the first time. This resulted in greater awareness among the African people about the situation in the West and relatively comfortable lifestyles that the Westerners enjoyed. Like in many countries, the explosion of media choices leads to a widening of the debate in politics, economics, and social sciences. This resulted in calls for greater freedom and better standard of living, which was manifested in the way the people in these countries started using the media to voice their concerns.

The media, in turn, were happy to be part of this attitudinal change. Television and satellite TV in particular was the game changer for many countries that were wholeheartedly embracing the Western way of life. It would suffice here to say that satellite TV played a prominent role in emancipation of women, more entertainment, and greater exposure to the youth resulting in the MTV Generation that was completely westernized and started to vote with their feet about the kind of products that they wanted to buy and consume.

The onset of the Global Village has meant that the vision of "One Market under God" has been realised and this has helped both the marketers who could market their products globally and the consumers who had more choices and a variety of options to choose from. Finally, it also resulted in greater political awareness and liberation of attitudes among the youth.

Q 2. Read carefully the passage given below and write your answers to the questions that follow in clear, correct and concise language: 15 × 5 = 75

The thought of Young Bengal (Pearychand Mitra, one of the circle, called it in 1877 'Young Calcutta') flowed through the fourth decade of the 19th century, arising in the late twenties and ebbing away after the mid-forties. Its inspirer was Derozio (1809-31), competent scholar, gifted writer, radical thinker, and the most famous of our teachers in the new education. It will be unusual to link with Young Bengal a second name, that of David Hare (1775-1841) who seems so different from Derozio in so many ways. Hare was indeed no professional instructor or intellectual, no man of letters or of academic learning. He had neither the brilliance nor the waywardness of his contemporary; unlike him he had become in diet and habits almost a half-Hindu. Yet between the two may be detected an underlying resemblance which furnishes a key to a proper estimation of Young Bengal.

Common to both was the passionate conviction that for India nothing was more essential than "a dissemination of European learning and science among her people." Both encouraged freedom of thinking and discussion and inspired a courage and personal integrity in their followers "to throw off the fetters of that antiquated bigotry which still clung to their countrymen." And unlike other leaders around them, both were 'godless' secularists with little faith in denominations or religious instruction, and yet staunch idealists. Nor can one forget that in the hour of trial, Hare tried to stand by Derozio and his maligned pupils about whom he declared – "your countrymen look upon you as – their reformers and instructors"' while the Derozians were the first to honour Hare publicly, and after his death they were in the forefront in the endeavour to perpetuate his memory, in the unique First of June anniversaries for 25 years without a break.

Henry Louis Vivian Derozio was a Calcutta Eurasian of Portuguese-Indian ancestry, the son of an officer in an English mercantile firm. (in the Hindu College Records of 1831, the name is occasionally spelt as De Rozio; Max Muller wrote D. Rozario). He was educated in one of the pioneer English-teaching private schools of the early 19th century, run by the Scotsman Drummond in the Dharmatala area. Drummond was a scholar-poet, and as a notorious free-thinker an exile from his native land. It may safely be conjectured that Derozio derived from Durmmond his taste in literature and philosophy, his love of Burns, his faith in the French Revolution and English Radicalism.

Derozio's youthful critique on Kant was considered as something which "would not disgrace even gifted philosophers"; his translation of a French essay on Moral Philosophy was printed posthumously. The fame already won secured him an appointment as teacher to the senior classes in the Hindu College before he had ended his 'teens'.

Derozio's personality brought "a new era in the annals of the College", the youthful teacher drawing the senior boys "like a magnet" round him. According to his biographer "neither before, nor since his day has any teacher, within the walls of any native educational establishment in India, ever exercised such an influence over his pupils." Not alone in the classrooms, but outside the hours as well, he strove with success "to broaden and deepen the knowledge of his pupils" in Western thought and literature, the new fountain which emancipated and intoxicated. The College students clustered round him and very many of them carried down to their last days the deep impress stamped on them by their Master. This was the cementing link which held together the Young Bengal group, the memory which made a close-knit fellowship of affection and friendship even in later life.

Unlike most teachers, Derozio encouraged his students to debate freely and question authority. He urged them to think for themselves, "to be in no way influenced by any of the idols mentioned by Bacon-to live and die for truth". One of his pupils, Radhanath Sikdar, said of him: "he has been the cause and the sole cause of the spirit of enquiry after truth, and that contempt of vice – which cannot but be beneficial to India." Another, Ramgopal Ghosh, held up the motto: "He who will not reason is a bigot; he who cannot is a fool, and he how does not is a slave."

Questions

(a) Which of the period when the thought of Young Bengal, the youthful band of reformers flourished in Bengal? Who were the two main teachers of the new education and in what ways were they different from each other?

Ans. *The period for "The Thought of Young Bengal," when the youthful brand of reformers flourished in Bengal was roughly the second quarter of the 19th Century. The two main teachers, competent scholars and radical educationists were Derozio (1809-1831) and David Hare (1775-1841). The two seem to be different from each other as unlike Derozio, David Hare was neither a professional instructor or intellectual, nor a man of letters. David Hare had neither the brilliance nor the waywardness of Derozio: unlike Derozio, Hare had become in diet and habits almost a half-Hindu.*

(b) What was common to both these teachers? How did they support each other?

Ans. *Despite the differences between Derozio and Hare there were certain underlying commonalities between them. Both had a passionate conviction for dissemination of European learning and study of science among Indian people. Both encouraged free* *thinking, courage, personal integrity in their fellow beings to throw of the fetters of antiquated bigotry. Both were secularists and staunch idealist. They supported each other and try to stand by each other on the issues of reforms and the renaissance that Bengal was to undergo.*

(c) Comment on the education of Derozio. Did Drummond have any influence on him? Justify your answer.

Ans. *Derozio was a Calcutta Eurasian of Portuguese Indian ancestry and the son of an officer in an English mercantile firm. He was educated in a pioneer English teaching private school, run by the Scotsman Drummond in the Dharmatala area of Calcutta. Drummond had heavily influenced Derozio in his taste in literature and philosophy, his love of Burns, his faith in the French Revolution and English Radicalism.*

(d) What kind of influence did Derozio have on his pupils i.e., the Young Bengal Group?

Ans. *Derozio had tremendous influence on his pupils i.e. the Young Bengal Group. His personality brought a new era in the annals of the college. Derozio tried with success to broaden and deepen the knowledge of his pupils in western thought and literature, and this new wave emancipated and intoxicated his students.*

(e) 'He has been the cause and the sole cause of the spirit of enquiry after truth'. Explain the significance of the statement by Radhanath Sikdar.

Ans. *Radhanath Sikdar's statement about Derozio that "He has been the cause and the sole cause of the spirit of enquiry after truth," underscores the point that students must debate freely and question authority and not to be influenced by any of the idols. Only the spirit of inquiry can be beneficial to India.*

Q. 3. Make a précis of the following passage in about one-third of its length. Do not give a title to it. The précis should be written in your own language. 75

India is essentially a land of knowledge and it must rediscover itself in this aspect. Once this rediscovery is done, it will not require much struggle to achieve the quality of life, strength and sovereignty of a developed nation.

Knowledge has many forms and it is available at many places. It is acquired through education, information, intelligence and experience. It is available in academic institutions, with teachers, in libraries, in research papers, seminar proceedings and in various organizations and workplaces with workers, managers, in drawings, in process sheets and on the shop floors. Knowledge, though closely linked to education, comes equally from learning skills such as those possessed by our artists, craftsmen, hakims, vaidyas, philosophers and saints, as also our housewives. Knowledge plays a very important role in their performance and output too. Our heritage and history, the rituals, epics and traditions that form part of our consciousness are also vast resources of knowledge as are our libraries and universities. There is an abundance of unorthodox, earthy wisdom in our villages. There are hidden treasures of knowledge in our environment, in the oceans, bioreserves and deserts, in the plant and animal life. Every state in our country has a unique core competence for a knowledge society.

Knowledge has always been the prime mover of prosperity and power. The acquisition of knowledge has therefore been the thrust area throughout the world. Additionally, in India, there has been a culture of sharing it, not only through the traditions of guru-shishya but also by its spread to neighbouring countires through travelers who came to Nalanda and other universities drawn by their reputation as centres of learning. India is endowed with natural and competitive advantages as also certain distinctive competencies. But these are scattered in isolated pockets and the awareness of these is inadequate. During the last century the world has changed from being an agricultural society, in which manual labour was critical factor, to an industrial society where the management of technology, capital and labour provide the competitive advantage. In the twenty-first century, a new society is emerging where knowledge is the primary production resource instead of capital and labour. Efficient utilization of this existing knowledge base can create wealth for us in the form of better health, education and other indicators of progress. The ability to create and maintain the knowledge infrastructure, to enhance skills and increase productivity through the exploitation of advances in various fields will be the key factors in deciding the prosperity of this society.

The knowledge society has two very important components driven by societal transformation and wealth generation. The societal transformation is in respect of education, healthcare, agriculture and governance. These will lead to employment generation, high productivity and rural property.

The task of wealth generation for the nation has to be woven around national competencies. The TIFAC task team has identified core areas that will spearhead our march towards becoming a knowledge society. The areas are: information technology, biotechnology, space technology, weather forecasting, disaster management, telemedicine and tele-education, technologies utilizing traditional knowledge, service sector and infotainment which is the emerging area resulting from convergence of information and entertainment. These core technologies, fortunately, can be interwoven by IT, a sector that took off only due to the enterprising spirit of the young.

Thus there are multiple technologies and appropriate management structure that have to work together to generate a knowledge society. With India carving a niche for itself in information technology, the country is uniquely placed to fully capitalize on the opportunity to quickly transform itself into a knowledge society.

The Planning Commission has taken a lead in generating a roadmap for transforming India into a knowledge society.

Evolving suitable policy and administrative procedures, changes in regulatory methods, identification of partners and most important, creation of young and dynamics leaders are the components that have to be put in place. In order to generate wealth, which is the second component for establishing a knowledge society, it is essential that simultaneously a citizen-centric approach to shaping of business policy, user-driven technology generation and intensified industry-lab-academic linkages have also be the established.

A knowledge society has a two-dimensional objective of societal transformation and wealth generation, and a third dimension emerges if India is to transform itself into a knowledge superpower. This is knowledge protection and it entails a tremendous responsibility. It is very important that our communication network and information generators are protected from electronic attacks through surveillance and monitoring. There should be a focused approach to intellectual property rights and related issues, and our ancient knowledge and culture too are part of our resource base and need to be protected as such. **(776 words)**

PRECIS

Since times immemorial, India has been unfolding as a knowledge society. It now needs to rediscover and underscore this distinction, and metamorphise into a strong, sovereign and developed nation, ensuring quality life to its citizens. Knowledge – possessed by India's artists, craftsmen, *vaidyas*, philosophers, saints and housewives, etc. and stored in heritage, history and tradition shaping and enriching our consciousness— is closely linked to education, skills, intelligence and experience and play key roles in enhancing performance and output of the Indians. The entire country including villages, oceans, deserts, plants and animal life has immense potential and competency for the creation of a knowledge society. Knowledge as the prime mover and indicator of power, prosperity, progress health and education, needs to be exploited and appropriated to make advances in the agricultural and industrial society of India simultaneously. The societal transformation with regard to education and healthcare and agriculture, governance and wealth generation through the tapping of core technologies coupled with the utilisation of traditional wisdoms are the two key components of the knowledge society. The transformation of India into a knowledge society can be expedited by capitalizing on multiple technologies and appropriate management.

The TIFAC task team has identified core areas that will spearhead our march towards becoming a knowledge society. The Planning Commissions emphasises on the creation of young and dynamic leaders involving suitable policies and administrative procedures, evolving a citizen centric approach to shape user-driven technology. The establishment of intensified industry-lab-academia linkage may be revolutionized towards the creation of a knowledge society in India. Insuring intellectual property rights, i.e. the protection of knowledge in all forms and manifestations including ancient wisdom and culture, through monitoring and surveillance is an act of tremendous responsibility and this must be ensured by all means. **(290 words)**

Q 4. (a) Rewrite the following sentences after making necessary corrections. Do not make unnecessary changes in the original sentences. **1 × 10 = 10**

(i) I request your favour to grant me leave.

Ans. *I request you to grant me leave.*

(ii) He lived there for a day.

Ans. *He lived there for one day.*

(iii) He is the fastest runner and he came last.

Ans. *He is the fastest runner but he came last.*

(iv) They know each other since January.

Ans. *They have known each other since January.*

(v) All the patients have been admitted and received attention.

Ans. *All the patients were admitted and received attention.*

(vi) They didn't see any movies since March.

Ans. *They haven't seen any movies since March.*

(vii) We shall go on a tour as soon as the schools will close.

Ans. *We shall go on a tour as soon as the schools close.*

(viii) Each of the answers was not correct.

Ans. *Every answer was not correct.*

(ix) If we had had money we would go shopping.

Ans. *If we had money we would go shopping.*

(x) I wanted that he should get leave.

Ans. *I wanted him to get leave.*

(b) Supply the missing words. **1 × 5 = 5**

(i) The scene ________ us is magnificent, isn't it?

Ans. *The scene around us is magnificent, isn't it?*

(ii) ________ your proposals, we shall meet later.

Ans. *Put up your proposals, we shall meet later.*

(iii) You can't climb ________ that high roof.

Ans. *You can't climb up that high roof.*

(iv) He pushed his way ________ the crowd of people.

Ans. *He pushed his way through the crowd of people.*

(v) She ________ in with the wrong group of friends in her teens.

Ans. *She was in with the wrong group of friends in her teens.*

(c) Use the correct forms of the verbs given in brackets: **1×5=5**

(i) All our plans of starting a new venture ________ up in smoke. (end)

Ans. *All our plans of starting a new venture ended up in smoke.*

(ii) Men of straw are not ________ in the society. (respect)

Ans. *Men of straw are not respected in the society.*

(iii) He got angry before I ________ a word. (say)

Ans. *He got angry before I said a word.*

(iv) Later on he ________ his mistake. (realize)

Ans. *Later on he realized his mistake.*

(v) Television is a powerful means of ________ knowledge. (diffuse).

Ans. *Television is a powerful means of diffusing knowledge.*

(d) Write the antonyms of the following: **1 × 5 = 5**

(i) Awkward **Ans.** *Elegant*

(ii) Diligently **Ans.** *Lazily*

(iii) Persist **Ans.** *Resist*

(iv) Traitor **Ans.** *Patriot*

(v) Enrich **Ans.** *Impoverish*

Q 5. (a) Rewrite each of the following sentences as directed without changing the meaning: **1 × 10 = 10**

(i) I have many debts to repay. (Change into a complex sentence)

Ans. *I have many debts that I would have to repay.*

(ii) He hasn't been informed. (Change into active voice)

Ans. *Nobody has informed him.*

(iii) He wanted to get a raise. He had to study Accounting. (Use 'in order to')

Ans. *He had to study Accounting in order to get a raise.*

(iv) He didn't complain at all. He was kind. (Rewrite the sentence starting with 'It')

Ans. *It was kind of him not to have complained at all.*

(v) Arvind said, "I must write it". (Change into indirect speech)

Ans. *Arvind said that he must write that.*

(vi) I didn't meet the government official from France. I didn't meet his friend too. (Rewrite using 'neither ….. nor')

Ans. I neither met the government official from France nor his friend.

(vii) He didn't describe it well. He was very excited. (Use 'too')

Ans. *He was too excited to describe it well.*

(viii) People respect politicians only when they change their ways. (Rewrite the sentence using 'unless')

Ans. *Unless politicians change their ways people don't respect them.*

(ix) We seldom see them nowadays, ________? (Supply an appropriate question tag)

Ans. *We seldom see them nowadays, do we?*

(x) The girl worked hard but she didn't succeed. (Change into a simple sentence)

Ans. *Despite hard work the girl didn't succeed.*

(b) Use the following words to make sentences that bring out their meaning clearly. Do not change the form of the words. (No marks will be given for vague and ambiguous sentences). **1 × 5 = 5**

(i) Nebulous

Ans. I had no concrete plan but rather a *nebulous* idea to write a book.

(ii) Expeditious

Ans. We need a fair and *expeditious* justice delivery system.

(iii) Contiguous

Ans. North America and Canada are *contiguous* countries.

(iv) Fastidious

Ans. Kapil always had a *fastidious* approach in his work.

(v) Proscribe

Ans. ISIS is a *proscribed* organisation all over the world.

(c) Choose the appropriate word to fill in the blanks: 1 × 5 = 5

(i) We are ________ to learn that the President has given his assent to the act. (gratified/ grateful)

Ans. We are gratified to learn that the President has given his assent to the act.

(ii) He did not make a single ________ to the examination results in his speech. (illusion/ allusion)

Ans. He did not make a single allusion to the examination results in his speech.

(iii) Make a ________ selection of the books in this library. (judicial/ judicious)

Ans. Make a judicious selection of the books in this library.

(iv) The sight of home gave the boys the ________ to walk fast. (impetus/ impetuous)

Ans. The sight of home gave the boys the impetus to walk fast.

(v) The lawyer used many ________ arguments which did not deceive the Judge. (specious/ spacious)

Ans. The lawyer used many specious arguments which did not deceive the Judge.

(d) Use these idioms/phrases in sentences of your own to bring out their meaning clearly. Do not change the form of the words: 1 × 5 = 5

(i) with impunity

Ans. If an official discharges his duty *with impunity,* then his acts are not questionable.

(ii) under a cloud

Ans. The corrupt officer is *under a cloud.*

(iii) loaves and fishes

Ans. Nowadays everybody is running after *loaves and fishes.*

(iv) a leap in the dark

Ans. The act of demonetization is considered by many to be *a leap in the dark* in the fight against corruption.

(v) yeoman service

Ans. When plague broke out in the state, the NGOs did *yeoman service.*

UPSC (MAIN) EXAM – 2015
ENGLISH
(Compulsory)

Time allowed: 3 hours *Maximum Marks: 300*

Candidates should attempt all questions.

The number of marks carried by each question is indicated at the end of the questions.

Answer must be written in English.

Q 1. Write an essay in about 600 words on any one topic: (100)

(a) Impact of politics on society

(b) E-commerce : A win-win situation for all

(c) Harassment of women at workplaces

(d) Does Indian cinema reflect social reality?

ESSAY

Does Indian Cinema Reflect Social Reality?

Cinema and society mirror each other. The social patterns, lifestyles, traditions, cultures, customs and value systems have a great impact on cinema and its makers. In equal measure, cinema has a similar impact on society too. It launches new fashions and trends, highlights the social evils and social problems and problems related to women like rape, molestation, dowry deaths etc. It exposes gender bias and the unholy nexus between the politicians and criminals, and raises various issues of governance from time to time. Cinema and society has had a close relationship since the inception of cinema about 100 years ago.

Cinema is one of the biggest sources of entertainment for the people of all ages, strata and sections of the society throughout the length and breadth of the country. All sections of the society rich or poor, young or old, literate or illiterate – are crazy about watching movies. Cinema is a main source of entertainment for the poorer sections of the society. Catchy dialogues and lilting songs and powerful dialogues in Indian movies is a great attraction for movie lovers.

Bollywood is a live example of a vibrant and composite culture. All the artists, actors, directors, producers and technicians work in close tandem and deep harmony irrespective of caste, class, religion, region or gender. The love and admiration for the trilogy of Khans i.e., Shah Rukh Khan, Salman Khan and Aamir Khan by millions of Indians in India and abroad is a symbol of national integration. The doyen of the Hindi cinema Dilip Kumar (who is actually a Muslim) is equally venerated in Muslim and non-Muslim world for his immense contribution. Amitabh Bachchan is an icon of Hindi cinema and is one of the most prominent faces of Bollywood. Cinema cutting across the barriers of caste, class, religion, region and gender is one of the greatest binding force for national integration. It crosses international barriers and boundaries, languages and cultures promotes universalism, humanism and universal brotherhood and fraternity.

Cinema is a source of employment and revenue generation. It boosts the flow of money within the country and also earns millions of dollars through exports.

Cinema owes a great social responsibility and social obligation. It can become a tool of education, information and awareness spreading the message of humanity, equality, brotherhood. But nowadays some undesirable tendencies are creeping into the making of cinema. The degradation and dehumanization of women portraying them as sex symbols and tools of enjoyment and exploitation is quite demeaning and an extremely unhealthy trend. The film makers should also try to minimize the glorification and magnification of negative characters. They should try to discourage smoking, drinking and other such like negative activities. The shortcuts to money making, name and fame should not be euologised, rather should be strongly discouraged. They should try to promote the values of honesty, sincerity, discipline, hard work, ethics, morality and other values of secularism, humanism, liberalism and democracy. Like Mary Kom and Milkha Singh, film makers should try to make films on the life histories of eminent people and sportspersons who have risen from humble backgrounds to reach the highest summit.

Q 2. Read carefully the passage given below and write your answers to the questions that follow in clear, correct and concise language. **15 × 5 = 75**

A desert is a barren area of land where little precipitation occurs and consequently living conditions are threatening for plant and animal life. The lack of vegetation exposes the vulnerable surface of the ground to the processes of denudation. About one-third of the land surface of the world is arid or semi-arid. Deserts are usually hot and barren places; yet they are also beautiful. A few plants, rocks and dusty red-brown soil make up the ingredients of most North American deserts where there is sufficient food and water for certain animals to survive. Deserts cover more than one-fifth of the Earth's land and they are found on every continent. A place that receives less than 10 inches of rain per year is normally considered a desert. They are part of a wider classification of regions called "dry land". These areas exist under a moisture deficit, which means they repeatedly lose more moisture through evaporation than they receive from annual precipitation.

Deserts are biologically rich habitats with a vast array of animals and plants that have adapted to harsh conditions there. Some deserts are among the planet's last remaining areas of total wilderness. Yet more than one billion people, one-sixth of the Earth's population, actually live in the desert regions.

Despite the common notion of deserts as dry and hot, there are cold deserts as well. One famous dry and hot place in the world with no visible rock or plant and barely any water is the Sahara desert. It is the largest hot desert in the world that reaches temperatures of up to 122 degrees Fahrenheit during the day. Some deserts are very cold, like the Gobi desert in Asia and the desert on the continent of Antarctica. Only about 10 percent of deserts are covered by sand dunes. The driest deserts get less than half an inch of precipitation each year and that is from condensed fog.

Desert animals have adapted ways to help them keep cool when the going gets tough. Camels also have thick hair in their ears for keeping out sand; they also sport closable nostrils, an eye membrane, and wide feet that act like snow-shoes in the land. Desert plants may have to go without fresh water for years at a time. Some plants have adapted to the arid climate by growing long roots that tap water from deep underground. Other plants, such as cacti, have special means of storing and conserving water. Many desert plants can live to be hundreds of years old.

Some of the world's semi-arid regions are turning into deserts at an alarming rate. This process, known as "desertification", is not caused by drought, but usually arises from the demands of human population that settles on the semi-arid lands to grow crops and graze animals. The pounding of the soil by the hooves of livestock may degrade the soil and encourage erosion by wind and water. Global warming also threatens to change the ecology of deserts. Higher temperature may produce an increasing number of wildfires that alter desert landscape by eliminating slow-growing trees and shrubs and replacing them with fast-growing grasses.

Questions:

(a) Explain what you understand by 'barren and dry land'.

(b) What do you understand by rich habitats?

(c) How have desert animals and plants in arid climate adapted themselves to the use of less water?

(d) Describe the process of desertification.

(e) What are the camel's two most visible features that make it perfect for deserts?

Ans.

(a) A barren and dry land is the land where little precipitation occurs and which doesn't provide living conditions for plant and animal life.

(b) Rich habitat is an area with vast array of animals and plants that have adapted to harsh conditions.

(c) Desert animals have adapted ways to help them keep cool when the going gets tough. Desert plants may have to go without fresh water for years at a time. Some plants have adapted to the arid climate by growing long roots that tap water from deep underground. Other plants, such as cacti, have special means of storing and conserving water. Many desert plants can live to be hundreds of years old.

(d) Some of the world's semi-arid regions are turning into deserts at an alarming rate. This process, known as "desertification", is not caused by drought, but usually arises from the demands of human population that settles on the semi-arid lands to grow crops and graze animals.

(e) Camels also have thick hair in their ears for keeping out sand; they also sport closable nostrils, an eye membrane, and wide feet that act like snow-shoes in the land.

Q 3. Make a precis of the following passage in about one-third of its length. Do not give a title to it. The precis should be written in your own language. 75 marks

The means may be equated to a seed, the end to a tree; and there is just the same inviolable connection between the means and the end as there is between the seed and the tree. I am not likely to obtain the result flowing from the worship of God by laying myself prostrate before Satan. If, therefore, anyone were to say; 'I want to worship God; it does not matter that I do so by means of Satan', it would be set down as ignorant folly. We reap exactly as we sow.

If I want to deprive you of your watch, I shall certainly have to fight for it; if I want to buy your watch, I shall have to pay you for it; and if I want it as a gift, I shall have to plead for it; and according to the means I employ, the watch is a stolen property, my own property, or a donation. Thus we see three different results from three different means. Will you still say that means do not matter?

Let us proceed a little further. A well-armed man has stolen your property; you have harboured the thought of his act; you are filled with anger; you argue that you want to punish that rogue, not for your own sake, but for the good of your neighbours; you have collected a number of armed men, you want to take his house by assault; he is duly informed of it, he runs away; he, too, is incensed. He collects his brother-robbers, and sends you a defiant message that he will commit robbery in broad daylight. You are strong, you do not fear him, you are prepared to receive him. Meanwhile, the robber pesters your neighbours. They complain before you. You reply that you are doing all for their sake, you do not mind that your own goods have been stolen. Your neighbours reply that the robber never pestered them before, and that he commenced his depredations only after you declared hostilities against him. You are between Scylla and Charybdis. You are full of pity for the poor men. What they say is true. What are you to do? You will be disgraced if you now leave the robber alone. You, therefore, tell the poor men: 'Never mind. Come, my wealth is yours. I will give you arms. I will train you how to use them; you should belabour the rogue; don't you leave him alone.' And so the battle grows. The robbers increase in numbers; your neighbours have deliberately put themselves to inconvenience. Thus the result of wanting to take revenge upon the robber is that you have disturbed your own peace; you are in perpetual fear of being robbed and assaulted; your courage has given place to cowardice. If you patiently examine the argument, you will see that I have not overdrawn the picture. This is one of the means.

Now let us examine the other. You set this armed robber down as an ignorant brother, you intend to reason with him at a suitable opportunity; you argue that he is, after all, a fellow man; you do not know what prompted him to steal. You, therefore, decide that when you can, you will destroy the man's motive for stealing. Whilst you are thus reasoning with yourself, the man comes again to steal. Instead of being angry with him, you take pity on him. Henceforth, you keep your doors and windows open, you change your sleeping place, and you keep your things in a manner most accessible to him. The robber comes again and is confused as all this is new to him; nevertheless, he takes away your things. But his mind is agitated. He enquires about you in the village, he comes to learn about your broad and loving heart; he repents, he begs your pardon, returns you your things, and leaves off the stealing habit. He becomes your servant, and you find for him honourable employment. This is the second method.

Thus, you see, different means have brought about totally different results. I do not wish to deduce from this that robbers will act in the above manner or that all will have the same pity and love like you. I only wish to show that fair means alone can produce fair results, and that, at least in the majority of cases, if not indeed in all, the force of love and pity is infinitely greater than the force of arms. There is harm in the exercise of force, never in that of pity.

PRECIS

The given write up is about the intricate connection between the means and the end likening it to the connection between the seed and the tree. One cannot obtain the godly results by satanic means. We reap exactly as we sow. The 'means' matter a lot in the attainment of the 'end'. For instance, one's act of punishing a rogue who has done lot of wrongs by means of violence, may lead to the disturbance of one's own peace of mind. The same person (rogue) by subjecting him to different treatment i.e. by being nice to him and in trying to understand his motives for becoming rogue, will help the man in correcting him. He may start repenting and seeking your pardon and may end up leaving his wrong doings. Thus it will not be incorrect to say that fair means alone can lead to fair results in majority of cases if not in all. Love and sympathy are definitely greater and fairer than the power of sword. The use of force may lead to one's harm but never in that of love and care. Thus, it can be concluded by saying that the means justifies the end and not the vice-versa.

Q 4. (a) Rewrite the following sentences after making necessary corrections. Do not make unnecessary changes in the original sentence. 10 marks

(i) He enjoyed during the holidays.

Ans. *He enjoyed himself during the holidays.*

(ii) Whoever works hard he will win.

Ans. *Whoever works hard will win.*

(iii) The man who knocked at the door was stranger.

Ans. *The man who knocked at the door was a stranger.*

(iv) I asked my colleague when was he going to his home town.

Ans. *I asked my colleague when he was going to his home town.*

(v) Besides clothes, the shopkeeper deals with cosmetics too.

Ans. *Besides clothes, the shopkeeper deals in cosmetics too.*

(vi) He is desirous for joining the army.

Ans. *He is desirous of joining the army.*

(vii) The judge said that the truth always triumphed.

Ans. *The judge said that the truth always triumphs.*

(viii) One should help his friend in difficulty.

Ans. *One should help one's friend in difficulty.*

(ix) Sachin Tendulkar is the best batsman India has produced, isn't it?

Ans. *Sachin Tendulkar is the best batsman India has produced, isn't he?*

(x) More you read less you understand.

Ans. *The more you read, the less you understand.*

(b) Supply the missing words. 1 × 5 = 5

(i) Mr. Sharma is senior__________ Mr. Verma.

Ans. *Mr. Sharma is senior <u>to</u> Mr. Verma.*

(ii) He is ____________ poor to afford travelling by air.

Ans. *He is <u>too</u> poor to afford travelling by air.*

(iii) More than 160 million people suffer__________malaria.

Ans. *More than 160 million people suffer <u>from</u> malaria.*

(iv) Beware__________ pickpockets.

Ans. *Beware <u>of</u> pickpockets.*

(v) Time and__________wait for none.

Ans. *Time and <u>tide</u> wait for none.*

(c) Use the correct forms of the verbs given in brackets: **1×5=5**

(i) Your friends__________ for you for over an hour, (wait)

Ans. *Your friends <u>waited</u> for you for over an hour.*

(ii) It is not worth__________ so much money for this concert. (pay)

Ans. *It is not worth <u>paying</u> so much money for this concert.*

(iii) When I reached the station, the train__________. (leave)

Ans. *When I reached the station, the train <u>had left.</u>*

(iv) I __________ the Taj Mahal last month. (visit)

Ans. *I <u>visited</u> the Taj Mahal last month.*

(v) The criminal__________the victim with a blunt object. (attack)

Ans. *The criminal <u>attacked</u> the victim with a blunt object.*

(d) Write the antonyms of the following: **1 × 5 = 5**

(i) Arrival **Ans.** *Departure*

(ii) Introvert **Ans.** *Extrovert*

(iii) Ascend **Ans.** *Descend*

(iv) Save **Ans.** *Spent*

(v) Mortal **Ans.** *Immortal*

Q 5. (a) Rewrite each of the following sentences as directed without changing the meaning: **1 × 10 = 10**

(i) He is too arrogant to listen to advice. (Change into a complex sentence)

Ans. *He is so arrogant that he cannot listen to advice.*

(ii) He said to me, "What is your name?" (Change into indirect speech)

Ans. *He asked me what my name was.*

(iii) My mother asked me if I had finished my breakfast. (Change into direct speech)

Ans. *My mother said to me, "Did you finish your breakfast."?*

(iv) The people will make him president. (Change into passive voice)

Ans. *He will be made President by the people.*

(v) My pocket has been picked. (Change into active voice)

Ans. *The pick pocket has picked my pocket.*

(vi) He confessed that he was guilty. (Change into a simple sentence)

Ans. *He confessed his guilt.*

(vii) He ran fast to reach the bus stop. (Change into an interrogative sentence)

Ans. *Did he not run fast to reach the bus stop?*

(viii) To the best of my knowledge, he is a vegetarian. (Begin the sentence : As far as ...)

Ans. *As far as I know, he is a vegetarian.*

(ix) A.R. Rehman is a versatile music composer,_______? (Supply an appropriate tag question)

Ans. *A.R. Rehman is a versatile music composer, isn't he?*

(x) It is a pity that a noble person should suffer. (Change into an exclamatory sentence)

Ans. *What a pity that a noble person suffers!*

(b) Use the following words to make sentences that bring out their meaning clearly. Do not change the form of the words. **1 × 5 = 5**

(i) drought

Ans. *Drought – Farmers are under heavy debts because of drought for the second consecutive year.*

(ii) profitable

Ans. *The coaching classes is quite a profitable profession.*

(iii) plunge

Ans. *The value of the gold has plunged to the lowest ebb nowadays.*

(iv) deformity

Ans. *The physical deformity could not stop Yadwinder to become an IAS Officer.*

(v) restraint

Ans. *A public figure should speak with restraint.*

(c) Choose the appropriate word to fill in the blanks: **1 × 5 = 5**

(i) Slow and ________ wins the race. (study/steady)

Ans. *Slow and <u>steady</u> wins the race.*

(ii) The farm scientists have discovered a new ________ to combat soil erosion. (device/devise)

Ans. *The farm scientists have discovered a new <u>device</u> to combat soil erosion.*

(iii) Going back on your word is a _______ of trust. (breach/break)

Ans. *Going back on your word is a breach of trust.*

(iv) A_______ of cars was following the minister. (fleet/float)

Ans. *A fleet of cars was following the minister.*

(v) The businessman tried to _______ a deal with inspector. (strike/stroke)

Ans. *The businessman tried to strike a deal with inspector.*

(d) Use these idioms/phrases in sentences of your own to bring out their meaning clearly. Do not change the form of the words: 1 × 5 = 5

(i) in spite of

Ans. *In spite of the fact that Subhash had a very shady past, the company gave him one more chance.*

(ii) a bed of roses

Ans. *The position of Prime Minister of India is not a bed of roses.*

(iii) cold war

Ans. *USA and USSR had a cold war for a long period.*

(iv) to rule with an iron hand

Ans. *Sardar Patel believed in ruling with an iron hand and that is why he earned the epithet 'Iron Man of India'.*

(v) to make haste

Ans. *Joshi is very unpopular for making haste and spoiling everything all the time.*

UPSC (MAIN) EXAM – 2014

ENGLISH

(Compulsory)

Time allowed: 3 hours **Maximum Marks: 300**

Candidates should attempt all questions.

The number of marks carried by each question is indicated at the end of the questions.

Answer must be written in English.

Q 1. Write an essay in about 600 words on any one topic: (100)

(a) What kind of crisis in India facing – moral or economic?

(b) Participating in sports helps develop good character.

(c) Should students be allowed to grade their teachers?

(d) Not everything that can be counted counts, and not everything that counts can be counted.

ESSAY

Not Everything that can be counted Counts, and not Everything that Counts can be counted.

Not everything that can be counted counts and not everything that counts can be counted, which means very often things which seem important for us today turn out to be not important later on in life and things which seem insignificant today, assumes importance later on. Many times in our childhood we have felt depressed when things did not happen the way we wanted it or we did not get what we asked for. Later on when we look back, we find that our worries and anxieties on such issues were unnecessary. Many of those issues would seem trivial today.

The beauty of life is unpredictable. The very unpredictability and uncertainty of life is the real challenge. Time is the most important blessing in life and life in itself is a great blessing. If we make a flashback, then we can realise that in the depression of the past and the anxiety of the future, we have lost the present. To be present to the present and remain present in the present can make us feel that not everything that can be counted counts, and not everything that counts can be counted.

Life is a pendulum between full of success and failure, hopes and disappointments but the most important thing in life how we look at all these things and make a differentiation between important and unimportant things at various stages of life. The other most important thing is our attitude towards life and our response to all the good and bad things of life.

Health is the greatest wealth because a healthy mind resides in a healthy body and produces healthy ideas. Translating those ideas into action makes our life meaningful. Lethargy, idleness and drudgery are the greatest demotivators in life. To keep moving, and keeping pace with the pace of life, is the most important thing. But man loses health to gain wealth, and then loses wealth to regain health. Here lies the tragedy of life.

Man doesn't try to recognise what he can control and what he cannot control. He overlooks the hairline difference between important and unimportant things in life and his blind ambitions, incessant craze for money, his unrealistic inclination for materialism and his mental slavery to excessive consumerism make his life miserable.

At the end, when he realises the futility of the so called worldly attainments, it becomes already too late and goes beyond repair and cure.

There are people who first watch their parents making this useless rat race but they do not learn any lesson. Rather they knowingly/ unknowingly start their own rat race, and if they turn out to be winner on worldly fronts, then they compel their children to run the same rat race to maintain and aggrandize them. If per chance their children fail, then they impose their failures, fractured dreams and frustrations on them and this race goes on and on incessantly.

Ultimately what matters are not external achievements, although they are necessary, but man's spiritual growth and journey. Material comforts and achievements must be considered as a stepping stone to the ultimate aim of man's continuous journey to achieve enlightenment.

So to sum up, it is very important in life to understand priorities and not to let the life meander meaninglessly.

Q 2. Read carefully the passage below and write your answers to the questions that follow in clear, correct and concise language: 15×5 = 75

A complete reading programme, therefore, should include four factors: at least one good book each week, a newspaper or news magazine, magazines of comment and interpretation, and book reviews. If your keep feeding your intelligence with these four foods, you can be sure that your brain cells will be properly nourished. To this must be added the digestive process that comes from your own thinking and from discussion with individuals or groups.

It is often desirable to make books that you own personally, part of your mind by underlining or by marking in the margin the more important statements. This will help you to understand the book as you first read it, because out of the mass of details you must have selected the essential ideas. It will help you to remember better the gist of the book, since the physical act of underlining, with your eyes on the page, tends to put the thought more firmly into your brain cells. It will save time whenever you need to refer to the book.

Above all, never forget that creative intelligence is correlation of facts and ideas, not mere memorising. What counts is what you can do with your knowledge, by linking it with other things you have studied or observed. If you read Plutarch's life of Julius Caesar, think how his rise to political power paralleled the technique of Adolf Hitler, or that of your local political boss. If you read a play by Shakespeare, think how his portrayal of the characters helps you to understand someone you know. In everything you read, keep at the back of your mind what it means to your life here and now, how it supports or challenges the things you were taught in school, in church and at home, and how the wisdom you get from books can guide you in your thinking, in your career, in your voting as a citizen and in your personal morals.

Questions:

(a) What are the four things required for a complete reading programme and why?

Ans. *Reading of a good book each week, a newspaper, magazines and book-reviews go into making a complete reading programme. This is so because these reading activities give food for thought and thus contribute to the growth of our psyche and intelligence.*

(b) What else is required to feed your intelligence?

Ans. *To feed our intelligence, critical thinking and constructive discussion with individuals and groups are indispensable.*

(c) Why does the writer recommend underlining or marking in the margin the more important statements?

Ans. *While engaged with reading, underlining or marking in the margin is important as it is quite helpful in remembering the core message of the book. It also saves time whenever the book is referred to in future.*

(d) What use can you put your knowledge to?

Ans. *Knowledge acquired though the act of memorisation is not of much significance. It matters when it is linked with the things we study or observe. In other words, the knowledge should give a better understanding of life and the society in which we live.*

(e) How can what you learn from books help you in your life?

Ans. *Knowledge that we acquire through books must help us in conducting and organising ourselves in better terms, than those who are ignorant and unknowledgeable. It should help us in facing head on the challenges of our life.*

Q 3. Make a précis of the following passage in about one-third of its length. Please do not give a title to it. Précis should be written in your own language. 75

If this century has, in the famous phrase, made the world safe for democracy, the next challenge is to make a world safe for diversity. It is in India's interest to ensure that the world as a whole must reflect the idea that is already familiar to all Indians – that is shouldn't matter what the colour of your skin is, the kind of food you eat, the sounds you make when you speak, the God you choose to worship (or not), so long as you want to play by the same rules as everybody else, and dream the same dreams. It is not essential in a democratic world to agree all the time, as long as we agree on the ground rules of how we will disagree. There are the global principles we must strive to uphold if we are to be able to continue to uphold them securely at home.

We want a world that gives us the conditions of peace and security that will permit us to grow and flourish, safe from foreign depredations but open to external opportunities. Whether global institutions adapt and revive will be determined by whether those in charge are capable to showing the necessary leadership. Right now many of us would suggest that there is a global governance deficit. Reversing it would require strong leadership in the international community by a number of powers, including the emerging ones. India is an obvious contender to provide some of that leadership. India should aim not just at being powerful – it should set new standards for what the powerful must do.

This is a huge challenge, and one to which India must rise. An analogy from another field is not encouraging; many would argue that India has not acquitted itself well when given the change to have global impact in one domain – that of the sport of cricket, where India accounts for more than 80 percent of the game's revenues and perhaps 90 percent of its viewership, giving it an impact on the sport that no country can rival. Clearly, international opinion does not believe that in its domination of world cricket, India has set new standards for what the powerful must do. Broadening the analogy to global geopolitics, one could well say: India, your world needs you.

So India must play its due part in the stewardship of the global commons (including everything from the management of the Internet to the rules governing the exploitation of outer space). We can do it. India is turning increasingly outwards as a result of our new economic profile on the global stage, our more dispersed interests around the world, and the reality that other countries, in our neighbourhood as well as in Africa, are looking to us for support and security. India has the ability and the vision to promote global partnerships across the broad range of its interests; it only needs to act.

The world economic crisis should give us an opportunity to promote economic integration with our neighbours in the subcontinent who look to the growing Indian market to sell their goods and maintain their own growth. But as long as South Asia remains divided by futile rivalries and some continue to believe that terrorism can be a useful instrument of their strategic doctrines that is bound to remain a distant prospect. We in South Asia need to look to the future, to an interrelated future on our subcontinent, where geography becomes an instrument of opportunity in a mutual growth story, where history binds rather than divides, where trade and cross-border links flourish and bring prosperity to all our peoples.

PRECIS

After securing democracy, the establishment of diversity is the next challenge in this century. India has already given a roadmap of the diversity to the world through its plural principles, including the diverse range of coloured people, food habits, multiple spoken languages and numerous religious faiths. Global principles must be adhered to secure safety and order at local levels. To create favourable conditions for securing peace and security, capable and strong leadership is indispensable and India is striving as a strong contender to realise this objective. India as a powerful nation for instance, has set a new standards for the world in the field of cricket accounting for 80 percent of the game's revenue and 90 percent of its viewership. In addition, the country has also set various landmarks in the field of management of internet, exploitation of outer space and through its new economic profile and vision has turned out to be a major promoter of global economy. To beat the economic crisis and to promote economic integration, many countries including the neighbourers look forward to India. These goals including the promotion of mutual growth could be realised sooner and better if futile rivalries, terrorism and many other divisive activities could be countered internationally in unison. Nations of the world acting as instruments of opportunities, promotion of international trade and flourishing of cross-border links are essential for bringing prosperity to peoples across the globe.

Q 4. (a) Rewrite the following sentences after making necessary corrections. Please do not make unnecessary changes in the original sentence. 10

(i) School is very near my home.

Ans. *School is very near to my home.*

(ii) They never fail who die in great cause.

Ans. *They never fail who die for a great cause.*

(iii) It rained an hour before.

Ans. *It has rained an hour before.*

(iv) He wrote a most complete account of his travels.

Ans. *He wrote a complete account of his travels.*

(v) Either of these three answers is incorrect.

Ans. *Anyone of these three answers is incorrect.*

(vi) You will be late until you hurry.

Ans. *You will be late unless you hurry.*

(vii) He is seldom or ever absent from school.

Ans. *He is seldom or never absent from school.*

(viii) The colours so passed off one another that she could not distinguish them.

Ans. *The colours so matched that she could not distinguish them.*

(ix) The general as well as his soldiers were killed in the battle.

Ans. *The general as well as his solders was killed in the battle.*

(x) The boat was drowned.

Ans. *The boat was sunk.*

(b) Supply the missing words: **5**

(i) If you see him give him __________ message.

Ans. *my*

(ii) I hope to reach the station __________ an hour at the outside.

Ans. *within*

(iii) __________ Rustam and Sohrab, there were three other boys present.

Ans. *Besides*

(iv) Invalids are not capable __________ continued exertion.

Ans. *of*

(v) __________ he had not paid his bill, his electricity was cut off.

Ans. *As*

(c) Use the correct forms of the verbs in brackets: **5**

(i) His company is greatly __________ after. (seek)

Ans. *sought*

(ii) His courage __________ him. (forsake)

Ans. *forsook*

(iii) The terrified people __________ to the mountains. (flee)

Ans. *fled*

(iv) The police __________ no stone unturned to trace the culprits. (leave)

Ans. *left*

(v) The robber __________ him a blow on the head. (strike)

Ans. *struck*

(d) Write the antonyms of the following: **5**

(i) Ability	**Ans.** *Inability*
(ii) Precise	**Ans.** *Exhaustive*
(iii) Constructive	**Ans.** *Destructive*
(iv) Extravagant	**Ans.** *Frugal*
(v) Pretentious	**Ans.** *Humble*

Q 5. (a) Rewrite each of the following sentences as directed without changing the meaning: **10**

(i) He finished his exercise and put away his books. (Change into simple)

Ans. *Having finished his exercise, he put away his books.*

(ii) In the event of his being late, he will be punished. (Change into compound)

Ans. *He should not be late, otherwise he will be punished.*

(iii) He said to me, "I have often told you not to play with fire". (Change into indirect speech)

Ans. *He told me that he had often said to me not to play with fire.*

(iv) He said that he had come to see him. (Change into direct speech)

Ans. *He said, "I have come to see you".*

(v) He drove too fast for the police to catch. (Remove 'too')

Ans. *He drove so fast that the police could not catch.*

(vi) The audience loudly cheered the Mayor's speech. (Change into passive voice)

Ans. *The Mayor's speech was loudly cheered by the audience.*

(vii) A reward was given to him by the Governor. (Change into active voice)

Ans. *The Governor gave him a reward.*

(viii) Sita is not one of the cleverest girls in the class. (Change into comparative degree)

Ans. *There are many girls in the class cleverer than Sita.*

(ix) I was doubtful whether it was you. (Change into negative form)

Ans. *I was not sure whether it was you.*

(x) It is sad to think that youth should pass away. (Change into exclamatory sentence)

Ans. *How sad it is to think that youth should pass away!*

(b) Use each of the following words to make a sentence that brings out their meaning clearly. Do not change the form of the words. **5**

(i) gratitude — **Ans.** *I expressed my sense of gratitude to the college authorities for granting me a scholarship.*

(ii) flavour — **Ans.** *Anaadi likes strawberry flavour of ice-cream.*

(iii) explosion — **Ans.** *The explosion of the bomb created terror in the minds of the people.*

(iv) dismal — **Ans.** *What a dismal scene it was!*

(v) clumsy — **Ans.** *I do not like the clumsy way he was doing the job.*

(c) Choose the appropriate world to fill in the blanks. **5**

(i) He got a __________ blow from his enemy. (deadly/ deathly)

Ans. *deadly*

(ii) The __________ of his speech was very lucid and natural. (delivery/ deliverance)

Ans. *delivery*

(iii) I do not know how to express my gratitude; you have been __________to me. (beneficial/ beneficent)

Ans. *beneficent*

(iv) My friend will __________ me to the hospital. (accompany/ escort)

Ans. *accompany*

(v) We sat in the __________ of a tree and relaxed a while. (shadow/ shade)

Ans. *shade*

(d) Use these phrases in sentences of your own to bring out their meaning clearly. Do not change the form of the words. **5**

(i) According to

Ans. *According to me, democracy is the best form of government.*

(ii) All of a sudden

Ans. *All of a sudden the day turned stormy.*

(iii) Ready money

Ans. *Everybody is in the pursuit of ready money.*

(iv) A burning question

Ans. *Nowadays, women's safety is a burning question.*

(v) Ins and outs

Ans. *I know the ins and outs of the share market.*

UPSC (MAIN) EXAM – 2013
ENGLISH
(Compulsory)

Time allowed: 3 hours **Maximum Marks: 300**

Candidates should attempt all questions.

The number of marks carried by each question is indicated at the end of the questions.

Answer must be written in English.

Q 1. Write short essays in about 300 words on each of the following: 100

(a) We Indians are hypocrites

(b) Fitness and healthcare – Latest fad in urban India

ESSAY 1

We Indians are hypocrites

There will be no exaggeration in saying, "hypocrisy thy name as well as nature: both are Indian". We Indians, with very few exceptions, are by and large by nature and by compulsion hypocrites is a blatant truth.

Majority of us are hypocrites by nature. A few are hypocrites because of social taboos, social compulsions and personal or professional bindings. A few inherit it, learn it, imbibe it, nourish it, theorize it and practise it religiously. A great many relish it and take pride in it. A few who condemn it and discourage it are called impractical, nincompoops, buffoons and unfit and mismatch for the society.

It goes without saying that Indians have double standards. Duality of character is the only singularity most commonly found amongst majority of Indians. We adore martyrs and patriots but indulge in the most antinational activities. At the same time there is no denying the fact that India gave birth to Patel, Bose, Bhagat Singh and innumerable legendary patriots and martyrs.

In the name of humanity, we indulge in the most inhuman activities but adore people like Mother Teresa, Kailash Satyarthy, Gandhi, Periyar, Jyotibha Phule, Vivekanand who are great altruists and philanthropists.

We claim, profess and try to be a socialist, secular democracy but examples of most undemocratic activities are umpteen. India faced a large number of communal riots since independence but the epitomes of secularism like Gandhi, Nehru, Maulana Azad, are also there.

India has the largest number of laws in the world. But lawlessness is the order of the day. But legal gems like Krishna Iyer, Palkiwala, PN Bhagwati, Justice Verma, are also the pride of India.

Hypocrisy is a dominant trait because we suffer from crises of character, credibility, leadership, transparency and accountability. We can spend anything in the name of religion, superstition and obscurantism, but we are not willing to spend a rupee for the needy and the helpless.

We adore women as goddesses but newspaper headlines of crime against women speak about the intensity of our hypocrisy. We worship many goddesses but female feoticide, female infanticide and abortions is a common story.

We instruct our children to respect elders but we cannot afford to look after even our parents in their old age. We profess humanity, integrity, truthfulness but the history of our political journey shows how dishonest, corrupt our rulers have been. Our nationalism is most vocal at the time of Indo-Pak match, but otherwise nation and nationalism stand nowhere on our priorities.

“Honesty is the best policy, “Hard work pays in the long run” are all beautiful terms buried under the garbage of sycophancy, hatred, opportunism and hypocrisy.

ESSAY 2

Fitness And Healthcare – A Latest Fad In Urban India

It is indeed a fact that fitness and healthcare is a latest fad in urban India. India’s exposure to the global market and products, the IT revolution and the upwardly mobile middle class has led to huge awareness about fitness and healthcare.

People, especially urban Indians, have become health conscious and fitness freaks. Hollywood and Bollywood have also played a great role. Earlier, people were not much aware about diseases, medical techniques, scientific discoveries and innovations, health management strategies. But now the spread of knowledge and awareness about these things have given boost to fitness and healthcare among urban Indians. They have started managing their health with inputs from medical experts, physical fitness experts, physiotherapists.

Now a large number of urban Indians can be seen in parks and playgrounds in the morning and evening sessions for walking, running, hopping, jumping, playing exercises etc.

One the one hand, people have been addicted to junk foods and consequent ailments. But at the same time they resort to fitness programmes and healthcare management strategies to reduce the risk factors to their lives.

The levels of stress/ tension have been growing manifold because of blind ambition, craze for money, and insatiable thirst for recognition, unquenched jealousies and many other things.

Their stress/ tension is the biggest cause of concern and also a source of a number of serious ailments like blood pressure, hypertension leading to heart attacks, brain seizure and many others.

So to manage and balance these things, fitness and healthcare is becoming the focus of attention. People are advised to maintain the balance between their personal and professional life, control their dietary habits, have regular medical check ups and devote time for physical fitness. A healthy mind resides in a healthy body.

Q 2. Read carefully the passage given below and write your answers to the questions that follow in clear, correct, and concise language of your own: 50

In barely one generation, we’ve moved from exulting in the time – saving devices that have so expanded our lives, to trying to get away from them – often, in order to make more time. The more ways we have to connect, the more of us seem desperate to unplug. Like a teenager, we appear to have gone from knowing nothing about the world to knowing too much, all but overnight.

The average person spends at least eight and a half hours a day in front of the screen. The average teenager spends or receives 75 text messages a day. Since luxury, as any economist will tell you, is a function of scarcity, the children of tomorrow will crave nothing more than freedom, if only for a short while, from all the blinking machines, streaming videos and scrolling headlines that leave them feeling empty, and too full all at once. The urgency of slowing down – to find the time and space to think – is nothing new, of course, and wiser souls have always reminded us that the more attention we pay to the moment, the less time and energy we have to place it in some larger context. Even half a century ago, Marshall McLuhan warned, "When things come to you very fast, naturally you lose touch with yourself".

Yet few of those voices can be heard these days, precisely because 'breaking news' is coming through perpetually on the news channels, and Meena is posting images of her summer vacation and the phone is ringing. We barely have enough time to see how little time we have. And the more that floods in on us, the less of ourselves we have to give to every snippet.

We have more and more ways to communicate, as Thoreau noted, but less and less to say. Partly because we are so busy communicating, and as he might also have said – we are rushing to meet so many deadlines that we hardly register that what we need most are lifelines. So what to do? The central paradox of the machines that have made our lives so much brighter, quicker, longer and healthier is that they cannot teach us how to make the best use of them; the information revolution came without an instruction manual. All the data in the world cannot teach us how to sift through data; images don't show us how to process images. The only way to do justice to our onscreen lives is by summoning exactly the emotional and moral clarity that cannot be found on any screen.

Maybe that is why more and more people, even if they have no religious commitment, seem to be turning to yoga or meditation, or tai chi; these are not New Age fads so much as ways to connect with that what could be called the wisdom of old age. A series of tests in recent years has shown that after spending time in a quiet rural setting, subjects "exhibit greater attentiveness, stronger memory and generally improved cognition. Their brains become both calmer and sharper." More than that, empathy, as well as deep thought, depends on neural processes that are "inherently slow". The very ones our high-speed lives have little time for.

Questions:

(a) According to the author, what is likely to become a scarcity in the future?

Ans. *According to the author, on account of excessive dependence on machines, the scarcity would be to get freedom from all sorts of gadgets and machinery.*

(b) What ability have people lost thanks to the constant inflow of data?

Ans. *People have lost the capacity to think, thanks to the constant flow of data.*

(c) Why does the author say, "We have more and more ways to communicate, but less and less to say"?

Ans. *The author says that we have more and more ways to communicate but less and less to say because we are highly busy with communicating through various medium, but not able to articulate our thoughts and express them.*

(d) Why are people taking an active interest in old-age fads?

Ans. *People are taking active interest in old-age fads as the latter give ways to people to get connected with the wisdom of the age.*

(e) Why is modern man unable to empathise with others?

Ans. *The very high-speed lives or life-styles leave little time for empathy as the latter requires a deep emotional connect.*

Q3. (a) Make a précis of the following passage in about one-third of its length. Please do not suggest a title. 60

Honesty in business dealings in or other areas are not the only measures of morals and values. The strength of character of a person is also measured by uncompromising aversion to cowardice, intrigue, envy, ambiguity, falsehood, disloyalty, treachery, in short, all undignified actions. There are, in reality, few human beings endowed with a truly spotless character. This is because an almost immaculate character does not exist until the last lives in human form. Educated individuals are not necessarily endowed with good morals and values. Infact, some of them use education and their intellect as a tool for deceit. However, the advantages and the need for education and culture cannot be denied. They contribute largely for the development of intellectual ability and the power to reason, which are the means by which the spirit analyses, compares, infers and arrives at conclusions in the search for truth about the meaning of life. The most precious assets of the soul are its morals and values, but they are not easy to build. The character of each person requires longer periods of thoughtfulness, reasoning and the practice of those values, during many reincarnations, in the course of which, ideas sink in under life experiences. It is only after enduring much disillusionment, grief, injustice and ingratitude for many successive corporeal lives, that a person will be able to measure, in the innermost recesses of his soul, the extent of human moral misery. Then, disgusted, he rebels against it and opens the door to a more ethical and honourable life. Thus, having known and experienced suffering, the spirit, in countless reincarnations, gradually frees itself from evil actions, and through enlightenment and conviction follows the rigid tracks of a flawless conduct. It is of great significance to talk about morals and values and it is also crucial to define the lines of character that everyone should consider in their lives. Some of the most important ones are: good judgement, fairness, common sense, punctuality, loyalty, courage, magnanimity, dignity, gratitude, politeness, faithfulness, moderation, truthfulness, self-respect, respect for others, etc. All these qualities, if properly cultivated, compose a prime set of dignifying virtues which accounts for a refined character. For example, we all make mistakes and to err is human. However, once an honest person is advised and becomes convinced of his mistake, he should admit it and try not to repeat it. Unfortunately it is common practice to conceal one's mistakes, instead of avoiding them. This is very detrimental to spiritual growth. Most people seldom use impartiality and justice in the innermost evaluation of their own actions. Even those who are too harsh in the judgement of other people's action, for whom they always have words of criticism and reproach, do not escape the usual tendency. When their own faults are concerned, they find a full, lenient, absolvent justification. In this way, not only it denotes lack of character, but mistakes often end up incorporated to human habits. By acting this way, an individual loses his self-respect and his sense of character and dignity and becomes corrupted. What everyone should do, is to face up his mistakes and avoid new mistakes, by improving his sense of morals and values, with the help of his will-power.

PRECIS

Not only in business dealings or activities, but also in day-to-day life, honesty is indispensable for the strong character building of a person. Such a man makes no compromises with such false values as cowardice, intrigue, envy, falsehood, disloyalty treachery or any other indignified action. There are very few human beings blessed with unblemished character. Even educated ones are no exception. Education, no doubt, helps in the development of intellectual ability and the power to reason, yet it cannot ensure that the educated people have good character. Thoughtfulness, reason and the practise of values under varied and long life experiences are essential for the making of an ethical soul. Experience of suffering is a must for understanding the pain of others. Reflection and practise of such dignifying virtues as fairness, judgement, loyality, courage, magnanimity, gratitude, politeness, moderation, truthfulness, self-respect and respect for others are essential for a refined character. The acts of concealing one's mistakes or not admitting them have fatal consequences for the spiritual growth. Fairness and impartiality are must, be it a case of self evolution or that of others. Parameters and yardsticks of judgement should remain the same, otherwise the person is nothing less than a corrupt one. Strong will power is a mandate for improving one's sense of morals and values.

(b) Make a précis of the following passage in about one-third of its length. Please do not suggest a title. 40

People write and publish autobiographies and autobiographical sketches for a number of reasons. One of these reasons is to put on record the events of a famous or influential career. But not all autobiographies, not even the autobiographies most frequently and widely read, are by famous or extraordinary men. Another reason is to hand on to others, wisdom won through experience and hard labour. Yet many fine autobiographers seem to have little concern to teach or to persuade. A third reason is to distill from past experience events, persons, and situations which hold a firm place in memory, and to put true values on them. In this sense, autobiography is, as Somerset Maugham has said, a 'summing-up' and its first utility is to its author himself.

Whatever its purpose or the fame of the man who writes it, autobiography is a thing created out of the recollections of life. It is not life itself. Whether it be valuable or useless depends upon whether it is well-or ill-made. Good autobiographies can be mined from inconspicuous lives.

For, autobiography is the inclusive and summary form of what we call 'themes of experience'. It may contain reminiscences, descriptions of places, of animals, of people, the identification of characteristics preferences and prejudices, and other matters as well. It has the traits of all these minor forms.

An autobiography is objectively true, but is not indiscriminately inclusive. It presents a selection of detailed episodes with sufficient fullness to preserve their essential qualities. It is usually written within the framework defined by a consistent point of view. It presents its subject in more than two dimensions, fusing the person and his actions with setting, manner and purpose. One further trait of autobiographical writing raises a few special problems: by its nature autobiography tempts its author to proceed chronologically. The events sort themselves by the calendar, and it is a natural impulse of every autobiographer to begin with the words "I was born on ..."

Strict chronological arrangement poses a discipline of some force. It is by no means easy to "being at the beginning, go until you come to the end, and then stop." Considerations other than the calendar have a way of forcing their way to notice. With due care, however, a chronological autobiography can be accomplished.

It is important to remember that chronology is not the only principle by which autobiography can be organized. Benjamin Franklin, whose procedure in his autobiography is basically chronological, does not hesitate to recognize the Philadelphia girl who laughed at him as the very one who subsequently became his wife. Joseph Conrad prefers the patter of walking tour to that of the calendar, and his richly imaginative account is stored with pertinent associations of the past with the present and future. Often, to the autobiographer, it seems that life does not pass so much as it accumulates. Qualities emerge as identities independent of time. For this reason, we should not as we write feel compelled to maintain a steady rate of advance through the time marks or our stories. Like Hazlitt on his journey, we linger over a choice adventure or a valued friend, and then, if we choose, we skip a few years to catch up.

Precis

Autobiographies are written with numerous purposes. Record of life of an influential career, sharing wisdom gained through life experienced, or to sum up, significant experiences of one's past are the key reasons for writing autobiographies. Autobiographies are a kind of reminiscence. Even so called insignificant lives could be source of good autobiographies. Life accounts are primarily a summary of one's life experiences. They are not all inclusive, being a selection of episodes of one's life and need not necessarily be a chronological account of one's life. It may be an account of one's natural impulses bereft of objectivity and strictly arranged chronological sequences of one's life. Great writers like Benjamin Franklin, Joseph Conrad and Hazlift have compromised with chronology in their illuminating autobiographies, yet have got prominence by highlighting the other dimensions of autobiographies such imagination, adventures, journeys, identities and accumulative experiences.

Q 4. (a) Use each of the following words to make sentences that bring out their meaning clearly. Do not change the form of the words. 10

(i) Desultory

Ans. Desultory – After riots, the town bore a desultory look.

(ii) Grapevine

Ans. Disclosing the secrets of the company, he came to be notorious as a grapevine.

(iii) Holistic

Ans. Dalai Lama has a holistic outlook towards life.

(iv) Insidious

Ans. Cancer is an insidious disease.

(v) Intransigence

Ans. The habit of intransigence is not good for the healthy growth of one's personality.

(vi) Paradigm

Ans. There was a paradigm shift in Kejriwal's strategy in 2015 Delhi elections.

(vii) Susceptible

Ans. *A weak person becomes susceptible to many diseases.*

(viii) Ubiquitous

Ans. *Media is very ubiquitous nowadays.*

(ix) Voracious

Ans. *Khuswant Singh was a voracious reader.*

(x) Venerable

Ans. *As a leader of the chain of schools, he held a venerable position amongst the student community.*

(b) Correct the following sentences without changing their meaning. Please do not make unnecessary changes in the original sentence. 10

(i) One must do what he thinks best.

Ans. *One must do what one thinks is best.*

(ii) He will surely not do that, did he?

Ans. *He will surely not do that, will he?*

(iii) Can I leave the room now, Sir?

Ans. *May I leave the room now, Sir?*

(iv) My neighbour, along with two friends, was pushing his car which is stalled.

Ans. *My neighbour, along with two friends, was pushing his car which was stalled.*

(v) I thought to help him, but he did not welcome my suggestion.

Ans. *I thought of helping him, but he did not welcome my suggestion.*

(vi) When I was a child, I enjoyed to eat ice cream in the bench.

Ans. *When I was a child, I enjoyed eating ice cream in the bench.*

(vii) The Principal, along with the teachers, are planning to apply for a leave.

Ans. *The Principal, along with the teachers, is planning to apply for a leave.*

(viii) Do you have an idea who is that man?

Ans. *Do you have an idea who that man is?*

(ix) Unemployment as well as poverty influence the votes.

Ans. *Unemployment as well as poverty influences the votes.*

(x) When I woke up, the man already disappeared after committing murder in the running train.

Ans. *When I woke up, the man had already disappeared after committing the murder in the running train.*

(c) Rewrite each of the following sentences as directed without changing the meaning: **10**

(i) No one dares to criticise her for what she says. (Rewrite the sentence starting with 'No matter')

Ans. *No matter what she says no one dare criticise her.*

(ii) Radha was the eldest. She had to look after her parents. (Combine to form a single sentence)

Ans. *Radha being the eldest had to look after her parents.*

(iii) She decorated the room. The purpose was to make it look beautiful. (Combine using 'so that')

Ans. *She decorated the room so that it looked beautiful.*

(iv) "What a beautiful day!", said the young tourist. (Change the narration)

Ans. *The young tourist exclaimed with wonder that the day was very beautiful.*

(v) The one-man committee determined there was no need to take action. (Rewrite using passive structure)

Ans. *It was determined by the one-man committee that no action need to be taken.*

(vi) The proud father remarked, "What a wonderful batsman my son is!" (Change into indirect speech)

Ans. *The proud father exclaimed with pride what a wonderful batsman his son was.*

(vii) My mother remarked, "Aren't the children lovely?" (Change into indirect speech)

Ans. *My mother asked if the children weren't lovely.*

(viii) Cricket fans filled the streets during the World Cup. (Rewrite using passive structure)

Ans. *The streets were filled with cricket fans during World Cup.*

(ix) It would be wonderful if we could go the Shimla. (Change into an exclamatory sentence using 'how')

Ans. *How wonderful it would be if we could go to Shimla!*

(x) I could have finished the work. But I would have had to go out early. (Combine into one sentence beginning with 'Had')

Ans. *Had I gone out early, I could have finished the work.*

(d) Fill in the blanks using one of the following linkers: **5**

In case, but, even, though, so provided, as

(i) _______ he was late for the meeting, his boss didn't get angry.

Ans. *Though he was late for the meeting, his boss didn't get angry.*

(ii) _______ he was late for the meeting, his boss became angry.

Ans. *As he was late for the meeting, his boss became angry.*

(iii) I'll not get angry, _______ you are not late for the meeting.

Ans. *I'll not get angry, though you are late for the meeting.*

(iv) I started early _______ I was still late for the meeting.

Ans. *I started early but I was still late for the meeting.*

(v) I'll give you her telephone number _______ you have problems finding her place.

Ans. *I'll give you her telephone number in case you have problems finding her place.*

(e) Rewrite the following sentences using 'it' at the beginning of the sentence. **5**

(i) Impressing Ramesh Mohan would be a piece of cake.

Ans. *It would be a piece of cake impressing Ramesh Mohan.*

(ii) Visiting old people in hospitals is a very good idea.

Ans. *It is a very good idea visiting old people in hospitals.*

(iii) To smoke 20 cigarettes a day is bad for your health.

Ans. It is bad for your health to smoke 20 cigarettes a day.

(iv) Chatting with strangers on the computer can be very dangerous.

Ans. *It can be very dangerous chatting with strangers on the computer.*

(v) My father says, keeping the computer on, all day, is a waste of electricity.

Ans. *It is a waste of electricity my father says, keeping the computer on all day.*

(f) Choose the appropriate word to fill in the blanks. **5**

(i) My teacher said that I need to _______ (practice, practice) more.

Ans. *My teacher said that I need to practise more.*

(ii) The hot weather _______ (affects, effects) people in different ways.

Ans. *The hot weather affects people in different ways.*

(iii) Wouldn't it be nice if we had to work only on _______ (alternative, alternate) days?

Ans. *Wouldn't it be nice if we had to work only on alternate days?*

(iv) Our politicians are known to _______ (avoid, evade) taxes.

Ans. *Our politicians are known to evade taxes.*

(v) The Principal _______ (complimented, complemented) the students on their find performance.

Ans. *The Principal complimented the students on their fine performance.*

(g) Write the opposite of the following words: **5**

(i) Amateur **Ans.** *Professional*

(ii) Modesty **Ans.** *Snobbery*

(iii) Shallow **Ans.** *Deep*

(iv) Conceited **Ans.** *Humble*

(v) Atheist **Ans.** Theist

UPSC (MAIN) EXAM – 2012
ENGLISH
(Compulsory)

Time allowed: 3 hours ***Maximum Marks: 300***

Candidates should attempt all questions.

The number of marks carried by each question is indicated at the end of the questions.

Answer must be written in English.

Q1. Write an essay in about 300 words on any one of the following: (100)

(a) Indian women in international sports.

(b) Cultivation of organic foods.

(c) Foreign Direct Investment in retail – boon or bane?

(d) How effective are our systems and institution in dealing with disasters?

(e) Food security – legislation and implementation

ESSAY

Foreign Direct Investment in retail – Boon or Bane?

FDI in retail has always been a matter of debate in our country. One school of thought favours it, while another is not in favour of it. Actually, a middle path is the need of the hour. A synthesised and harmonious policy should be preferred. All the pros and cons should be considered carefully.

The recent FDI reforms will have implications in future. The clearance of 51 per cent FDI in multi-brand retailing in September 2012 is a big step and will change the way business is conducted in India. The assured supply chains of organized multi-brand retailing would offer better varieties of products at lower and stable prices to consumers. Further, big retailers would buy products directly from farmers and producers, cutting middlemen, and making way for better price realisation since competition would increase manifold offering alternative opportunities to producers.

The provision of 50 per cent FDI fund going to back-end infrastructure such as storage, logistics and better extension services would substantially reduce wastage and trade and transaction costs. The provision of 30 per cent sourcing from SMEs in India would help them to expand capacity, improve quality, and be exposed to international supply chains. FDI would be very useful in the civil aviation sector which is short of capital and on the verge of collapse. Any FDI inflow into the sector, affected by crisis in two of its largest airlines, Kingfisher and Air India, would not only improve connectivity but also boost technology upgradation and management practices.

An early clearance of 49 per cent FDI in the insurance sector will assure international investors that India is committed to reforms to attract investment. Another indicator that shows that the insurance sector is underdeveloped is insurance density (per capita premium). IRDA estimates that insurance companies require Rs.61, 200 crore to deliver innovative insurance products, better distribution networks and risk management. The increased FDI cap can finance this requirement and will bring better insurance products, technological capabilities, awareness efforts, and expertise and skills in underwriting, actuarial, claims management and data standardisation to India.

Q 2. Read carefully the passage below and write your answers to the questions that follow in clear, correct and concise language. **5 × 15 = 75**

Oratory demands enthusiasm, which can spring only in an earnest soul; and neither beauty of composition nor graceful delivery can compensate for want of passion. To be able to interest people without tiring them is a prime test of oratory. It is a gift that may draw valuable aid from such natural advantages as a noble figure, handsome countenance, and pleasant voice. But there has been no lack of eminent orators of ungainly men at any time. Few have equaled Sir Robert Peel in skillful management of the House of Commons, but he often assumed very undignified postures standing with his hands behind his coat tails, or thumbs buried in the pockets of his waistcoat, and threw one leg over the other in attitudes of nonchalance. The composition of his speeches was slovenly and they were noted for the disorder of their contents. Oliver Cromwell was one of the most influential speakers of his day, but he rarely wore clean linen and his voice was "harsh and untuneable."

The indispensable requisite of oratory is a mind well-stored with knowledge and information, sound reasoning, wit and humour, vehemence, fire, and imaginative insight all conducive to enhance the power of eloquence; but the same speakers are not able to make the same impression in all places, nor secure the same effect at all times. The pinnacle of triumph of oratory is reached when a speaker is able to magnetise his hearers into thinking as he thinks, and feeling as he feels. When Sheridan had concluded his famous speech in Parliament on the "Begum Charge", so great was the excitement caused by it that the Minister concerned besought the House to adjourn the decision of the question, "as being incapacitated from forming a just judgment under the influence of such powerful eloquence."

It is clear that there is a rivalry between the orator and the occasion and the dazzling effect of the moment does not always endure through later cool reflection.

The world moves in continual cycles of action and reaction, and the homage paid to speakers is followed by tests in the course of which there is unrelenting research as to what extent precept and example tally. When there is no wide gulf between the two, further speeches are listened to with increased respect.

Questions:

(a) What are the most important qualities required for becoming a good orator?

(b) What was the effect created by Sheridan's speech?

(c) How can one judge the true effect of a good oration?

(d) What research does the audience do when they listen to speakers?

(e) Which speeches are not taken seriously by an audience?

Ans. ***(a)*** *Good oratory requires enthusiasm, passion, knowledge, reasoning, wit and humour, vehemence, fire and imaginative insights.*

(b) *The effect of Sheridan's speech caused excitement which dumbed the nerves of the concerned Minister to form a just judgment.*

(c) *One can judge the true effect of a good oration when a speaker is able to mesmerize his listeners to think as he thinks, and feel as he feels.*

(d) *There is unrelenting research as to what extent precept and example tally.*

(e) *The speeches which exhibit shallowness and hollowness are not taken seriously.*

Q 3. Make a precis of the following passage in about 200 words. It is not necessary to suggest a title. Failure to write within the word limit may result in deduction of marks. The precis must be written on the separate precis sheets provided which must then be fastened securely inside the answer-book. 75

Taking into account the compelling and inescapable reality of an increasingly resource-constrained world, India needs to link the aspirations of the people and its prospects for accelerated growth to what I would call a "resource-frugal" instead of a "resource-intensive" strategy of development. I believe that such a strategy would enable India to sustain a high rate of growth over a more extended period of time, delivering affluence without waste, and current welfare without sacrificing the welfare of future generations. I will touch upon just a few illustrative examples.

The notion of frugality is current in some sectors of our economy and has been successful enough to attract international attention. "Frugal manufacture" is already acclaimed as Indian industry's contribution to innovative production processes. This involves the stripping down of complex machinery or devices, to their most essential applications without frills. An example is the cost-effective, easy to use, hand-held ECG machine, which is a major contribution to public health. The other is the use of the mobile telephone to deliver information, services as funds on a low-cost and widely spread platform. Even in agriculture, there have been significant successes in promoting production processes which are dramatically economical in the use of water, dispensing with the use of costly chemical fertilizers and pesticides of G.M. seeds and still deliver high agricultural output, ensuring food security. This is frugal agriculture. What should be appreciated is that these innovations, by making products affordable, lead to significant market expansion. This in turn brings economies of scale, further lowering of costs and generating even greater demand in a virtuous, self-reinforcing circle.

The hallmark of any modern society is its ability to deliver rapid affordable and efficient means of mobility to its people. Enabling people to exercise their right to mobility is a critical state responsibility. However, mobility is linked to the use of energy and the use of scarce land, both of which are in short supply in our country. It follows, therefore, that we must have a transport strategy that ensures the most economical use of these resources. The continued expansion of private vehicular transportation is not sustainable. If the density of private car ownership in India were to approach U.S. or European levels, we would be using liquid fuels far in excess of the total consumption of all such fuels globally today. Just as the space required for parking a billion cars and constructing highways for them to run on, would occupy land on a scale that would leave little space for any other activity. Therefore, shifting resources from private transportation to public transportation and investing in the latter to make them convenient, comfortable and cost-effective is another essential component of a "resource-frugal" strategy. Greater mobility ensures a more productive population and a more efficient distribution of goods and services. This is what can ensure a sustained and high rate of growth.

If frugal process is what India is good at, it can add value to each of the sectors of its economy by leveraging its proven strengths in information and communications technology. The systems which make modern economies run, whether these are the power supply networks, the transportation system, the distribution of goods and services, the water supply system, to name only a few, are being transformed through the use of modern data analytics. The placement of sensors at critical points in any economic process generates massive and continuous mass of real time data, which high powered computers, using sophisticated software can analyse in considerable detail and propose what are called "smart" solutions. This reduces waste to the minimum, eliminates redundancies in processes and improves efficiencies all around. This, too, is an example of "resource- frugality". It is India which can provide the biggest market for such value-added services, which can act as a multiplier across the board in a range of sectors in the Indian economy. What is important to appreciate here is that such services are really the hallmark of a flat world because they can add value in developing societies as they can in advanced ones.

The purpose of providing these examples is to add some substance to the overall optimism I retain about our future as a plural, democratic and innovative society, despite the seeming gloom around us.

What is more, each of these innovations enables inclusive growth, because they empower the poor; they profit from leveraging the power of numbers. What we need is to upscale these successes from the margin to the mainstream, from the local to the national level.

PRECIS

India must take recourse to the resource-frugal strategy of development to meet the aspirations of people living in a resource constrained world. Such a strategy of development would help India sustain long term high rate growth of material production leading to affluence and prosperity. Frugal manufacturing, an innovative contribution of Indian industry, needs to be promoted as it is economical and easy to use, and effective in many sectors such as public health, agriculture, information technology etc. It provides people rapid and affordable mobility and thereby supporting the state's responsibility for fast growth of the country's economy. Fast, economical and convenient mobility of people sustained by public transportation, an essential component of a resource frugal strategy, ensures productivity of people and distribution of goods and services. This frugal process is good and adds value of the various sectors of the country's depending upon information and communication technology. High powered computers with sophisticated software acting as a means of smart solutions, reduces the waste to the minimum, eliminates redundancies and improves efficiencies all around. Such a mode of production, as illustrated above ensures not only the establishment of plural, democratic and innovative society, but it also empowers the poor, the marginalised. As a result the excluded sections stand included.

Q4. (a) Rewrite the following sentences after making necessary corrections, if any.(10)

1. The vehicular pollution causes serious harm to human beings.

   Ans. *Vehicular pollution causes serious harm to human beings.*

2. Both Ashish and Smita came late to college today.

   Ans. *Today, both Ashish and Smita came to college late.*

3. There is many problems relating to this matter.

   Ans. *There are many problems relating to this matter.*

4. Not only David passed but got a distinction.

   Ans. *David not only passed but also got a distinction.*

5. We'd like some informations about the types of cars available.

   Ans. *We'd like some information about the types of cars available.*

6. I prefer to pay by cash.

   Ans. *I prefer to pay in cash.*

7. My uncle has proposed me a job in his company.

   Ans. *My uncle has proposed to me a job in his company.*

8. All of a sudden she burst in tears.

   Ans. *All of sudden she burst into tears.*

9. I enjoy this type of music still now.

   Ans. *I enjoy this type of music even now.*

10. The teacher said me to submit the assignment the next day.

    Ans. *The teacher said to me to submit the assignment the next day.*

(b) Rewrite the following sentences inserting suitable article(s), wherever necessary. **(5)**

1. Oranges and lemons are citrus fruits.

   Ans. *Oranges and lemons are the citrus fruits.*

2. Aijaz is tallest boy in class.

   Ans. *Aijaz is the tallest boy in class.*

3. She teaches at University in Indiana but I don't know which one it is.

   Ans. *She teaches at a University in Indiana but I don't know which one it is.*

4. New teacher seems to be very strict.

   Ans. *The new teacher seems to be very strict.*

5. It was beautiful sight to see.

   Ans. *It was a beautiful sight to see.*

(c) Rewrite the following sentences inserting suitable prepositions in the blank spaces. **(5)**

1. The Minister gave _______ the prizes on the annual day.

   Ans. *The Minister gave <u>away</u> the prizes on the annual day.*

2. Seeing the children playing, brought _______ memories of my childhood games.

   Ans. *Seeing the children playing brought <u>about</u> memories of my childhood games.*

3. Randhir is always ready to take _______ any responsibility.

   Ans. *Randhir is always ready to take <u>up</u> any responsibility.*

4. The members decided to deal ______ the problem collectively.

   Ans. *The members decided to deal with the problem collectively.*

5. I hope the picnic will not be called ______.

   Ans. *I hope the picnic will not be called off.*

(d) Give the antonyms of the following words. (5)

1. useful — ***Ans.*** *Useless*
2. active — ***Ans.*** *Inactive*
3. encourage — ***Ans.*** *Discourage*
4. rational — ***Ans.*** *Irrational*
5. timely — ***Ans.*** *Untimely*

Q 5. Answer as directed.

(a) Rewrite the following sentences using the passive structure. (5)

1. They have permitted me to leave.

   Ans. *I have been permitted to leave by them.*

2. The rains have completely ruined the roads.

   Ans. *The roads have been completely ruined by the rains.*

3. Why did you close the door?

   Ans. *Why was the door closed by you?*

4. History records his great achievements.

   Ans. *His great achievements are recorded in history.*

5. They awarded her the degree at the convocation.

   Ans. *She was awarded the degree at the convocation by them.*

(b) Change the following sentences into indirect speech. (5)

1. Anil to Ajay, "Why don't you join us for a party on Saturday?"

   Ans. *Anil asked Ajay why he did not join them for a party on Saturday.*

2. Mrs. Nair to Mr. Shah, "Good morning! There's a small problem I want to speak to you about."

   Ans. *Mrs. Nair wished good morning to Mr. Shah and said she wanted to speak to him about a small problem.*

3. Jack to Parimala, "How was your trip to the National Park?"

   Ans. *Jack asked Parimala how her trip to the National Park was.*

4. Mr. Patil to the cashier, "Do you have change for five hundred rupees?"

   Ans. *Mr. Patil asked the cashier if he had change for five hundred rupees."*

5. Sushil to Prasad, "Congratulations! I'm so glad you received the young scientists' award."

   Ans. *Sushil congratulated Prasad and expressed his joy as the latter had received the young scientists' award.*

(c) Use the correct form of the verb in brackets to fill in the blanks. **(5)**

1. The first such prize _______ in 1999. (AWARD)

   Ans. *The first such prize was awarded in 1999.*

2. The computer is a complex gadget and _______ of many parts. (CONSIST)

   Ans. *The computer is a complex gadget and consists of many parts.*

3. I _______ the groceries for you tomorrow. (BRING)

   Ans. *I will bring the groceries for you tomorrow.*

4. Jacob _______ his report already. (COMPLETE)

   Ans. *Jacob had completed his report already.*

5. The postman _______ his bag and left. (COLLECT)

   Ans. *The postman collected his bag and left.*

(d) Supply the missing words. **(5)**

1. The music was too loud _______ she adjusted the volume.

   Ans. *The music was too loud so she adjusted the volume.*

2. _______ the technician worked for an hour, he was unable to repair the machine.

   Ans. *Although the technician worked for an hour, he was unable to repair the machine.*

3. _______ you pay attention you are likely to miss the important points.

   Ans. *Unless you pay attention you are likely to miss the important points.*

4. Raju calls his mother _______ he finds it difficult to manage on his own.

   Ans. *Raju calls his mother as he finds it difficult to manage on his own.*

5. Leave a wide margin _______ the tutor's comments can be written in it.

   Ans. *Leave a wide margin so the tutor's comments can be written in it.*

(e) Rewrite the following sentences using 'It' in the beginning as a preparatory subject. **(5)**

1. Finding fault with someone is easy.

   Ans. *It is easy to find fault with someone.*

2. For them to close down the family business would be right.

   Ans. *It would be right for them to close down the family business.*

3. To clean your car yourself would be a good idea.

   Ans. *It would be a good idea to clean your car yourself.*

4. To eat alone was embarrassing for her.

   Ans. *It was embarrassing for her to eat alone.*

5. Shouting out to someone across the room is rude.

   Ans. *It is rude to shout out at someone across the room.*

UPSC (MAIN) EXAM – 2011

ENGLISH

(Compulsory)

Time allowed: 3 hours **Maximum Marks: 300**

Candidates should attempt all questions.

The number of marks carried by each question is indicated at the end of the questions.

Answer must be written in English.

Q 1. Write an essay in about 300 words on any one of the following: (100)

(a) The Predicaments of Indian Democracy.

(b) In India when inflation rises governance stalls.

(c) Modern world's fears about Nuclear Energy.

(d) Information Technology Transforming the Indian Society.

(e) Invention Generate Necessity.

Model Answer: 1. d

ESSAY

Information Technology Transforming Indian Society

In the past few decades, there has been a revolution in computing and communications, and all indications are that technological progress and use of information technology will continue at a rapid pace. Accompanying and supporting the dramatic increase in the power and use of new information technologies has been the declining cost of communication as a result of technological improvements and increased competition.

These advancements present many significant opportunities but also pose major challenges. Today, innovations in information technology are having wide-ranging effects across numerous strata of society, and policy makers are acting on issues involving economic productivity, intellectual property rights, privacy protection, and affordability of and access to information. Choices made now will have long-lasting consequences, and attention must be paid to their social and economic impacts. One of the most significant outcomes of the progress of information technology is probably electronic commerce over the Internet, a new way of conducting business. Though only a few years old, it may radically alter economic activities and the social environment. Already, it affects such large sectors as communications, finance and retail trade and might expand to areas such as education and health services. It implies the seamless application of information and communication technology along the entire value chain of a business that is conducted electronically.

Although distance learning has existed for some time, the Internet makes possible a large expansion in coverage and better delivery of instruction. Owing to the Internet's ease of access and convenience for distance learning, overall demand for such programmes will probably expand, leading to growth in this segment of e-commerce.

The internet, facebook, whatsapp, e-mail, mobiles, computers, laptops, tabs, ipods have revolutionised modern society. Our thinking pattern, priorities and attitudes have undergone a drastic change

The ongoing computing and communications revolution has therefore numerous economic and social repercussions on modern society and requires serious study and investigation which can be done through the subject of social science. Such a work would be valuable for both social policy and health of society.

Q 2. Read carefully the passage below and write your answers to the questions that follow in clear, correct and concise language. (5 × 15 = 75)

Water is the basis of all life. Every animal and every plant contains a substantial proportion of free or combined water in its body, and no kind of physiological activity is possible in which the fluid does not play an essential part. Water is, of course, necessary for animal life, while moisture in the soil is equally imperative for the life and growth of plants and trees, though the quantity necessary varies enormously with the species. The conservation and utilisation of water is thus fundamental for human welfare. Apart from artesian water, the ultimate source in all cases is rain or snowfall. Much of Indian agriculture depends on seasonal rainfall and is therefore very sensitive to any failure or irregularity of the same. It is clear that the adoption of techniques preventing soil erosion would also help to conserve and keep the water where it is wanted. In other words, on and in the soil, such techniques therefore serve a double purpose. It is evident however that in a country having only a seasonal rainfall, an immense quantity of rain-water must be necessarily run off the ground. The collection and utilisation of water is therefore of vital importance. Much of it flows down into the streams and rivers and ultimately finds its way to the sea. The harnessing of our rivers, the waters of which now mostly run to waste, is a great national problem which must be considered and dealt with on national lines. Closely connected with the conservation of water supplies is the problem of afforestation. The systematic planting of suitable trees in every possible or even in impossible areas and the development of what one can call civilized forests as distinguished from wild and untamed jungle is one the most urgent needs of India. Such plantation would directly and indirectly prove a source of untold wealth to the country. They would check soil erosion and conserve the rainfall of the country from flowing away to waste and would provide the necessary supplies of cheap fuel and thus stop unnecessary waste of farmyard manure.

Questions:

1. Where does the world get water from?
2. What is the national problem relating to our rivers?
3. What are the benefits of afforestation?
4. What is fundamental for human welfare?
5. What are the advantages of preventing soil erosion?

Ans. *1. The world gets its water mainly from rainfall, snowfall and artesian wells.*

2. *The harnessing of our rivers is a great national problem. The waters of many rivers now are mostly wasted. The problem must be dealt on national lines.*
3. *Afforestation would check soil erosion and. conserve the rainfall of the country from flowing away and would provide the necessary supplies of cheap fuel and thus stop unnecessary waste of farmyard manure.*
4. *The conservation and utilisation of water is fundamental for human welfare. The moisture in the soil is equally imperative for the life and growth of plants and trees as well.*
5. *The adoption of techniques preventing soil erosion would help to conserve and keep the water where it is wanted. In other words, such techniques serve a double purpose collection and utilization of water.*

Q3. Make a precis of the following passage in about 200 words. It is not necessary to suggest a title. Failure to write within the word limit may result in deduction of marks. The precis must be written on separate precis sheets provided, which must then be fastened securely inside the answer book. (75)

While all the religious teachers tell us that compassion gives us a motive for existence, a guide for action and a reason for courage would help us to diminish the sum of human suffering. In the very name of God, who is all compassionate, abominable crimes have been committed in the world. It is not enough to believe in God of love but we must love. The saints are the masters who are not stained-glass figures, remote and ethereal in their sanctity. There is nothing in them, which we would not like to spread everywhere in the world. It is there but what it is, we cannot say. It is there in their blood and bones, in the breath of their speech, in the lights and shades of their speech, in the lights and shades of their personalities, a mystery that can be lived but not spoken in words.

On the rock of moral law, and not on the shifting sands of political or economic expediency, can be built a civilised society with individual freedom, social justice and political equality. Truth, freedom and righteousness are essential to peace. The Evangelist tells us how 'the devil taketh him up into an exceeding high mountain, and showeth him all the kingdoms of the world, and the glory of them. And saith unto him, 'All these things will I give thee, if thou wilt fall down and worship me'. Then saith Jesus unto him, Get thee hence, Satan; for it is written, Thou shalt worship thy Lord, thy God and Him alone shalt thou serve'.

In the new society, we need a new universal religion. By it we mean not a uniform religion, but a religion of awareness and love of wisdom and compassion, prajna and karuna of truth and love. Religions must be cured of their provincialism and made to reveal their universality. This does not mean spiritual vagueness or ambiguity.

Tolerance implies an elementary right belonging to the dignity of every man. The right to believe, like the right to live a free, unfettered life is fundamental to the concept of brotherly love. We have had in our country peaceful co-existence of different religions. It is not more passive co-existence but an active fellowship, a close inter-relation of the best of different religions. Co-existence is the first step and fraternity is the goal. We have not adhered steadfastly to these ideals and have suffered often. Yet the ideal has been kept in view and supported by great leaders like Ram Mohan Roy, Ramakrishna, Tagore and Gandhiji.

The view of tolerance is based on the conviction that all transcendental use of the logical categories, all attempts to submit the transcendent to the finite are wrong. Nature and history announce God's presence but do not disclose his whole nature. Religions are cut off from one another by mutual incomprehensiveness. We are born or trained in certain traditions of religion. Loyalty to tradition does not mean imprisonment within it. We adopt different symbolic representations of the supreme determined by our age, circumstances, upbringing and by narrower loyalties of caste, class, race or nation. Whatever progress we make at the expense of those values is morally wrong.

The seers of all religions affirm that the various peoples of the world form a community with a common purpose and a common destiny. It is said that the whole world is the fatherland of a noble soul. The application of this universality of spirit requires us to look upon our common enemies not as monsters of evil but as misled by their obsessions and as capable of change.

PRECIS

One of the highest virtues of man compassion, a motive for existence, guide for action and a reason for courage, is very much godly, as it brings an end to human suffering. We must love people to make the world free from hatred and heinous crimes. An enlightened and civilised society can be built on the principles of individual freedom, social justice, political equality, truth, freedom, and peace. As Jesus Christ and many other illustrious saints did, the world could be redeemed from various crimes, sins, evils and ills through acts of devotion, dedication, compassion and love.. Ideals of tolerance, brotherhood, peaceful co-existence are the foundational principles of all religions of the world. The great leaders like Ram Mohan Roy, Ramakrishna, Tagore and Gandhiji set luminous examples for us by living their lives guided by such virtues. The practice of tolerance based on this conviction helps us rise above the divisive lives of caste, class, race or nation. The whole world is a valley of soul- making and the entire world a community as is affirmed by the seers of all religions. Those who are misled by their obsession, should not be treated as enemies or monsters, even they are capable of transformation.

Q4. (a) Rewrite the following sentences after making necessary corrections (10)

1. Saints desire nothing to the society.

   Ans. *Saints desire nothing from the society.*

2. I regret at the delay in doing this.

   Ans. *I regret the delay in doing this.*

3. I congratulate you for your success.

   Ans. *I congratulate you on your success.*

4. Ram as well as Mohan have gone.

   Ans. *Ram as well as Mohan has gone.*

5. He has passed order on my application.

   Ans. *He has passed order against my application.*

6. He is more intelligent than any boy.

   Ans. *He is more intelligent than any other boy.*

7. What will be ensued on this?

   Ans. *What will be ensued after this?*

8. This is high time that we should change the bike.

   Ans. *It is high time that we should change the bike.*

9. I did nothing but laughed.

   Ans. *I did nothing but laugh.*

10. I informed him, "Leave the room."

    Ans. *I told him to leave the room.*

(b) Supply the missing words: **(5)**

1. The wages of sin __________ death.

   Ans. *The wages of sin is death.*

2. I trust __________ God.

   Ans. *I trust in God.*

3. I have no fondness __________ music.

   Ans. *I have no fondness for music.*

4. I have no doubt __________ your honesty.

   Ans. *I have no doubt about your honesty.*

5. I am conscious __________ my duties.

   Ans. *I am conscious of my duties.*

(c) Use the correct forms of the verbs in brackets: **(5)**

1. I remember __________ her when she was a little girl. (SEE)

   Ans. *I remember seeing her when she was a little girl.*

2. You will __________ twenty-four hours to consider your decision. (GIVE)

   Ans. *You will be given twenty-four hours to consider your decision.*

3. Can you hear what he __________? (SAY)

   Ans. *Can you hear what he is saying?*

(d) Write the opposites of the following: **(5)**

1. Notorious ***Ans.*** *Reputable*
2. Legitimate ***Ans.*** *Illegitimate*

3. Responsible **Ans.** *Irresponsible*
4. Satisfaction **Ans.** *Dissatisfaction*
5. Promotion **Ans.** *Demotion*

Q5. Answer as directed:

(a) Rewrite the following sentences removing 'too ….. to'. **(5)**

1. He is too honest to steal.

   Ans. *He is so honest that he cannot steal.*
2. He is too weak to run.

   Ans. *He is so weak that he cannot run.*
3. She is too shy to sing.

   Ans. *She is so shy that she cannot sing.*
4. He was too shocked to speak.

   Ans. *He was so shocked that he could not speak.*
5. The matter will be too complicated to resolve.

   Ans. *The matter will be so complicated that it may not be resolved.*

(b) Rewrite the following sentences using 'It' in the beginning as a subject. **(5)**

1. To scold the boys would be foolish.

   Ans. *It will be foolish to scold the boys.*
2. Smoking is bad for him.

   Ans. *It is bad for him to smoke.*
3. To call after ten was unusual for him.

   Ans. *It was unusual for him to call after ten.*
4. Keeping the windows open on the roadside does not look decent.

   Ans. *It does not look decent to keep the windows open on the road side.*
5. To play games on Sundays is not allowed.

   Ans. *It is not allowed to play games on Sundays.*

(c) Combine each pair of sentences using one of the words: 'nor', 'and', 'but', 'if' or 'when'. Use each word only once. **(5)**

1. He turned pale. He saw me.

   Ans. *He turned pale when he saw me.*
2. They are poor. You consider their bank balance.

   Ans. *They are poor if you consider their bank balance.*

3. She wanted to make a speech. She did not know how to begin.

   Ans. *She wanted to make a speech but did know how to begin.*

4. He took a pen. He started writing.

   Ans. *He took a pen and started writing.*

5. She doesn't like Rakesh. She doesn't like Mohini.

   Ans. *She doesn't like Ramesh or Mohini.*

(d) Change the narration of the following sentences. **(5)**

1. The teacher said to me, "Why are you late?"

   Ans. *The teacher asked me why I was late.*

2. He said that his mother was just then absent from home.

   Ans. *He said "my mother is just now gone from home".*

3. A wrote to B, "Your letter reached me here early this morning."

   Ans. *'A' wrote to 'B' that his letter has reached him there early that morning.*

4. Ramesh requested his sister, "Please keep my things ready when I return from my trip tomorrow."

   Ans. *Ramesh requested his sister to keep his things ready when he returns from his trip the next day.*

5. He said, "What a strange man you are!"

   Ans. *He wondered what a strange man I was.*

(e) Rewrite the following sentences using the passive voice structure. **(5)**

1. He gave her a book to read.

   Ans. *A book was given to her to read by him.*

2. Even a child can handle this machine.

   Ans. *This machine can be handled even by a child.*

3. Who has put the book on the shelf?

   Ans. *By whom has the book been put on the shelf?*

4. Everyone rejected the bold idea.

   Ans. *The bold idea was rejected by everyone.*

5. Ramesh is driving Sunita's car.

   Ans. *Sunita's car was driven by Ramesh.*

UPSC (MAIN) EXAM – 2010

ENGLISH

(Compulsory)

Time allowed: 3 hours   ***Maximum Marks: 300***

Candidates should attempt all questions.

The number of marks carried by each question is indicated at the end of the questions.

Answer must be written in English.

Q 1. Write an essay in about 300 words on any ONE of the following: 100

(a) "Increasing consumerism in the middle class in India".

(b) Are traditional forms of protest no longer effective?

(c) The Nuclear Civil Liability Bill.

(d) "To feed our increasing population, forest areas need to be cleared to increase land area available for cultivation." Do you agree?

(e) Need to check politicization of Sports bodies in India.

ESSAY

Consumerism in Middle Class in India – 2010

Since the 1990s, after the onset of liberalisation, consumerism in India particularly among middle class has assumed new dimensions and proportions. The approach and outlook of the Indian middle class consumers have undergone drastic changes. India opened up to the global market, global trends and global fashion. With rapid influence of western culture, the major brands of the world made an entry into India. So the middle class consumers in India got exposure to a wide range of consumer products.

The economy got a new lease of life. Foreign investment, foreign companies, corporate houses expanded business in India and gave stimulus to business opportunities generating large scale employment as well. The purchasing power of the middle class enhanced. With enhanced purchasing power, the middle class started looking for a better way of life. They switched over to new gadgets, a new style of life with plethora of choices at their disposal.

The new gadgets, especially electronic gadgets like TV, refrigerators, washing machines, AC, microwaves etc. have made life of the middle class less stressful. The recent stimulus to online shopping has also contributed to increasing consumerism. The online players like Flipkart, Amazon, Snapdeal etc, have not only brought the market at the doorsteps of the consumers, but also made them cheaper with heavy discounts.

The global exposure, the international connectivity, the rise of the corporate world, the sprawling malls, the IT revolution, media, Hollywood and Bollywood, and the latest online shopping fad have captivated the imagination of consumers. The consumer is caught in a whirlwind of such a consumerist atmosphere.

So to sum up, multiple brands, easy availability, competitive prices, corporate culture, western life styles, IT revolution, media promotion, online shopping, sprawling malls, foreign investments, global exposure, increasing business opportunity, new job avenues, and enhanced purchasing power are some of the prominent reasons of growing consumerism in India.

Q 2. Read the following passage carefully and based on it, answer the questions given below it in clear, correct and concise language: (5 × 15 = 75)

According to the findings of a recent government survey, there are an estimated 3.3 million registered NGOs working in the country – one for every 400 Indians. Not only has the number of NGOs in India risen dramatically, but so has their influence. In some of India's flagship development efforts –the National Rural Employment Guarantee Act, the National Rural Health Mission, the Right to Education or even the draft Right to Food Act – NGOs have been at the forefront, both in formulating these laws and policies and in implementing them. NGOs have helped voice the concerns of some of India's most vulnerable groups and focus the attention of the government of critical, social and development issues. They have also spearheaded efforts to expose corruption and maladministration in government bringing in much needed transparency.

But despite the growing influence of NGOs in India today, we know very little about them: their structure, activities, sources of funding and, more importantly, how accountable they are to the people they represent. This is alarming, given the crores of rupees in development aid that NGOs receive from the government and from donors every year. Ironically, though NGOs have been watchdogs of the government for many year, there has been little regulation or monitoring of their own activities. Leading many to ask a very fundamental question" who watches the watchers?

Interestingly, although India has probably the world's highest NGO population, the debate on NGO accountability is still in its nascent stages. Across the world, NGOs have been experimenting with different ways of addressing the issue of accountability; Indian NGOs would do well by learning from these efforts. For example, NGOs in Kenya are legally required to comply with the Code of Conduct for NGOs developed by the National council of NGOs, a self-regulatory body set up under the NGO Coordination Act in 1990. The code ensures that NGOs comply with basic ethical and governance standards. Similarly, in Uganda, the NGO Quality Assurance Mechanism (QuAM) certifies NGOs against a set of quality standards designed to ensure NGO credibility. In Chile, Chile Transparent has developed transparency standards for NGOs which require organisations to publish online information about their mission, vision, activities, staff, details of funding etc.

Questions:

(a) What are India's important schemes?

Ans. *India's important development schemes are National Rural Employment Guarantee Act, the National Rural Health Mission, the Right to Education and draft Right to Food Act.*

(b) How do NGOs help 'vulnerable groups' in India?

Ans. *NGOs raise and agitate the concerns of some of India's most vulnerable groups and focus the attention of the government on serious, social and economic issues.*

(c) What do we know about the structure, activities and sources of funding of the NGOs in India?

Ans. *NGOs' structure, activities, sources of funding and their accountability are not largely known.*

(d) Whom does the author describe as watchers? Why?

Ans. *Author describes NGOs as watchers as they are called watchdogs. NGOs have been at the forefront influencing government to make law and policies and implement them.*

(e) How do the NGOs in other nations deal with the issue of accountability?

Ans. *NGOs in Kenya are legally required to comply with the code of conduct developed by National Council of NGOs; in Uganda, the NGO Quality Assurance Mechanism (QuAM) certifies their conduct, in Chile, Chile Transparent has developed transparency standards for NGOs. In short, they have self-regulatory mechanisms to ensure the transparency of the NGOs.*

Q 3. Make a précis of the following passage in about 210-230 words. Failure to write within the stipulated word limit may result in deduction of marks. The précis must be written on the separate prices sheets provided, which must be then fastened securely inside the answer book. (75)

In many respects "Shakuntala" is comparable to the more idyllic comedies of Shakespeare, and Kanva's hermitage is surely not far from the Forest of Arden. The plot of the play, like many of Shakespeare's plots, depends much on happy chances and on the supernatural, which, of course, was quite acceptable to the audience for which Kalidasa wrote. Its characters, even to the minor ones, are happily delineated individuals. Kalidasa makes no pretence to realism, but his dialogue is fresh and vigorous. In fact the dialogue of the better Sanskrit plays generally seems did not demand the conflict of feelings and emotions which is the chief substance of serious European drama, but Kalidasa was quite capable of portraying such conflict effectively. His beauties and merits are tarnished by many translations, but the few who can read him in the original would doubt that, both as poet and dramatist, he was one of the great men of the world.

There were many other dramatists. Sudraka, probably Kalidasa's approximate contemporary, has left only one play "The Little Clay Cart" (Mrcchakatika). This is the most realistic of Indian dramas, unraveling a complicated story, rich in humour and pathos and crowded with action, of the love of a poor Brahman, Charudatta, for the virtuous courtesan Vasantasena; this story is interwoven with one of political intrigue, leading up to the overthrow of the wicked king Palaka, and the play contains a vivid trial scene, after which the hero is saved from execution at the last moment. It is notable for its realistic depiction of city life, and for its host of minor characters, all of whom are drawn with skill and individuality. It has more than once been performed in translation on the European stage, and, to a Western audience is certainly the most easily appreciated of Indian plays.

Visakhadatta (6th century) was the dramatist of politics. His only complete surviving play, "The Minister's Signet Ring" (Mudrarakshasa), deals with the schemes of the wily Chanakya to foil the plots of Rakshasa, the minister of the last of the Nandas, and to place Chandragupta Maurya firmly on the throne. The plot is exceedingly complicated, but is worked out with great skill, and the play is beautifully constructed to lead up, like "The Little Clay Cart" to a pathetic scene, where one of the chief characters is saved from death by impalement at the last moment.

Second only to Kalidasa in the esteem of the critics was Bhavabhuti, who lived at Kanyakubja in the early 8th century. Three of his plays survive – "Malati and Madhava", "The Deeds of the Great Hero" (Mahaviracharita), and "The Later deeds of Rama" (Uttararamacarita). The first is a love story with a pseudo-realistic background, full of incident of an exciting or horrific type, in which the heroine is more than once rescued from death, while the two latter plays tell the study of Rama. By Western standards, as a dramatist, Bhavabhuti falls short of those we have mentioned earlier. His plots are weakly constructed and his characters lack individuality. His greatness rests on his deep understanding of sorrow; in his treatment of the pathetic and the terrible, he perhaps excels Kalidasa.

Precis

Comparable to the comedies of Shakespeare, *Shakuntala*, a play by Kalidasa, is a masterpiece with complex plot, nicely developed characters, vigorous and fresh dialogues, use of supernatural imagery, refined and exquisite idiomatic expressions. An original poet and dramatist, Kalidasa was capable of portraying conflict and tensions effectively in his plays, though many qualities and beauties of his plays are lost when rendered in translation from Sanskrit. A contemporary of Kalidasa and a dramatist, Sudraka, wrote *The Little Clay Cart* (Mrcchakatika), depicting city life, rich in humour and pathos. Dealing with the theme of love between a poor Brahman and a virtuous courtesan, Vasantasena, the text is interwoven with political intrigue. The play has been appreciated by the western audience when staged, rendered in translation. A dramatist of politics, Visakhdatta's *Mudravakasosa* deals with the schemes of Chanakya to place on throne Chandragupta Maurya. A beautiful classic worked out with great skill. The play has a pathetic sense when one of the chief characters is saved from death by impalement at the last moment. Second only to Kalidasa, the 8th century dramatist Bhavabhuti wrote such great plays as *Malati* and *Madhava*, *Uttarramacharita*, the latter dealing with the story of Rama. Though poor in terms of plot construction, Bhavbhuti's plays excel in deep understanding of human sorrow and in the skillful treatment of pathos.

Q 4. (a) Rewrite the following sentences after making necessary corrections, if any: (10)

(i) I live half of a mile from here.

Ans. *I live half a mile from here.*

(ii) "Do you like music?" "I like"

Ans. *"Do you like music?" "I do."*

(iii) Do you like some more coffee?

Ans. *Would you like some more coffee?*

(iv) He worked like a waiter for two years.

Ans. *He worked as a waiter for two years.*

(v) Like what does she look?

Ans. *What does she look like?*

(vi) I know him since 1960.

Ans. *I have known him since 1960.*

(vii) I wasn't used to drive a big car.

Ans. *I wasn't used to driving a big car.*

(viii) He suggested me to try the main car park.

Ans. *He suggested me to try the main car park.*

(ix) I have never met so nice person.

Ans. *I have never met such a nice person.*

(x) Too many Mathematics is usually taught in schools.

Ans. *Too much mathematics is usually taught in schools.*

(b) Rewrite following sentences inserting suitable article(s), wherever necessary: **(5)**

(i) My grandfather had had hard life.

Ans. *My grandfather had had a hard life.*

(ii) She hit him in stomach.

Ans. *She hit him in the stomach.*

(iii) Queen had dinner with president.

Ans. *The Queen had dinner with the president.*

(iv) My friend is in hospital

Ans. *My friend is in the hospital.*

(c) Rewrite the following sentences inserting suitable prepositions in the blank spaces: **(5)**

(i) I am angry ....her ....lying.

Ans. *I am angry with her for lying.*

(ii) I was red ....anger at his remarks.

Ans. *I was red with anger at his remarks.*

(iii) Could you explain this rule ....me please?

Ans. *Could you explain this rule to me please?*

(iv) People have always been kind ....me.

Ans. *People have always been kind to me.*

(d) Give the antonyms of the following adjective: **(5)**

(i) common **Ans.** *Uncommon*

(ii) loyal **Ans.** *Disloyal*

(iii) formal **Ans.** *Informal*

(iv) mature **Ans.** *Immature*

(v) sensitive **Ans.** *Insensitive*

Q 5. Answer as directed:

(a) Rewrite the following sentences using the passive structure: **(5)**

(i) She gave her sister the car.

Ans. ***The car was given by her to her sister.***

(ii) I had already shown the suspect's photograph to the policewoman.

Ans. ***The policewoman was already shown the suspect's photograph by me.***

(iii) They believe him to be dangerous.

Ans. ***He was believed to be dangerous by them.***

(iv) They made him tell them everything.

Ans. ***Everything was made to be told to them by him.***

(v) They elected me President.

Ans. ***I was elected President by them.***

(b) Change the following sentences into indirect speech: **(5)**

(i) He wrote in his letter, "I saw Poonam at the theatre a couple of days ago."

Ans. *He wrote in his letter that he saw Poonam at the theatre a couple of days ago.*

(ii) The forecast says, "It will rain tomorrow."

Ans. *The forecast said that it would rain the next day.*

(iii) He said to me, "It would be nice if I could see you again."

Ans. *He told me it would be nice if he could see me again.*

(iv) I said, "If I had any money I'd buy you a drink."

Ans. *I told him if I had had any money I would buy him a drink.*

(v) The teacher said, "Why don't you work harder?"

Ans. *The teacher asked me why I did not work harder.*

(c) Rewrite the following sentences, changing them into simple ones: **(5)**

(i) I wonder who I should invite.

Ans. *Whom should I invite?*

(ii) Show him what he should do.

Ans. *What should he do?*

(iii) She couldn't decide whether she should answer his letter.

Ans. *Should she answer his letter?*

(iv) He didn't know where he should park his car.

Ans. *Where should he park his car?*

(v) Tell me when I should pay.

Ans. *When should I pay?*

(d) Add a tag question at the end of each of the following sentences: **(5)**

(i) Pooja can speak French.

Ans. *Pooja can speak French. Can't she?*

(ii) The meeting is at ten.

Ans. *The meeting is at ten. Is it not?*

(iii) You didn't speak to Mohan.

Ans. *You didn't speak to Mohan. Did you?*

(iv) She wouldn't like a pet.

Ans. *She wouldn't like a pet. Would she?*

(v) Harish gave you a cheque.

Ans. *Harish gave you a cheque. Did he not?*

(e) Rewrite the following sentences using 'it' in the beginning as a preparatory subject: **(5)**

(i) To make mistakes is easy.

Ans. *It is easy to make mistakes.*

(ii) To wait for people who were late made him angry.

Ans. *It made him angry to wait for people who were late.*

(iii) My ambition was to retire at thirty.

Ans. *It was my ambition to retire at thirty.*

(iv) Your task is to get across the river without being seen.

Ans. *It is your task to get across the river without being seen.*

(v) For you to ask Ramesh would be a big mistake.

Ans. *It would be a big mistake on your part to ask Ramesh.*

UPSC (MAIN) EXAM – 2009
ENGLISH
(Compulsory)

Time allowed: 3 hours | ***Maximum Marks: 300***

Candidates should attempt all questions.

The number of marks carried by each question is indicated at the end of the questions.

Answer must be written in English.

Q 1. Write an essay in about 300 words on any one of the following: **100**

(a) Why are our farmers committing suicide?

(b) Ragging: should it be distinguished from brutality or criminality?

(c) "Sweet are the uses of adversity."

(d) Reform of sports bodies in our country.

(e) Alternative sources of energy for our country.

ESSAY

Ragging Should be Distinguished from Brutality and Criminality

Ragging in India is a damaging form of interaction of the seniors with the juniors, new comers of first year freshers in college or school, newcomers or first year freshers. It involves insults (simple or suggestive, sexual, sarcastic and even physical), running errands for seniors, and many other activities that are generally aimed at humiliating the new comer. Even reputed Indian colleges have a dark history of ragging, especially in engineering and medical colleges. It has become a big cause of concern to the management of the institutes due to complaints of serious injury to the victims. In the light of these incidents, there are now strict laws regarding ragging. Ragging is now defined as an act that violates or is perceived to violate an individual student's dignity.

The practice of ragging started off as a harmless way to familiarise beginners to their seniors and to ensure a cordial atmosphere in the campus. But its gradual misuse has turned it into a potent tool for ill-treating and punishing the new students if they fail to obey their seniors. Under the pretext of fun, the victims are often assaulted, sometimes even stripped and intimidated by his seniors. This ritualised torture leaves an indelible impression on his mind. The chilling incident continues to haunt him throughout his life, and he unknowingly develops various psychological disorders. After experiencing the evil of ragging, a student develops a feeling of revenge for his 'unjustified harassment' and in turn derives pleasure in ragging his juniors. So this vicious trend goes on and on. Those newcomers who refuse to follow their diktats are subjected to barbaric and brutal treatment such as being paraded naked, standing upside down, shaving their heads etc. The situation sometimes turns so bad that it compels the ragging victim to commit suicide.

However there is a positive argument being expressed regarding ragging. A section of students feel that light ragging should be allowed in educational institutes.

But there can be no two views on distinguishing ragging from brutality/criminality.

Those who are in favour of ragging should be made clear of the distinction between ragging and brutality/ criminality. They should be made to realise that their momentary fun is not more important than human life itself. Stricter laws and strictest punishments is the need of the hour. Execution of laws is more important than codification of laws. Some psychological workshops should also be conducted with help of a few legal legendaries. They should be made to realise the legal consequences of their action. The media can play a great role. The sports stars, the film stars, and other corporate magnets who are role model for youngsters should be made ambassadors to spread message against ragging.

Q 2. Read carefully the passage below and write your answers to the questions that follow, in clear, correct and concise language: 5 × 15 = 75

The altogether new thing in the world then was the scientific method of research, which in that period of Galileo, Kepler, Descartes, Harvey and Francis Bacon was advancing with enormous strides. All walls, all the limitations, all the certainties of the ages were in dissolution, tottering. In fact this epoch, in which we are participating still, with continually opening vistas, can be compared in magnitude and promise only to that of the 8th to the 4th millenniums B.C.: of the birth of civilization in the Near East, when the inventions of food production, grain agriculture and stockbreeding, released mankind from the primitive condition of foraging and so made possible an establishment of soundly grounded communities: first villages, then towns, then cities, kingdoms, and empires. Leo Frobenius wrote of that age as the Monumental Age, and of the age now dawning as the Global:

"In all previous ages, only restricted portions of the surface of the earth were known. Men looked out from the narrowest, upon a somewhat larger neighbourhood, and beyond that, a great unknown. They were all, so to say, insular: bound in. Whereas our view is confined no longer to a spot of space on the surface of this earth. It surveys the whole of the planet. And this fact, this lack of horizon, is something new."

It is chiefly to the scientific method of research that this release of mankind is due, and every developed individual has been freed from the once protective but now dissolved horizons of the local land, local moral code, local modes of group thought and sentiment. Not only in the sciences, but in every department of life the will and courage to credit one's own senses and to honor one's own decisions, to name one's own virtues and to claim forces of the new age. There is a growing realisation even in the moral field that all judgments are (to use Nietzsche's words) "human, all too human."

Questions:

1. What is the "epoch in which we are participating still"?

   Ans. *We are participating in the age of scientific discoveries and advancements.*

2. In what way is it comparable to the period of the 8th to the 4th millenniums B.C.?

   Ans. *Mankind today is also engaged in establishing the settlements across the globe continuing the job his ancestors took up between the 8th to the 4th millennium BC, the period considered as the birth of civilization where man transformed from a food gatherer to a food producer.*

3. What is meant by the new "lack of horizon"?

Ans. *This refers to the vastness of the areas that modern man is exploring. The modern man is no more confined to specific spots on the planet, but the whole planet is his field of exploration, so much so, that he is even exploring the other worlds in the universe.*

4. What do you think is implied by "all the certainties of the ages" that were "in dissolution" during the period of Galileo and his fellow scientists?

Ans. *The new method of scientific research opened up the mental abilities of man. There was no limitation to experimentation. There occurred advancement in every field of life and nothing remained confined to closed spheres. It is because of the scientific research that this period introduced men of substance like Galileo, Kepler, Descartes, Harvey and Francis Bacon.*

5. What is the new freedom we have found, and why does it require courage?

Ans. *The lack of horizons or today's dissolved horizons has lifted man out of the shackles of confinement to the new age of scientific research. He could recognise and realise his potential and decide according to his own will and ability. All this needed his courage. It is only because of this courage that man today is a master not only in science, but also in other aspects of his life.*

Q 3. Make a précis of the following passage in about 235 words. It is not necessary to suggest a little. Failure to write within the word limit may result in deduction of marks. The précis must be written on the separate precis sheets provided, which must then be fastened securely inside the answer book. 75

There are, of course many motivating factors in human behavior, but we would claim that nationalism is particularly worthy of study. Why is it particularly significant? Its significance lies in its power to arouse passionate loyalties and hatreds that motivate acts of extreme violence and courage, people kill and die for their nations. Of course it is not alone this; people are driven to similar extremes to protect their families, their extended families of 'tribes', their home areas with their populations, and their religious groups and the holy places and symbols of their religions,. However, these other loyalties are often rather easier to understand than nationalism. Parents making supreme sacrifices for their children can be seen as obeying a universal imperative in life forms, the instinct to protect one's own genetic material. This instinct can also be seen at work in the urge to protect one's extended family; but then the extended family, or on a slightly larger scale the 'tribe', can also be seen, in perhaps the majority of circumstances in which human beings have existed, as essential for the survival of the individual and the nuclear family. The nation is not generally essential to survival in this way. Of course, if the entire nation were to be wiped out, the individuals and their families would die, but the disappearance of the nation as a social unit would not in itself pose a threat to individual or family survival; only if it were to be accompanied by ethnic violence or severe economic collapse would it be life threatening, and such cataclysmic events are an inevitable consequence of the loss of political independence. Conversely, there is no logical connection between the gaining of political independence by a subject nation and increased life chances for its citizens. In many, perhaps the vast majority, of modern nations there is likewise no defending one's own genetic material; the notion that the citizens of modern nations are kinsfolk, while the citizens of (potentially) hostile neighbours are aliens makes no sense in view of the highly varied genetic make-up of most modern populations.

Devotion to one's religious group, like support for one's nation, is much less obviously to the individual's advantage than is defence of the family, but we would maintain that it can be more comprehensible than nationalism. It can be seen in ideological terms as the defence of a world views and its symbols against rival world views, which are considered to conquered to act in ways abhorrent to their beliefs. While the defence of one's nation has often been seen as the defence of one's religion, and while modern hostilities between nations frequently do have a religious dimension, there are many serious national conflicts that have no clear religious element, the two World Wars were fought in Europe with Catholic France, Protestant Britain, and Orthodox Russia opposing Germany with its mixed Catholic and Protestant population. Thus, while modern nationalisms may be linked to religion many cases can be found without any clear religious dimension. Not only do modern nationalism lack a religious element, there is often (to outsiders) no obvious ideological difference between rival nations. Hence, while defence of one's religion can be seen as defence of an entire system of beliefs, a world view, it is true of the defence of one's nation. There is in fact a good case for seeing nations as 'imagined communities', and such would be the view of some commentators.

Such imagined communities could not, of course, exist unless they fulfilled a need. We can postulate that the need to belong to a community of some kind is a fundamental human characteristic, and that nations have arisen to fulfill this need, as earlier more primary communities – local, 'tribal', and religious – have lost their significance through economic and social change. But why should this need be fulfilled by nations, rather than some other type of unit? There is strong support in the literature for a view of nations as products of particular social and economic conditions operating from around the mid-eighteenth century, as products of 'modernization'.

Precis

Of the many motivating factors, nationalism is the most significant one which instigates and inspires people to fight and even die for their nations. The motivation to protect one's family, tribe, religious groups and holy symbols and places seem to be less important and easier to understand than nationalism. Parents protecting their children can be seen as a universal instinct to preserve one of their own, which may further stretch upto one's extended family or tribe. Nation as a social unit, on the other hand, is not directly related with the survival of individuals and communities. The wiping out of nations by means of ethnic violence or economic collapse, however poses threat to life of its citizens together with a loss to the political independence of the nation. On the contrary, gaining political independence does not increase the life expectancy of the citizens of subject nations. In the highly varied modern society, the notion of universal kinsfolk holds no good.

The defence of a family assumes more importance than the defence of religion. For the nations, however the clash is among the difference in world views. It is presumed that defending nationalism is synonymous to defending religion but looking at two World Wars – they were not fought over religious ideologies-- since the Allies in the World War were Catholic Britain, Protestant France and Orthodox Soviet Union who were opposing the mixed Catholic – Protestant Germany. Thus modern nationalism lacks the element of religion. With economic and social change, nations have taken over the role of local tribes and religious communities to a great extent. So nations can be said to be the product of modernisation.

Q 4. (a) Rewrite the following sentences after making necessary corrections: **10**

1. The bear has a ring on it's nose.

   Ans. The bear has a ring on its nose.

2. This shirt is too lose for me.

   Ans. *This shirt is too loose for me.*

3. This coat looks a bit small – I'd like to try on it.

   Ans. *This coat looks a bit small – I 'd like to try it on.*

4. Let's listen the music.

   Ans. *Let's listen to the music.*

5. Do you know what is the answer?

   Ans. *Do you know the answer?*

6. The weather today is too good.

   Ans. *The weather is very good today.*

7. I saw him yesterday only.

   Ans. *I saw him only yesterday.*

8. Who you want to see?

   Ans. *Whom do you want to see?*

9. The ice cream's good-may I please have little more?

   Ans. *The ice cream's good – may I please have a little more?*

10. His office is quite opposite to my house.

    Ans. *His office is opposite to my house.*

(b) Supply the missing word: **5**

1. The shopkeeper refused to bargain....... the customer.

   Ans. *The shopkeeper refused to bargain with the customer.*

2. He did not believe .... bargaining.

   Ans. *He did not believe in bargaining.*

3. He had already decided .... a fair price.

   Ans. *He already decided on a fair price.*

4. The customer was looking .... a bargain.

   Ans. *The customer was looking for a bargain.*

5. They argued .... the price for a long time.

   Ans. *They argued upon the price for a long time.*

(c) Use the correct form of the verb in brackets: **5**

1. I do not usually ……. an umbrella but today I'm ……. one. (CARRY)

   Ans. *I do not usually carry an umbrella but today I'm carrying one.*

2. She never ……. about her children (WORRY)

   Ans. *She never worries about her children.*

3. That child always ……. when he has a bath. Listen, he's ……. now. (CRY)

   Ans. *That child always cries when he has a bath. Listen, he's crying now.*

(d) Form the opposite of these words by adding a prefix: **5**

1. do -----

   Ans. *do undo*

2. credible -----

   Ans. *credible incredible*

3. ambiguous -----

   Ans. *ambiguous unambiguous*

4. lawful -----

   Ans. *lawful unlawful*

5. legal -----

   Ans. *legal illegal*

Q 5. (a) Combine the following sentences using too ……to **5**

1. The coffee was hot. We could not drink it.

   Ans. *The coffee was too hot for us to drink.*

2. You are now old. You cannot continue to work.

   Ans. *You are too old to continue working.*

3. The child was very small. It could not walk.

   Ans. *The child was too small to walk.*

4. This book is heavy. I cannot carry it.

   Ans. *This book is too heavy for me to carry.*

5. She was shocked. She did not react.

   Ans. *She was too shocked to react.*

(b) Rewrite these sentences so that they begin with the word *it*. **5**

1. To talk like that is silly.

   Ans. *It is silly to talk like that.*

2. To hear your voice was good.

   Ans. *It was good to hear your voice.*

3. To tell the truth is essential.

   Ans. *It is essential to tell the truth.*

4. To have friends is better than money.

   Ans. *It is better to have friends than money.*

5. To think for yourself is difficult.

   Ans. It is difficult to think for yourself.

(c) Combine these sentences using one of the words *although, but, so, or, because.* Use each word only once. **5**

1. They were tired. They worked late into the night.

   Ans. *They were tired because they worked late into the night.*

2. He slept early. He woke up late.

   Ans. *He slept early but woke up late.*

3. He was on medication. He felt drowsy.

   Ans. *He was on medication, so he felt drowsy.*

4. She was very angry. She said nothing

   Ans. *She was very angry although she said nothing.*

5. The engine stopped. It has heated up.

   Ans. *The engine stopped because it has heated up.*

(d) Combine the following sentences using *enough to.* **5**

1. The wind was strong. It could blow people away.

   Ans. *The wind was strong enough to blow people away.*

2. The print was clear. We could read it easily.

   Ans. *The print was clear enough to be read easily.*

3. It was hot. We could cook food with the sun's rays.

   Ans. *It was hot enough to cook food with the sun's rays.*

4. You are old. You should know better.

   Ans. *You are old enough to know better.*

5. The essay was good. It earned full marks.

   Ans. *The essay was good enough to earn full marks.*

(e) Rewrite these sentences, using a form of the word *get* and a suitable preposition or prepositions instead of the word(s) underlined. **5**

1. Has the company recovered from its losses?

   Ans. *Has the company got over from its losses?*

2. I'd like to continue with my cooking now, if I may.

   Ans. *I would like to get on with my cooking now, if I may.*

3. How do you manage with so little to eat?

   Ans. *How do you get by with so little to eat?*

4. Did you establish a connection with New York on the telephone?

   Ans. *Did you get through a connection with New York on the telephone?*

5. Put the milk away where the cat can't reach it.

   Ans. *Put the milk away where the cat can't get it.*

UPSC (MAIN) EXAM – 2008
ENGLISH
(Compulsory)

Time allowed: 3 hours **Maximum Marks: 300**

Candidates should attempt all questions.

The number of marks carried by each question is indicated at the end of the questions.

Answer must be written in English.

Q 1. Write an essay in about 300 words on any one of the following: 100

(a) The impact of liberal economy on Indian Industry

(b) Terrorist attacks on civilian population

(c) Uses of mobile phones

(d) Is dual citizenship good for an individual?

(e) Global warming and the future of mankind

ESSAY

Uses of Mobile Phones

Cell phones are influencing and impacting our lives like never before. It has revolutionised communication and information transfer in ways that no one could have dreamt of, even just before five years. In particular, the advent of smart phones has entirely changed the dynamics of modern life. Indeed, it is a resource that gives its user unprecedented benefits and advantages. It is now an indispensable part of modern society. Interestingly, its influence cuts across all barriers of society. From information to entertainment, the mobile is now a one-stop solution to the needs of today's under-25 generation.

From the industy and economy point of view, cell phone companies (communication industry) is flourishing, with market capital in billions. This is a good thing for the economy. Nowadays, cell phones are not just phone calls; they're about messaging, video, songs, games, alarm clock, notes, calendar, reminder, etc. One piece of equipment, lots of uses.

Yet, as is seen with all forms of technology, cell phones are also prone to misuse and can cause problems in families and society in general.

Parents can be worried about their kids being constantly on their mobile. If you're net-savvy, you have Internet handy all the time, you are prone to become an internet addict. . Some people (especially teens) get so much addicted to cell phones for video, games, etc that they forget the real purpose of the phone and waste a large part of their time in an unhealthy addiction to their cell phones. The health of those living in the vicinity of cell phone towers is becoming a growing concern. The towers emit strong electromagnetic signals, which can be a health hazard for those living nearby and who are getting exposed to strong radiations continuously during a good span of their lives.

Mobiles can also be annoying at times. For example, when you are on vacation, you get calls from your office that spoils the mood of your vacation. Use of hands-free (wired/blue-tooth) can at times, pass on loud sounds to our ears, which can result in weakening of eardrums. Nowadays, one can download many songs, so keeping the hands-free glued inside your ears for long hours can really affect the sensitivity of ears in the long run of life. There have been cases of cell phone blasts, due to the excessive heating up of its battery. This can be a fatal issue; although rare. The surface of a cell phone has millions of bacteria and virus on it and that can be a strong reason of immediate skin problem on face or can result into other internal infections wherein the microbes creep inside the body through mouth or other openings.

A cell phone can be helpful while driving. But talking while driving can cause accidents because it deviates the attention of a driver. Mobiles can also be a big time distraction and nuisance in calm and silent places like libraries, cinemas, restaurants, etc. Some cell phone users lose the sense of context and can't decide when and where they can talk on the cell phone. Mobile phone advertisements through messages are becoming a pain for the cell phone users.

In short, there is no doubt that cell phone is one of the biggest boon for humanity in recent times. If used properly and sensibly, cell phones can be a wonderful piece of utility in life and most of its disadvantages will simply be insignificant.

Q 2. Read the passage carefully and write your answers to the questions that follow, in clear, correct and concise language: 15 x 5 = 75

Winning the war against France had been Herculean effort. The conventional wisdom, then and later, attributed final victory to sea power because, above all, it ensured that Britain stayed in the ring. The ships of the Royal Navy had prevented invasion; they had confined French power to Europe and allowed Britain to occupy nearly all the overseas possessions of her adversaries; they had guarded the convoys which sustained Wellington's army in the peninsula; and they had guaranteed the survival of Britain's global commerce, which generated the wealth needed to pay for her war effort, and underwrite those of the three big European powers with armies large enough to engage Napoleon on equal terms.

There were many reasons for the navy's success. The determination, self-confidence and professionalism of its officers and crews owed much to traditions established in the previous hundred years. Nelson was outstanding as a leader and tactician, but Duncan, Jervis and Collingwood also deserve high praise. All understood their country's predicament and how much depended on them, which was why, whenever the chance came for battle, they grabbed at it, regardless of the odds. In the decisive battle of Cape St. Vincent, Camperdown, Abukir Bay and Trafalgar the British fleets were outnumbered but trusting to superior seamanship and gunnery, their admirals took the offensive.

An aggressive, gambling spirit paid off. As Nelson famously observed, an officer who laid his ship alongside the enemy could never be in the wrong.

Much depended on the individual naval officer's instinctively correct response to an emergency, something which Nelson cultivated among his subordinates to the point where they knew without being told what he expected of them. This quality filtered downwards. During an engagement with the French frigate Topaze of Guadeloupe in January, 1809, Captain Willain Maude of the Jason saw no need to inform the commander of his consort, the Cleopatra, of his intentions. "I considered it unnecessary to make any signals to him, and he most fully anticipated my wishes by bringing his ship to anchor on the frigate's starboard bow and opening a heavy fire," Maude wrote afterwards. The action lasted forty minutes and was decided by superior broadsides aimed against the French ship's hull.

Questions:

1. How did the British navy defeat the French navy?

   Ans. *The victory through sea-power with the support of the Royal Navy enabled Britain to keep France confined to Europe and allowed Britain to occupy newly all the overseas possessions of her adversaries.*

2. What were the reasons for the British navy's success?

   Ans. *The determination, self-confidence and professionalism of its officers and crews were the key reasons for the success of the British Navy.*

3. How did the British navy win the battles of Cape St. Vincent, Camperdown, etc.?

   Ans. *The British Navy won the battles of Cape St. Vincent, Camperdown, etc. on account of its superior seamanship, gunnery, aggressive spirit.*

4. What did Nelson cultivate among his subordinates?

   Ans. *Keeping in view the predicament of the country, Nelson, an outstanding leader and tactician, cultivated among his subordinates the capacity to make instinctively correct response on emergency situations, like war.*

5. What was the reason for Captain William Maude's victory in January, 1809?

   Ans. *The reason for Captain William Maude's victory in January 1809 was his correct and spontaneous response to the situation of war. He acted and executed as per the requirement without wasting time in seeking the consent of his commanders.*

Q 3. Make a précis out of the following passage in about one-third of its original length. It is not necessary to suggest a title. Failure to write within the word limit may result in deduction of marks. The précis must be written on the separate précis sheets provided for the purpose; they must be securely fastened inside the answer-book: 75

Love of play is the most obvious distinguishing mark of young animals, whether human or otherwise. In human children, this is accompanied by an inexhaustible pleasure in pretence. Play and pretence are a vital need of childhood, for which opportunity must be provided if the child is to be happy and healthy, quite independently of any further utility in these activities. There are two questions which concern education in this connection : first, what should parents and schools do in the way of providing opportunity? and secondly, should they do anything more, with a view to increasing the educational usefulness of games?

Let us begin with a few words about the psychology of games. This has been exhaustively treated by Groos. There are two separate questions in this matter : the first is as to the impulses which produce play, the second is as to its biological utility. The second is the easier question. There seems no reason to doubt the most widely accepted theory, that in play, the young of any species rehearse and practice the activities which they will perform in earnest later on. The play of puppies is exactly like a dogfight, except that they do not actually bite each other. The play of kittens resembles the behaviour of cats with mice. Children love to imitate any work they have been watching, such as building or digging; the more important the work seems to them, the more they like to play at it. And they enjoy anything that gives them new muscular facilities, such as jumping, climbing, or walking up a narrow plank-provided the task is not too difficult. But although this accounts, in a general way, for the usefulness of the play-impulse, it does not by any means cover all its manifestations, and must not for a moment be regarded as giving a psychological analysis.

Some psycho-analysts have tried to see a sexual symbolism in children's play. This, I am convinced, is utter moonshine. The main instinctive urge of childhood is not sex, but the desire to become adult, or, perhaps more correctly, the will to power. The child is impressed by his own weakness in comparison with older people, and he wishes to become their equal. I remember my boy's profound delight when he realized that he would one day be a man and that I had once been a child; one could see effort being stimulated by the realisation that success was possible. From a very early age, the child wishes to do what older people do, as is shown by the practice of imitation. Older brothers and sisters are useful, because their purposes can be understood and their capacities are not so far out of reach as those grown-up people. The feeling of inferiority is very strong in children; when they are normal and rightly educated, it is a stimulus to effort, but if they are repressed it may become a source of unhappiness.

In play, we have two forms of the will to power : the form which consists in learning to do things, and the form which consists in fantasy. Just as the balked adult may indulge in day-dreams that have a sexual significance, so the normal child indulges in pretences that have a power-significance. He likes to be a giant, or a lion, or a train; in his make-believe; he inspires terror. When I told my boy, the story of Jack the Giant-Killer, I tried to make him identify himself with Jack, but he firmly chose the giant. When his mother told him the story of Bluebeard, he insisted on being bluebeard, and regarded the wife as justly punished for insubordination. In his play, there was a sanguinary outbreak of cutting off ladies' heads. Sadism, Freudians would say; but he enjoyed just as much being a giant who ate little boys; or an engine that could pull a heavy load. Power, not sex, was the common element in these pretences. One day, when we were returning from a walk, I told him, as an obvious joke, that perhaps we should find a certain Mr. Tiddiewinks in possessions of our house, and he might refuse to let us in. After that, for a long time, he would stand on the porch being Mr. Tiddliewinks, and telling me to go to another house. His delight in this game was unbounded and obviously the pretence of power was what he enjoyed.

PRECIS

Love of play – common to the young ones of men and animals – and enhancing opportunities for the same is one of the most valuable duties of parents and educational institutions. Play and pretence, the most vital needs of childhood and an inexhaustible source of pleasure, must be supplied optimally for the happy and healthy growth of young ones. Playing has a biological utility. Young ones including that of animals build their body muscles by jumping, climbing, building, digging etc. Among the young of the species, there is also an impulse of rehearsing and practising the activities they will be performing later on. Children derive pleasure in imitating the work done by seniors and elderly ones. It is not sexual impulse behind the instinct of play, but the desire to become adult and the seeking power is the key driving urge for the love of play and pretence. They overcome their sense of inferiority by practising imitation of their own grown up people. Fantasy and learning to do things are the most powerful driving forces to indulge in pretences that have a power significance. Children's acts of posing themselves as a giant, a lion or a train, all symbolising power and their tendency to live in a make-believe world indicate their dissatisfaction with the current state of subordination and powerlessness. To be precise, children enjoy games immensely as it gives them the pretence of power.

Q 4. (a) Rewrite the following sentences after making necessary correction: 10

1. We reached at home at seven o'clock.

   Ans. *We reached home at seven o'clock.*

2. I am knowing him for many years.

   Ans. *I know him for many years.*

3. Vishal has watched this movie yesterday.

   Ans. *Vishal watched this movie yesterday.*

4. Where you have parked the car ?

   Ans. *Where have you parked the car?*

5. She will visit Chennai next month isn't it?

   Ans. *She will visit Chennai next month. Won't she?*

6. She knows when will Sushma reach Kolkata.

   Ans. *She knows when Sushma will reach Kolkata.*

7. Mukta's teaching made his disciple to think again.

   Ans. *Mukta's teaching made his disciple think again.*

8. Neither Lakshmi and her father have met the Director.

   Ans. *Neither Lakshmi nor her father has met the Director.*

9. I am seeing a man outside the door.

   Ans. *I am watching a man outside the door.*

10. If I were a Minister, I would have appointed you the Principal of this school.

    Ans. *If I were a Minister, I would have appointed you the Principal of the school.*

(b) Rewrite each one the following sentences inserting suitable articles wherever necessary: 5

1. She delivered __________ lecture on Shakespeare on Friday.

   Ans. *a*

2. Would you like __________ piece of cake?

   Ans. *a*

3. The University has decided to impart __________ free education.

   Ans. *Article is not necessary.*

4. Farida is ________ most talented girl in our office.

   Ans. *the*

5. Onkar was ________ first person to board the plane.

   Ans. *the*

(c) Give antonyms of the following adjectives: 5

1. possible **Ans.** *impossible*
2. complete **Ans.** *incomplete*
3. able **Ans.** *unable*
4. regular **Ans.** *irregular*
5. relevant **Ans.** *irrelevant*

(d) Change each of the following sentences into indirect speech: 5

1. Amrita said to me. "Why didn't you attend my class?"

   Ans. *Amrita asked me why I had not attended her class.*

2. My father said to me, "Wash your clothes".

   Ans. *My father instructed me to wash my clothes.*

3. Our teacher said, "The earth revolves around the sun."

   Ans. *Our teacher said that the earth revolves around the sun.*

4. Meera said, "The plane has landed."

   Ans. *Meera informed that the plane had landed.*

5. Our English teacher said to Mohan, "Open the window".

   Ans. *Our English teacher asked Mohan to open the window.*

Q 5. (a) Change each one of the following sentences, into their corresponding (1) Negatives and (2) Wh-questions: 10

1. Rakhi has passed the M.A. examination.

   Ans. *Negative: Rakhi has not failed in M.A. Examination.*

   Wh: Which examination has Rakhi passed?

2. India played twenty matches last year.

   Ans. *Negative: India did not play more than twenty matches last year.*

   Wh : How many matches did India play last year?

3. Her father constructed this building.

   Ans. *Negative: Her father has not destructed this building.*

   Wh: Who constructed this building?

4. This car runs on CNG.

Ans. *Negative: This car does not run on diesel.*

Wh: What does this car run on?

5. Kirti studies in that college.

Ans. *Negative: Kirti does not study in that college.*

Wh:l In which college does Kirti study?

(b) Change each of the following sentences into passive voice: **5**

1. They will not open the shop on Monday.

Ans. *The shop will not be opened on Monday by them.*

2. Mukesh caught the thief at the airport.

Ans. *The thief was caught by Mukesh at the airport.*

3. Someone has stolen my pen.

Ans. *My pen has been stolen by someone.*

4. One cannot solve the problem.

Ans. *This problem cannot be solved by anyone.*

5. Rajesh has opened the door.

Ans. *The door has been opened by Rajesh.*

(c) Make sentences using the following words as verbs: **5**

1. rebel

Ans. *The natives rebelled against the exploitation of foreign rule.*

2. export

Ans. *They export gold and diamonds.*

3. ring

Ans. *The telephone rang at five o'clock yesterday.*

4. warm

Ans. *Warm up your body before you start the exercise.*

5. experiment

Ans. *He experimented with his career by choosing the science stream.*

(d) Use the following phrases/idioms in your own sentences so as to bring out their meaning: **5**

1. to turn up

Ans. *The inspector turned up at the right time and solved the (reveal, discover) mystery of the case and caught the accused.*

2. to lose your grip

   Ans. *Continue revising or you will lose your grip.*

3. to go to your head

   Ans. *How can I go to your head to know what you are thinking?*

4. to carry out

   Ans. *It is duty of a servant to carry out (execute) his master's orders.*

5. to pull one's leg

   Ans. *He will not hesitate to pull your leg to progress in his business.*

UPSC (MAIN) EXAM – 2007
ENGLISH
(Compulsory)

Time allowed: 3 hours ***Maximum Marks: 300***

Candidates should attempt all questions.

The number of marks carried by each question is indicated at the end of the questions.

Answer must be written in English.

Q 1. Write an essay in about 300 words on any one of the following: 100

(a) Heritage Tourism is Good for Us

(b) Importance of a Work-Ethic

(c) Should mercy-Killing be Legalized for Terminally ill Patients?

(d) The Culture of Modesty

(e) "External Vigilance is the Price of Liberty"

ESSAY

Should Mercy Killing Be Legalised

Euthanasia or mercy killing, is bringing about a medically gentle death of a patient who is suffering from a painful, chronic and incurable disease. It is a practice of ending the life of a person or animal in a painless or minimally painful way. Euthanasia, an ancient Greek word literally means "Good Death" Terminally ill patients, be it cancer, AIDS, accidental or traumatic coma, the children, old women and men afflicted with the diseases undergo excruciating pain. In such a situation, if death is certain, but not imminent, the question arises why not the patient be artificially induced for a "good death", through proper medical and legal means.

Netherlands was one of the first countries to legalise euthanasia followed by Canada, state of Oregon in USA and Columbia. The state of Oregon has a 'Death with Dignity' law, which has been in place for almost 10 years. It has allowed terminally ill patients to take legal, proscribed medication to end their suffering. The legalising of euthanasia has been a cause of disagreement throughout the world and will continue to do so. No one has empathy with the person who is suffering unbearable pain and agony.. The view is that each individual should have at least the right to choose a graceful death for him or herself. Why should he/she be allowed to bear suffering day and night?

The essence of human life is to be able to live a dignified life, but when some law forces you to live in intense pain and humiliation, there is something wrong with our society. Who are we to prolong the life of one who is suffering and has decided without any undue pressure that he would like to be put to rest? Obviously, legalisation of euthanasia should not include anyone wanting to end their life at the flimsiest of excuses, but a patient must be allowed to decide when he has suffered enough.

Apart from the pain that the patient goes through, the trauma and the emotional turmoil his relatives go through is also immense. To see your close ones suffering and going through pain is not an easy sight. You wish the laws could be changed. After all as an individual, you decide whom to marry; you decide where to work, and at the last hurdle of your life, you should be allowed to choose how you want to end your life.

For the protagonists of mercy killing, this is perhaps the right cause and the perfect time to allow the patient to embrace death and put an end to his unbearable pain for an eternal peaceful abode. If human beings have the freedom to live with dignity, should they be deprived of their right to die in dignity?

Legalising mercy killing will help freeing a person from shackles of a life, which is not worth living. Sometimes, incurable medical conditions make life of a person and his near and dear-ones a living hell. Mercy killing should be legalised on humanitarian grounds, Solace, compassion; justice and humanism make euthanasia a legally permissible farewell to a life which is undergoing misery and desperation.

However, the issue of legalising euthanasia has been a cause of disagreement throughout the world and will continue to do so mainly due to fear of its misuse and/overuse. Critics have cited examples in cases where family members, to give consent to the ending of the patient's life, may coerce the patient. But this should not be an excuse for the law makers to take a backseat on this burning issue. Criticism is bound to pour in for every bold step you take. That does not mean that every move should come to a grinding halt.

Stringent laws and strict vigil by the administration in implementation of euthanasia should ensure safeguards against such a situation, and other instances of coercion and fraud.

Every case will have to be carefully monitored taking into consideration the point of views of the patient, the relatives and the doctors. This decision is based on the patient's rights and dignity, doctors' rights, religious beliefs, society's views, morality and other resolutions available.

Obviously, legalisation of euthanasia should not include anyone wanting to end their life at the flimsiest of excuses. Taking this into account the Kerala Law Reforms Panel (KLRP) suggested that mercy killing should be carried out with the written sanction of three state-recognised doctors certifying that the patient under consideration is a fit case for euthanasia.

Q 2. Read the passage carefully and write your answers to the questions that follow, in clear, correct and concise language: 15 x 5 = 75

An educated man should know what is first-rate in those activities, which spring from the creative and intellectual faculties of human nature, such as literature, art, architecture and music. I should like to add science and philosophy, but in these two subjects, it is difficult for any but the expert to estimate quality, and many educated people have not the close knowledge necessary to judge their real worth. On the other hand, everyone has close and daily contact with the other four. Architecture surrounds him in every city, literature meets him on every bookstall, music assails his ears on his radio set and from every jukebox; and art in its protean aspects of form and colour is a part of daily life. The architecture may often be bad, the literature and music often puerile, the art often undeserving of the name; but that is all the more reason why we should be able, in all of them, to distinguish good from bad.

To judge by the literature offered to us in hotel book-stands, and by most of the music played on the radio and by juke-boxes we might be more discriminating in these fields than we are. If it be said that music and art and literature are not essentials of life but its frills, I would reply that if so, it is curious, that they are among the few immortal things in the world, and that should a man wish to be remembered two thousand years hence, the only certain way is to write a great poem or book, compose a great symphony, paint a great picture, carve a great sculpture, or build a great building.

Questions:

1. What is it that is necessary for an educated person to know?

   Ans. *The first-rate understanding of literature, art, architecture and music is necessary for an educated person to know.*

2. Why does the author exclude science and philosophy from it?

   Ans. *The author excludes science and philosophy as essentials for an educated person as these two subjects are difficult, and many educated are not competent enough to judge their real worth.*

3. What makes it practically easy for an educated man to be able to know literature, art, architecture and music?

   Ans. *The knowledge of literature, art, architecture and music is practically easier than that of science and philosophy as with the former four subjects, every one has close and daily contact. These four subjects constitute an essential and integral ingredient of daily, mundane human existence.*

4. How does exposure to ordinary literature and music help us?

   Ans. *The exposure to ordinary literature and music helps up in cultivating a sense of distinguishing good from bad.*

5. What is the author's argument to prove that music, art and literature are the essentials of life?

   Ans. *Music, art and literature are essentials of life as the understanding of these subjects makes a man more discerning and distinctive. Knowledge becomes immortal and are remembered thousands of years even after their death. Those who acquire excellence in these departments of life, are remembered long even after their death.*

Q 3. Make a précis out of the following passage keeping the length within the limits of 230-240 words. It is not necessary to suggest a title. Failure to write within the word limit may result in deduction of marks. The précis must be written on the separate précis sheets provided for the purpose; they must be securely fastened inside the answer-book: 75

What part should reading play in our lives? It should certainly not be a substitute for action, not for independent thinking, nor for conversation; but it may be a help and stimulant to action; thought and talk; and it is capable of providing almost infinite pleasure. There on our bookshelves or on summons from a library, are wit, wisdom, adventure, romance from all ages and from all over the world. Is there any wonder that our eyes sometimes stray wistfully to the bookshelves and away from a dull visitor, or that we shirk a tiresome duty for an exciting book?

Books or people? Reading or conversation, listening in to a broadcast or watching a television programme? Which is the better way to gain knowledge or to spend your leisure? Some fortunate people seem always to find time for both and to enjoy both almost equally. My great friend, Arthur Wanchope, a fine soldier, an able administrator and a very gifted personality, was a constant reader, yet always ready to lay aside a book for talk.

The adventure of reading over talk are, of course, many. We can select the book that suits our mood, can go at our own pace, skip or turn back whereas we cannot turn over two pages of a tedious companion or close him or her, with a bang. But reading too has its own drawbacks. It lacks the human touch, the salt of life, and is therefore a dangerous substitute for thought or action. Bacon in one of his essays observes that reading maketh a full man; conference (that is talking) a ready man; and writing an exact man. One would like to be full of knowledge, ready in speech and exact by training. What short of books have impressed me and what books have found a permanent place on my bookshelves?

To begin with my profession – soldiering. I do not believe that soldiering, a practical business, in which human nature is the main element, can be learnt from text-books. But for those who have grasped the principles of war and have understood that the human factor is the most important element in it, there is military reading that is quite fascinating and valuable.

'Read and re-read the campaigns of the great commanders', said Napolean. I would venture to put it differently and would say that the lives and characters of the great commanders are what students of war should examine, since their campaigns are only incidents in them; and that the behaviour of leaders and of their men in the field is the real subject for study.

In my general reading, history, biography and travel occupy a prominent place; and since I have spent a considerable proportion of my life in the East, there are a good number of volumes on India and the Middle East. There is plenty of poetry on my shelves and a good deal of it is in my head. Poetry should dance in the mind, and blow one a kiss; or gallop to adventure with a cheer; or whisper gently of things past; not shuffle or slouch past with dark incomprehensible mutterings. Perhaps I am getting old, anyway I prefer the old poets.

Lastly comes what is sometimes called 'escapist' literature, the books we read with no other aim, than to rest or amuse the mind; to forget the day's chores and the morrow's anxieties. This is perhaps the most pleasant form of reading for most, and I suspect the only form of reading for many. The volume chosen may either be a thriller or soother; a thriller to bring sense of adventure into the dull daily routine or a soother to rest tired nerves. Our grandfathers in their leisurely days were content with the stately, comfortable three volume novel, but that had passed before the beginning of this century.

You will choose your books as you choose your friends, with taste and discrimination; I hope; because they can tell you something of your profession and interests, because they are wise and helpful, because they can stir your blood with tales of adventure, or because they are gay and witty. I can only wish you will get as much pleasure from them as I get from my books.

PRECIS

Though reading cannot be a substitute of independent thinking, conversation or action, yet it can be a great stimulant for all the three. The great call of books full of wit, wisdom, adventure, romance may keep us away from a dull visitor or tiresome duty. Successful people including soldiers, administrators and great personalities from various other fields, strike a balance between reading books for knowledge, leisure etc. and also engage in conversation, listen to broadcasts and watch T.V. programmes. Though reading has various advantages over conversation, as one can be selective and stop doing if the book turns out uninteresting and the same can't be done while engaging in conservation even to a tedious companion, yet reading can't provide the salt of life, the human touch and can never be an alternative to thought and action.

Reading can be highly valuable even for carrying out such practical business as fighting in a war. Lives, characters and behaviour of leaders and commanders and their man in the battle field are the great subject of study in view of the warrior, Napoleon. The narrator, finds immense pleasure in reading old poets, history, biography and gives prominence to adventurous travels. At times called 'escapist', literature is read with not clearly defined objective, other than just to rest or amuse the mind and to keep anxieties away. However, there is a sharp decline in leisurely reading of voluminous fictions in the new century, as the life in contemporary times has become too hectic and overbusy. Giving a piece of advice the writer suggest that we must exercise our sense and taste and discretion in selecting books as we do the same in selecting our friend. He wishes that the people do sustain their interest in reading.

Q4. (a) Rewrite the following sentences after making necessary correction of errors: 10

1. The Greeks were brave peoples.

   Ans. *The Greeks were brave people.*

2. His hat was blown off by the strong air.

   Ans. *His hat was blown off by the strong wind.*

3. I am the one who am to blame.

   Ans. *I am the one who is to be blamed.*

4. We should sympathies with blind.

   Ans. *We must sympathise with the visually impaired.*

5. I'd rather play cricket and not swim.

   Ans. *I'd rather play cricket than swim.*

6. Walking through the front door a wasp stung him.

   Ans. *While walking through the front door he was stung by a wasp.*

7. Two plus nine are eleven.

   Ans. *Two plus nine equals eleven.*

8. I have built the house in 1960.

   Ans. *I had built this house in 1960.*

9. Their wedding has not been a very happy one.

   Ans. *Their wedding has not been a very happy one.*

10. Choose only such friends whom you can trust.

    Ans. *Choose only such friends who are trustworthy.*

(b) Fill in the blanks with appropriate preposition/particle and *rewrite the complete sentences:* **5**

1. What kind of __________ animal is it?

   Ans. *an*

2. I will return in __________ hour.

   Ans. *an*

3. He is __________ richest man in our street.

   Ans. *the*

4. Gold is not __________ useful metal.

   Ans. *a*

5. While there is __________ life, there is hope.

   Ans. *a*

(c) Form Verbs from the following Nouns: **5**

1. Courage

   Ans. *encourage*

2. Memory

   Ans. *memorise*

3. Prison

   Ans. *imprison*

4. Class

   Ans. *classify*

5. Friend

   Ans. *befriend*

Q 5. (a) Use each of the following words in two separate sentences first as a Noun and then as a Verb: **10**

1. Bank

   Ans. *Noun: You should always have people on whom you can bank upon in times of distress.*

   Verb: Banking services is the must sought after services nowadays.

2. Battle

   Ans. *Noun: The Battle of Plassey gave a decisive edge to Britishers.*

   Verb: He has been battling with cancer.

3. Bite

   Ans. *Noun: The snakebite led to limb amputation of his foot.*

   Verb: The ferocious dog bit many children in the park.

4. Brave

Ans. ***Noun:*** *Modi is a brave statesman.*

Verb: Modi braved all odds & opponents.

5. Brush

Ans. ***Noun:*** *M.F. Hussain's brush became popular for Madhuri Dixit.*

Verb: The Prime Minister didn't brush aside the idea of going ahead with the nuclear deal.

(b) Change the following sentences into their corresponding (a) Negatives and (b) Questions: 10

1. Ram resembles his father.

Ans. ***Negative:*** *Ram does not resemble his father.*

Question: *Does Ram resemble his father?*

2. Raju Studies French.

Ans. ***Negative:*** *Raju does not study French.*

Question: Does Raju study French?

3. The bicycle costs Rs.500

Ans. ***Negative:*** *The bicycle does not cost Rs.500.*

Question: Does the bicycle cost Rs. 500?

4. The thief broke the window open.

Ans. ***Negative:*** *The thief did not break open the window.*

Question: Did the thief break open the window?

5. My mother has a beautiful umbrella.

Ans. **Negative:** *My mother does not have a beautiful umbrella.*

Question: Does my mother have a beautiful umbrella?

(c) Use the following phrases/idioms in sentences so as to bring out the meaning:5

1. The lion's share.

Ans. *In his partnership ventures, Ram always got a lion's share.*

2. Close shave

Ans. *When attacked by a shark during a diving exercise, Peter had a close shave with death.*

3. At daggers drawn

Ans. *Quarrelling over property issues, the brothers had daggers drawn at each other.*

4. (To) die in harness

   Ans. *The Government of India proposes to relax norms for providing employment to the next of kin of those who die in harness.*

5. eat one's words

   Ans. *One must not make such promises which will force him to eat one's words, later on.*

Q 6. Put the verbs in bracket in the correct tense and rewrite the following: 5

India (have) many calendars which Indians (use) since very early times. More than thirty (be) still in use. One difficulty about having so many calendars (be) that the same date (fall) on different days according to each.

Ans. India **has** many calendars which Indians **have used** since very early times. More than thirty **are** still in use. One difficulty about having so many calendars **is** that the same date **falls** on different days according to each.

UPSC (MAIN) EXAM – 2006
ENGLISH
(Compulsory)

Time allowed: 3 hours **Maximum Marks: 300**

Candidates should attempt all questions.

The number of marks carried by each question is indicated at the end of the questions.

Answer must be written in English.

Q 1. Write an essay in about 300 words on any one of the following: 100

(a) Social Impact of Black Money

(b) Women in Combat Forces

(c) Internet as Virtual Library

(d) Fashion Boom In India

(e) Are we Aggressive and Rude People?

ESSAY

Fashion Boom in India

India has been witnessing a fashion boom since the 1990s thanks to the era that heralded globalisation and economic liberalisation. The onset of globalisation and liberalisation helped India get exposure to the world market, the fashion trends prevailing at the international level, be it in textiles, shoes, electronics, food or any item of day to day use.

We can witness the fashion boom in a common Indian's life from dawn itself. Instead of local/ indigenous made products, Indians prefer to have bed tea with foreign branded biscuits, or breakfast with internationally recognised jams, pickles or cornflakes, oats etc. The foreign branded soaps, shampoos, pastes, oils, creams decorate our bathrooms. There has been a meteoric boom in textiles, dresses, shoes, neckties, hankies, socks.

The fashion boom can be seen in our lifestyles. Our lifestyles have undergone drastic changes. Our eating habits, our eating priorities, timings and tastes are based on western habits.

We prefer to wear western style clothes manufactured by western companies. We prefer pizzas, pastas, patties, burger, hotdogs etc. Interestingly, our local and indigenous industries are also getting updated, modernised on western lines. The electronic industry, information technology, media are the biggest sources of influences that make us fashion savvy resulting in fashion boom in India.

Bollywood and Hollywood are the main factors that boost the fashion industry in India. The fast growing consumerism, the shopping malls culture, the IT generation of youth, online shopping, social networking sites are the reasons as well as indicators of fashion boom in India.

Q 2. Read the passage carefully and write your answers to the questions that follow, in clear, correct and concise language: 15x5 =75

There is no reason to believe that there are fundamental differences between the East and the West. Human beings are everywhere human and hold the same deepest values. The differences which are, no doubt, significant, are related to external, temporary social conditions and are alterable with them. East and West are relative terms. They are geographical expressions and not cultural types. The differences among countries like China, Japan and India are quite as significant as those among European or American countries. Specific cultural patterns with distinctive beliefs and habits developed in different regions in relative isolation from one another. There were periods when China and India were pre-eminent in cultural affairs, others when Western nations became dominant. For the last four centuries, Western nations aided by scientific development have dominated the East.

The world has now reached a state of inter-communication. All societies are fast becoming industrialised and new sets of values are springing up. We are called upon to participate in the painful birth of a new civilisation. If we are to live together in peace, we must develop international cooperation and understanding.

It is for the political leaders to determine the practical steps by which the sources of power and communication now available to us can be used for closer cooperation and friendliness among the people of the world. No political understanding can be made permanent without understanding at the cultural level. Apart from its intrinsic importance, such understanding contributes to the enrichment of human experience. Facile generalizations are made by philosophers of history which are highly misleading. Hegel in his *Lectures on the Philosophy of History* says that 'Persia is the land of light; Greece the land of grace; India the land of dream; Rome the land of Empire.'

Questions:

1. What does the passage say about cultural differences in different regions?

   Ans. *Cultural differences in different regions are not fundamental and absolute. Human beings everywhere hold the same deepest values. However, it should not lead to the conclusion that there are no cultural differences and understanding the same are of no consequences.*

2. What comments does the author make about the similarities and dissimilarities between the East and the West?

   Ans. *According to the author, East and West have similarities, as the people of these geographical divisions hold some similar underlying deep values. However, the two regions are dissimilar on account of specific cultural patterns with distinctive beliefs and habits developed in different regions.*

3. What, according to the passage, is the role of communication in building up a new civilisation?

   Ans. *All societies are undergoing the experiences of industrialisation and new set of values are springing up. In this phase of transition leading to the creation of a new civilisation, the role of communication has increased manifold aiding international cooperation and understanding.*

4. How will cultural understanding at the international level benefit human societies?

   Ans. *No political understanding can be permanent without understanding at the cultural level for the promotion and establishment of cooperation and friendliness among the people of the world. Understanding of cultural differences and identities are of great significance.*

5. Why does the author call the statements of Hegel 'facile generalisations'?

Ans. *The author calls the statement of Hegel as facile generalizations as his statement about Persia, Greece, India and Rome involve superficial overgeneralisation. They exclude internal cultural differences pertaining to these nations, and the changes that these nations undergo with the passage of time.*

Q 3. Make a précis out of the following passage keeping the length within the limits of 230-240 words. It is not necessary to suggest a title. Failure to write within the word limit may result in deduction of marks. The précis must be written on the separate précis sheets provided for the purpose; they must be securely fastened inside the answer-book: 75

We all show our feelings on issues by the way we look and react. This has been referred to as body language. We tend to lean forward, hand on chin when we are interested, or turn away when disinterested. Our hands and arms can indicate we are open to what is being said by being relaxed, or show that we are not, by being clenched or crossed. We are, therefore, making body pictures of what we feel and think all the time. Indeed, people who are talking to us can often get as much information from our body posture as from what we say of how we say it. We might calmly but show we are anxious by moving from foot to foot or by blushing. It is hard to control one's behavioural reactions, for it is more of a stimulus response reaction than the words we use.

Nevertheless through training it is feasible to portray the image you want to show others. With the advent of television as a major political medium there is a lot of effort going into grooming representatives of organisations and particularly chief executives to control their gestures and gesticulations. All this may sound as if you need to be a good actor in order to be successful at conversation control. The answer is, in one sense, you do. There is no use in saying one thing and doing another. The actual visual behaviour of shaking you head, for example, while saying yes will deafen the words. Those who are effective at conversation control act in a congruent way. Their behaviour matches their words. You can see they mean what they say. They present an authentic picture because their visuals match their verbals.

With practice it is possible to improve performance in conversation without adding any more words. The improvement can come because you improve your visual gestures and gesticulations. For example, you can encourage another person by smiling when he/she says something that pleases you. Indeed the smile is a very powerful gesture. It can switch people 'on and off' if done at the appropriate time.

Psychologists refer to the laws of conditioning and reinforcement. To be skilled in conversation control you need to know and apply these laws. Conditioning means having an effect on someone's behaviour by introducing a condition that either encourages or discourages that behaviour. For example, we have all been conditioned to stop when we see a red light at a traffic intersection, and to proceed if we see a green light. People can be conditioned in conversation by such visual cues. For example, if you want someone to continue talking, smile and nod at regular intervals. The smile sets up the green light permission as a condition for the other person to speak. The nod reinforces what is being said and gives the unspoken permission to continue. People are very sensitive to such permission cues and clues. If you stop smiling and head nodding, they will usually stop and you can then contribute. Likewise you can influence the attention of people with whom you are talking by the way you use your eyes and hands, particularly when you are addressing a group. To exercise control it is important to make eye contact with one or more people. If it is a group, move your eye contact from time to time so that each person is being conditioned to the fact that it could be their turn next for you to speak to them.

Body language and the gestures and gesticulations you make are key aspects of conversation control. Many books have been written on the subject of how our body very often tells others what we are thinking before we have spoken. The visual clues get through much more quickly than the verbal ones. Also, use your hands to emphasise a point or get them to direct the listener's gaze where you want it to concentrate. The pointed finger or the open palm tells the story. Our task is to line up what we say with what we do and vice versa. If you do clench your fist and are angry, then your words should reflect this. If you are relaxed, happy and smiling, they say no.

PRECIS

People manifest their feelings the way they look at or react. This is called as body language. Learning forward or placing your hand on your chin shows one's interestedness and seriousness; being crossed or clenched indicates the opposite. Our body postures speak more than what we actually try to convey verbally. There must be maximum coordination between one's behavioural reactions and verbal responses. To create congruency between saying and doing (bodily gestures and gesticulations) with a view to more effective communication and reception is the need of the hour. Grooming (imparting training) representatives including chief executives in various organisations are a necessary step. They aim at utmost coordination between their visual and verbal responses. One can improve one's performance in conversation by improving one's visual gesture. Smiling is one of such powerful encouraging gestures. Psychological laws referred to as conditioning and reinforcement are of enormous value to understand human behaviour. To encourage someone to continue with one's conversation, smiles and nods at regular intervals are essential. Smiles and nods reinforce unspoken permission to continue with the same. People are very sensitive to such bodily and visual cues and clues. To be an effective and powerful communicator and conversationalist, one must make a point to establish a harmonisation between one's bodily gestures and gesticulations and intended verbal responses. The gulf between one's saying and behaviour will not have the desired effects.

Q 4. (a) Rewrite the following sentences after making necessary correction of errors: 10

1. Neither percept nor discipline are so forceful as example.

   Ans. *Neither percept nor discipline is as forceful as an example.*

2. Do you know if there is a house for letting in the neighbourhood?

   Ans. *Do you know if there is a house for to-let in the neighbourhood?*

3. Who you said was coming to see me in the morning?

   Ans. *Whom did you mention was coming to see me in the morning?*

4. He was finding it increasingly difficult to make his two ends meet.

   Ans. *He was finding it increasingly difficult to make both ends meet.*

5. The poor people of the village buy neither vegetables nor grow them.

   Ans. *The poor villagers neither buy vegetables nor grow them.*

6. On entering the hall, the number of visitors surprised me.

   Ans. *I was surprised to see the number of visitors after I entered the hall.*

7. The short story should not exceed more than two hundred words.

   Ans. *The short story should not exceed the limit of 200 words.*

8. Before giving the mixture to the child, shake it thoroughly.

   Ans. *Shake the mixture thoroughly before giving it to the child.*

9. Nothing has or could be more tragic than his death.

   Ans. *Nothing can or could be more tragic than his death.*

10. The reason that the students these days are so undisciplined is that they do not get any guidance from their parents.

    Ans. *The lack of discipline in students is due to the lack of guidance from their parents.*

(b) Fill in the blanks with appropriate preposition /particle and *rewrite the completed sentences*: **5**

1. I told him that he could not catch a big fish __________ a small rod.

   Ans. *with*

2. He was taken __________ task for shortage in cash balance.

   Ans. *to*

3. The father pulled __________ his son for his extravagant habits.

   Ans. *up*

4. He is so clever, it is difficult to see __________ his tricks.

   Ans. *through*

5. I have been invited by my friend __________ tea.

   Ans. *for*

(c) Choose the appropriative verb form to fill in the blanks and *rewrite* the sentences: **5**

1. The efficiency of a plant __________ by the load it can take.

   (a) knows (b) is known

   (c) has been known (d) has known

   Ans. *is known*

2. Every last week my aunt __________ a plate.

   (a) breaks (b) was broken

   (c) broke (d) has broken

   Ans *breaks*

3. If I __________ one more question, I would have passed.

   (a) had answered (b) would have answered

   (c) would answer (d) answered

   Ans. *had answered*

4. He promised __________ me a post in his department.

   (a) to have given (b) having given

   (c) have given (d) to give

   Ans. to give

5. Please don't __________, when you go out.

   (a) leave opening the door

   (b) leave the door open

   (c) leave the door opened

   (d) leave open the door

   Ans. *leave the door open*

(d) Change the following sentences into Indirect Speeches: 5

1. He said, "I will not approve of such a behavior in future."

   Ans. *He said that he would not approve of such a behavior in future.*

2. He said on the telephone, "We kept on doing our work till late night."

   Ans. *He conveyed on the telephone that he was working till late in the night.*

3. She said, "As your mother is ill, you must go home at once."

   Ans. *She asked him to go home as his mother was ill.*

4. Ram said to Sita, "Do you intend to come with me to the forest?"

   Ans. *Ram asked Sita whether she would accompany him to the forest.*

5. The child said to the Sherpa, "Why didn't you choose to climb to the Moon."

   Ans. *The child innocently asked the Sherpa as to why he did not climb to the moon.*

Q 5. (a) Fill in the blank with an appropriate derivation of the word given within brackets & rewrite the sentences: 10

For Example: It has been raining (continue) continuously for two days.

1. She had few rights but all the (responsible) __________ of her work.

   Ans. *responsibility*

2. Women chose not to vote (machine) __________ at the bidding of their menfolk.

   Ans. *mechanically*

3. In South Africa, certain areas are (exclude) __________ meant for white people.

   Ans. *exclusively*

4. The Pathans of the Frontier are (descend) __________ of Genghis Khan.

   Ans. *descendents*

5. The court ordered him a heavy fine and (prison) __________ of 3 years.

   Ans. *imprisonment*

6. India lodged a complaint with Pakistan for (courage) __________ terrorism in Kashmir.

   Ans. *encouraging*

7. Candidates with Graduate degrees in (Human) __________ and Arts prefer office jobs.

   Ans. *humanities*

8. Despite the call for ceasefire, the war continued (abate) __________.

   Ans. *unabated*

9. A creative person is known for his (source) __________ and flexibility.

   Ans. *resourcefulness*

10. The police could not control the situation as the protestors (number) __________ them manifold.

    Ans. *outnumbered*

(b) Make sentences using the following words *as directed* so as to bring out the meaning: **10**

1. Pitch (as noun and verb)

   Ans. ***Noun:*** *The cricket pitch was slippery because of drizzling.*

   Verb: BJP pitched Kiran Bedi against Kejriwal as CM candidate in Delhi.

2. Mirror (as noun and verb)

   Ans. ***Noun:*** *A driving mirror in the car enables the driver to see what is coming from behind.*

   Verb: *The trees were mirrored in the stillness of the lake.*

3. Humble (as adjective and verb)

   Ans. *Adj: He is so humble inspite of being from such a powerful family.*

   Verb: Winning the Oscar for A.R Rahman was an extremely humbling experience.

4. In (as adverb and preposition)

   Ans. **Adv:** *The running-in of a car's engine is essential for performance.*

   Pre.: *The highest mountain in the world is Mount Everest.*

(c) Use the following phrases/idioms in sentences so as to bring out the meaning: 5

1. bell the cat

   Ans. Everybody wants to teach a lesson to the erring boss, but nobody is ready to bell the cat.

2. thank one's stars

   Ans. Normally people thank their stars for all the best in life.

3. be on tenterhooks

   Ans. The thief kept the Chandigarh police on tenterhooks.

4. true to one's salt

   Ans. All Indians should try to be true to their salt.

5. come out with flying colours

   Ans. Pratibha came out with flying colours in the exam.

UPSC (MAIN) EXAM – 2005
ENGLISH
(Compulsory)

Time allowed: 3 hours **Maximum Marks: 300**

Candidates should attempt all questions.

The number of marks carried by each question is indicated at the end of the questions.

Answer must be written in English.

Q 1. Write an essay in about 300 words on any one of the following: 100

(a) Environment and Conservation

(b) Role of Women in Social Transformation

(c) Nuclear Energy in War and Peace

(d) India's Foreign Policy and World Power

(e) Television and its Impact on Youth

ESSAY

Television and Its Impact

Television is one of the most influential medium of communication in the 21st century. In today's world, whether it is a child, adult or an old man, everyone has some or other favourite show on television. Also, due to the upgradation of technology and competition among manufacturers, television is no more a commodity which is owned by only the urban populace.

Even rural families have access to television. Since it is reaching such a large number of people, it has a major impact on the lives of these people. As in any other medium of communication, television also has its pros and cons. Initially, when television shows were launched, one of the major impact was that it brought families close to each other. As TVs were a little expensive initially, and also with limited shows on air, people used to sit together. But slowly and steadily with the advent of technology and more and more choices available catering to the demands of every sector of the society, television sets reversed the above concept entirely. Now each room of a house may have a separate television set. Thus kids sit, watch, eat, drink, and play in their room and parents do the same in their room. Thus, television has both negative and positive effects on society.

All the children's programmes and cartoon channels are intermixed with advertisements. These advertisements have a definite influence on tender minds. How much impact TV has on children depends on many factors: how much they watch, their age and personality, whether they watch alone or with adults, and whether their parents talk with them about what they see on TV.

Also, television had a major impact on the youth in terms of violence, health and sex related issues. Over the past two decades, hundreds of studies have examined how violent programming on TV affects children and young people. While a direct "cause and effect" link is difficult to establish, there is a growing consensus that some people may be vulnerable to violent images and messages. Also, a check needs to be kept on kids who behave aggressively after watching a particular show. Since, these days' people are so much into television the biggest concern is that they sit in front of the TV set for hours thus most of their precious time is spent sitting and munching snacks without doing any physical activity because of which kids suffer from various health problems at a very young age. Kids today are bombarded with sexual messages and images in all media-television, magazines, advertisements, music, movies and the Internet. Parents are often concerned about whether these messages are healthy. While television can be a powerful tool for educating young people about the responsibilities and risks of sexual behaviour, such issues are seldom mentioned or dealt with in a meaningful way in programmes containing sexual content.

Television has both negative as well as positive effects. Television offers lots of benefits such as, sharing cultural experience with others, shared viewing gives a family some time together, parents can use television as a catalyst for reading by making them watch a particular show and then bringing books related to the same, improving the general knowledge, also helps in improving the social and communication skills of the kid.

The parents must go on talking to the child while watching TV, that is, they must explain the programme contents to the younger ones. This will help the children to make an important connection between actions and their consequences. Studies have shown that children whose parents explain events and clarify information tend to be more imaginative, less aggressive and less hyperactive and tend to understand the contents of the programme better. But at present, the parents do not spend time with children, nor do they discuss the values of the programme. Co-viewing can also help a child to cope with the impact produced by the programme. The rapport between the parents and children will also improve.

Thus, it is depends on us the kind of knowledge we want to gain from this medium. If we actually want to make this world a beautiful place to live in, we have to take a step ahead and decide what is good and what is not.

Q 2. Read the passage and answer in your own words the questions that follow:

15x5=75

It is wrong to believe that science has totally eclipsed literature with its inspiring zeal. That literature plays a subordinate role in science is equally untrue. Nevertheless, it is undeniable that science has comparatively a wider range, because of its impact on the physical world, than literature. But that does not mean that literature has been incorporated in the realm of science to the extent that it loses its distinct individuality. The reality is that both co-exist without the one overshadowing the other. Those who think that science has pushed literature into shade reducing it to a non-entity seem to be simply imaginative and illogical in the comparisons of their respective merits. It is no doubt unquestionable that products of science are of greater material value than those which make an emotional appeal, e.g., a bridge is of greater use to the public than a poem. But thereby one should not ignore the importance of a poem which will continue to appeal to human mind for time to come. It is indisputable that a scientific theory like the one propounded by Einstein is not without its philosophical import as it lays its impress on the future growth of literature. But to be effective in this respect, science should unfold its principles by appealing to human emotions and not through crude and concrete material facts. Darwin's theory of Natural Selection, in its exposition of the evolution of man by appeal to emotions and imagination of men, has been conducive to the growth of nineteenth century literature. Man's emotional attitudes to life and vicissitudes of his fortune are coloured not only by his inherited instincts and faith in his fate, but also by his hope in point of longevity of life and betterment of future prospects. Oriented by a scientific theory, they give colour to literature.

Literature feeds the emotional and imaginative hunger of man. In this perspective science will not oust literature but enrich it by its impact on human life. Science can provide amenities of life for human comfort but fails to lend or impart spiritual pleasure. Delight that literature instills in man far transcends the comforts which science provides.

Questions:

1. What is the basic contribution of science to humankind?

   Ans. *The basic contribution of science to human kind is to provide and enhance amenities of life for human comfort.*

2. What aspect of human life is fulfilled by works of literature?

   Ans. *The emotional and imaginative aspects of human life is fulfilled by literature. It imparts spiritual pleasures.*

3. How have Darwin's and Einstein's theories proved "conducive to the growth of literature?

   Ans. *Darwin's and Einstein's theories have philosophical foundations and import. Their theories have had great emotional and imaginative appeal and deeply impacted the growth of literature. These theories have given diverse colours to literary productions.*

4. How is science friendly and not hostile to the growth of literature?

   Ans. *Despite its emphasis on material aspects of life and producing greater material value, science has also played tremendous role to the growth of literature. Scientific discoveries and innovations have stirred human imagination and have had a great emotional appeal to the literary mind.*

5. Briefly enumerate the key ideas in the passage.

   Ans. *The passage accounts for a comparative study of the contribution of science vis-à-vis literature. If science matters to us because of its great material values and provides amenities of life, literature is of no less significance as it fulfills the emotional and imaginative needs of man by imparting the capacity to raise the spiritual quality of life to a different level.*

Q 3. Make a précis out of the following passage in your own words in about 220-240 words. Marks will be deducted if the précis is not written on the separate précis sheets provided and if it is longer or shorter than the prescribed limit. State the number of words used by you in the précis at its end and securely fasten the précis sheets inside the answer-book. 75

Gautama, the Buddha, has suffered as much as anyone from critics without a sense of history. He has been cried up, and cried down, with an equal lack of historical imagination. Buddhism came to be widely known in the west in the latter part of the 19th century, when a wave of scepticism spread over the world as a result of the growth of science and enlightenment. Positivism, agnosticism, atheism and ethical humanism found wide support. In much of the literature of doubt and disbelief, the name of Buddha is mentioned with respect. The humanists honour him as one of the earliest protagonists of their cause- the happiness, the dignity, and the mental integrity of mankind. Those who declare that man cannot know reality, and others who affirm that there is no reality to know, use his name. Agnostics quote his example. Social idealists, ethical mystics, rationalist prophets are all attracted by his teaching.

Great as is the value of the Buddha's teaching for our age, we cannot hope to understand its true significance without reference to the environment in which he lived. This effort of historical imagination is not easy. To view the Buddha as a thinker of the sixth century B.C., living, moving and teaching in its peculiar conditions, is a task of extreme difficulty and delicacy; and the work of reconstruction can never be complete. But we may be reasonably certain that it yields a picture which in its main outlines, at least, must correspond fairly well to the reality.

The supremacy of the ethical is the clue to the teaching of the Buddha. His conceptions of life and the universe are derived from his severely practical outlook. The existence of everything depends on a cause. If we remove the cause, the effect will disappear. If the source of suffering is destroyed, suffering will disappear. The only way in which we can remove the cause of suffering is by purifying the heart and following the moral law. Man is not divine but is to become divine. His divine status is something to be built up by good thoughts, good words, and good deeds. The ego consists of the feelings that burn us, of the passions we brood over, of the desires that hunt us and of the decisions we make. These are the things that give life its dramatic character. There is nothing absolute and permanent in them. That is why we can become something different from what we are. The reality of the person is the creative will. When we deny the clamour of emotions, stay the stream of things, siliencing the appetites of body, we feel the power of self within our own being.

For the Buddha, the impulse of dharma, to justice and kindliness is operative in things, and its efficient activity will mean the reduction of disorder, cruelty and oppression. Dharma is organic to existence and its implication of karma or right action is the builder of the world. There is not in the Buddha's teaching that demies that deep personal loyalty, passion of love, and intimate dialogue between soul and soul resembles closely in its expression of earthly love. And yet the essence of religion, the vision of a reality which stands beyond and within the passing flux of immediate things, the intuitive loyalty to something larger than and beyond oneself, is in him.

We find in Gautama, the Buddha, in powerful combination, spiritual profundity and moral strength of the highest order and a discreet intellectual reserve. He is one of those rare spirits who bring to men a realisation of their own divinity and make the spiritual life seem adventurous and attractive, so that they may go forth into the world with a new interest and a new joy of heart. While his great intellect and wisdom gave him comprehension of the highest truth, his warm heart led him to devote his life to save from sorrow the suffering humanity. The greatness of his personality, his prophetic zeal, and burning love for suffering humanity made a deep impression on those with whom he lived; but his true greatness stands out clearer and brighter as the ages pass, and even the skeptical minded are turning to him with a more real appreciation, a deeper reverence and a truer worship. He is one of those few heroes of humanity who have made epochs in the history of our race, with a message for other times as well as their own.

PRECIS

Gautam Buddha is often subjected to severe criticism without a sense of historical perspective.. His teachings became popular in the west in the latter half of the 19th century. When there was a wave of skepticism on account of progress in science and when such philosophies as positivism, agnosticism, atheism and ethical humanism were strengthening their grip over the world, his redemptive vision and liberating philosophy has been appropriated by all alike, including humanists, agnostics, idealists, mystics and rationalists attracted by his teachings. The value and significance of Buddhism cannot be comprehended properly without referring to the environment in which the Buddha lived in. Even the reconceiving and reconceptualizing of the sixth century conditions can never be easy and complete for the comprehensive understanding of the great seer. Buddha's vision of life and universe is predicted upon an ethical and pragmatic concern i.e. to make human beings free from sufferings and sorrows. Annihilating the root of man's suffering, i.e. the ego consisting of feelings, passions, craving and desires and replacing the same by good thoughts, good deeds and good words will lead to redemption. One can feel the power of self by controlling the clamour of emotions, the urge for things and silencing the appetite of body. Performing one's dharma coupled with an impulse to kindness and justice and loyality to something larger and beyond oneself, are the foundational principles of the Buddhist teachings. A rare but powerful combination of spiritual profundity, moral strength and discrete intellect, Buddha created an epoch in history with a profound message aimed at salvaging humanity.

Q 4. (a) Correct the following sentences: **10**

1. Too great a variety of studies destruct the mind.

   Ans. *Too much diversity in studies destructs the mind.*

2. The whole fleet of their ships were captured.

   Ans. *The whole fleet of ships was captured.*

3. Each of these students have done their work.

   Ans. *Each of these students has done his work*

4. None but fools has ever believed it.

   Ans. *Only fools have believed it.*

5. He is one of cleverest boy that has passed through the school.

   Ans. *He is one of the most intelligent students to have passed out of this school.*

6. My friend, philosopher and guide have come.

   Ans. *Here comes my friend, philosopher and guide.*

7. The majority are opposed to this proposal.

   Ans. *This proposal has been opposed by a majority of the members.*

8. He told me that he saw his father last month.

   Ans. *He informed me that he had seen his father last month.*

9. If he would have worked hard, he would have passed the examination.

   Ans. *He would have passed the examination only if he had worked hard.*

10. Unless he will be more careful, he will not recover.

    Ans. *He would not recover unless he becomes more careful.*

(b) Add the suffix 'able' or 'ible' to each of the following words making necessary changes in spelling. Write out the "new" words. 10

(i) Advice → Advisable
(ii) Contempt → Contemptible
(iii) Force → Forcible
(iv) Access → Accessible
(v) Value → Valuable
(vi) Reduce → Reducible
(vii) Discern → Discernable
(viii) Agree → Agreeable
(ix) Detach → Detachable
(x) Reverse → Reversible

(c) Use the following phrases in your own sentences so as to bring out their meaning: 5

1. Apple of discord

   Ans. *The Kashmir issue is the apple of discord between India and Pakistan.*

2. A bolt from the blue

   Ans. *Mahatma Gandhi's death was a bolt from the blue for the nation.*

3. A feather in one's cap

   Ans. *Bharat Ratna is another feather in Vajpayee's cap.*

4. Achilles' heel

   Ans. *Maths is the Achilles' heel for CLAT students.*

5. A man of letters

   Ans. *Khushwant Singh was really a man of letters.*

Q 5. (a) Which of the two words within brackets in the following sentences is correct in the context? 10

1. Poets often (sore, soar) to great heights of imagination.

   Ans. soar

2. Knowledge (proceeds, precedes) from the Goddess of Learning.

   Ans. proceeds

3. The tower was struck by (lightning, lightening) and fell down.

   Ans. *Lightning*

4. Kanpur lies on the air (rout, route) to Calcutta.

   Ans. *route*

5. Everyone is (jealous, zealous) of him.

   Ans. *jealous*

6. The crocodile emerged from the river and (seized, ceased) a goat.

   Ans. *seized*

7. He was found in (collusion, collision) with the plotters.

   Ans. *collusion*

8. Wicked persons are not (illegible, eligible) for responsible posts.

   Ans. *eligible*

9. He is a man of (lose, loose) character.

   Ans. *loose*

10. The Emperor is staying at the royal (mansion, mention)

    Ans. *mansion*

(b) Use each of the following words in two separate sentences, first as a noun and then as a verb: 10

1. Book

   Ans. Noun: *The book 'Inheritance of Loss' earned a Booker Prize.*

   Verb: They were booked for molestation.

2. Bare

   Ans. *Noun: He walked bare-footed.*

   Verb: He bared his soul to his beloved and told her the stark realities of his life.

3. Calm

   Ans. *Noun: He seemed cool and calm after the incident.*

   Verb: The storm gradually calmed down.

4. Drive

   Ans. *Noun: He went on a long drive.*

   Verb: His ambition of becoming an IAS officer has driven him to reach his goal.

5. Face

   Ans.*Noun: His face turned red with embarrassment when he was caught red handed with his girl friend.*

   Verb: Be ready to face the music.

(c) Change the following sentences into Indirect Speech: **5**

1. He said, "I am too ill to speak now."

   Ans. *He said he was too ill to speak then.*

2. The policeman said to the man, "Where are you going."

   Ans. *The policeman asked the man where he was going.*

3. She said to her children, Let me work undisturbed.

   Ans. *She requested her children to let her work undisturbed.*

4. He said to the students, "Do not sit here."

   Ans. *He asked the students not to sit there.*

5. He said, "May God pardon the sinner."

   Ans. *He begged God's pardon for the sinner.*

UPSC (MAIN) EXAM – 2004
ENGLISH
(Compulsory)

Time allowed: 3 hours ***Maximum Marks: 300***

Candidates should attempt all questions.

The number of marks carried by each question is indicated at the end of the questions.

Answer must be written in English.

Q 1. Write an essay in about 300 words on any one of the following: 100

(a) Indian Budget is a Gamble on the Monsoons

(b) Need of Water-Harvesting in India

(c) Social Harmony vs. Communal Frenzy

(d) Criminalisation of Politics

(e) 'All That Glitters Is Not Gold'

ESSAY

Criminalisation of Politics

The criminalisation of politics and politicisation of criminals seems to be a two-way traffic. The public perception is the politicians and criminals are hand in glove with each other and that both are thriving with the help of the 3 MP's: Muscle Power, Money Power and Mafia Power.

The Founding Fathers of our polity were patriotic men and women of great vision, wisdom and sagacity. They wanted to build a united nation, where despite differences of race, caste, ethnicity, religion, etc. all the citizens would live in peace and harmony. It was natural, therefore, that postulates of secularism were enshrined in the Preamble and in other Parts of the Constitution. Secular values in the Indian Constitution, however, never implied irreligion or disrespect to matters of the spirit.

The present electoral system may perhaps be one of the factors for many of debilitating ills afflicting our body politic today. The tattered social fabric, the fragmentation on narrow communal and caste grounds, the craze for separate identities and minority and backward status all have their source in the anxiety of politicians to build and preserve their distinct vote banks. Under the new standards, perhaps quite legitimately, politics is all about how to get to power, and if once there, how to stay on. The interest of the nation, public good or service to the people comes last, if at all, in the scheme of things.

Criminalisation of politics is not a new phenomenon. Perhaps Maulana Azad had a premonition of it when he said

"The palm of almost every politician bears the blood stains of a bleeding secularism. With the process of deideologisation nearing completion, casteism and communalism are bound to step in as successors, no matter how illegitimate they are. Now no party can think of setting up a candidate without any caste and communal considerations. In fact the spirit of nationalism has waned so precipitously under the impact of competitive politics of elections, that all kinds of particularistic trends are on the rise and Indians without denominational labels are a dying species".

The communal, racial or other ethnicity based conflictual situations, violence, terrorist activities, police atrocities, the spectacle in legislatures and in higher echelons of Government, many fissiparous and divisive tendencies raising their ugly heads here and there, rampant attempts by all parties and politicians to build political power bases and vote banks by dividing the people into narrow groups on the basis of religion, caste, region, language and the like, the general criminalisation of politics and politicisation of criminals and the all-round climate of corruption are an antithesis of all the citizenship values enshrined in the Constitution. The only hope for building a united and integrated nation with dignity of the individual lies in we, the citizens of India rising above petty self interests, identifying the hard core of citizenship values enjoined by the Constitution and making a determined bid to work together to protect and promote them by contributing all our mite.

All communalism/ casteism in public life is bad, whether of a majority or of a minority, whether the BJP variety or the Congress or the Muslim League variety. It becomes the constitutional duty of every citizen to question the ethicality of "inverted communalism" passing off as secularism, as well as the danger of encouraging minority communalism as a counter measure to majority communalism. The police-criminal nexus and political parties playing the communal card are by now well-known to be behind the communal riots. Police force is also said to be highly politicised and communalised. It is important for citizens of India to be alert and awake and break the unholy alliance between communal criminals and politicians and to stop political interference in law enforcement and to make the administration accountable for communal riots.

Politicians who are also first citizens of India than anything else seem to have forsaken all values of national interest. The highest value for them is that of somehow acquiring power and clinging to it.

The best way to protect secular values seems to be to create greater awareness among the citizens of the need on their part to neutralise the growing tendency among politicians and political parties of all hues to use religion and caste for political power ends.

Q 2. Read the passage and answer in your own words the questions that follow:

15 x 5 = 75

The flowering of Indian civilisation constitutes one of the most glorious chapters in the history of mankind. A culture, remarkable for its moral no less than for its material creativity, which has endured for three millennia and more, is necessarily a subject of great fascination. Yet over and above its longevity, Indian civilisation is also characterised by some other features which deserve to be highlighted in any reviews of its past. The ability of this civilisation to absorb alien cultures without losing its distinctive identity has intrigued scholars over the centuries; and this capacity for creative absorption is as much in evidence today, when India is undergoing a seminal transformation into a modern industrial community, as it was in the centuries past, when alien communities with novel ways of life migrated into the subcontinent, to be drawn into the living matrix of Indian society.

The continuity of Indian civilisation rests very substantially upon social institutions and upon the dissemination of a common corpus of religious values among different classes and communities in the subcontinent. This civilisation was also located in the plains of the Indus and the Ganga in the north; and those of the Mahanadi, the Godavari, the Krishna, and the Cauvery in the south. Over the centuries, the people living in these riverine regions had conjured into existence a round of economic activity and a set of social institutions, which were designed to produce the agricultural wealth which sustained life. Indeed, the structure of rural society, with a central place occupied by the cultivating classes, which were linked by ties of patronage and prescription to numerous artisanal and menial groups; and the fabric of caste society, with the interlocking institutions of Varna and Jati has to be looked upon as the historical answer of the Indian genius to the needs of sustaining production in a rural society. The striking feature of this social organisation was the premium which it put on self sufficiency and survival within the framework of an agrarian civilisation.

Questions:

1. What is the most distinctive feature of Indian civilisation?

   Ans. *The ability to absorb alien culture is the most distinctive feature of Indian civilisation.*

2. Which section of the society occupied a central place in Indian civilisation?

   Ans. *Along with people engaged with the dissemination of a common corpus of religious values among different classes and communities, the cultivating section – the backbone of Indian society – substantially determined the total ordering of society.*

3. Identify the great epicentres of Indian civilisation as narrated in the passage.

   Ans. *The great epicentres of Indian civilisation were located in the plains of the Indus and the Ganga in the north; and those of the Mahanadi, the Godavari, the Krishna and the Cauvery in the south.*

4. On what did the Indian social organisation lay emphasis?

   Ans. *The Indian social organisation laid emphasis on self-sufficiency and survival within the framework of an agrarian civilisation.*

5. What does the phrase "conjured into existence" mean?

   Ans. *To conjure means to evoke, to conceive or imagine and the phrases 'conjured into existence' means certain ideas, institutions and community organisations intricately connected with life and existence.*

Q 3. Make a précis out of the following passage in your own words in about 220-240 words. Mark will be deducted if the précis is not written on the separate précis sheets provided and if it is longer or shorter than the prescribed limit. State the number of words used by you in the précis at its end and securely fasten the précis sheets inside the answer-book. 75

There is some similarity between Italy and India. Both are ancient countries with long traditions of culture behind them, though Italy is a newcomer compared to India, and India is a much more vast country. Both are split up politically, and yet the conception of Italia, like that of India, never died, and in all their diversity the unity was predominant. In Italy the unity was largely a Roman unity, for that great city had dominated the country and been the fount and symbol of unity. In India, there was no such single centre or dominant city, although Benares might well be called the Eternal City of the East, not only for India, but also for Eastern Asia. But, unlike Rome, Benares never dabbled in empire or thought of temporal power. Indian culture was so widespread all over India that no part of the country could be called the heart of that culture. From Kanyakumari to Amarnath and Badrinath in the Himalayas, from Dwarka to Puri, the same ideas coursed, and if there was a clash of ideas in one place, the noise of it soon reached distant parts of the country.

Just as Italy gave the gift of culture and religions to Western Europe, India did so to Eastern Asia though China was as old and venerable as India. And even when Italy was lying prostrate politically, her life coursed through the veins of Europe.

It was Metternich who called Italy a "geographical expression", and many a would- be Metternich has used that phrase for India, and, strangely enough, there is a similarity even in their geographical positions in the two continents.

More interesting is the comparison of England with Austria, for has not England of the twentieth century been compared to Austria of the nineteenth, proud and haughty and imposing still, but with the roots that gave strength, shriveling up and decay eating its way into the mighty fabric.

It is curious how one cannot resist the tendency to give an anthropomorphic form to a country. Such is the force of habit and early associations. India becomes Bharat Mata, Mother India, a beautiful lady, very old but ever youthful in appearance, sad-eyed and forlorn, cruelly treated by aliens and outsiders, and calling upon her children to protect her. Come such picture, rouses the emotions of hundreds of thousands and drives them to action and sacrifice. And yet India is in the main, the peasant and the worker, not beautiful to look at; for poverty is not beautiful. Does the beautiful lady of our imaginations represent the bare-bodied and bent workers in the fields and factories? Or the small group of those who have from ages past crushed the masses and exploited them, imposed cruel customs on them and made many of them even untouchable? We seek to cover truth by the creatures of our imaginations and endeavour to escape from reality to a world of dreams.

And yet, despite these different classes and their mutual conflicts, there was a common bond which united them in India, and one is amazed at its persistence and tenacity and enduring vitality. What was this strength due to? Nor merely the passive strength and weight of inertia and tradition, great as these always are. There was an active sustaining principle, for it resisted successfully powerful outside influences and absorbed internal forces that rose to combat it. And yet with all its strength it could not preserve political unity. These latter do not appear to have been considered worth much trouble; their importance was very foolishly ignored, and we have suffered for this neglect. Right through history the old Indian ideal did not glorify political and military triumph, and it looked down upon money and the professional money-making class. Honour and wealth did not go together, and honour was meant to go, at least in theory, to the men who served the community with little in the shape of financial reward.

The old culture managed to live through many a fierce storm and tempest, but though it kept its outer form, it lost its real content. Today it is fighting silently and desperately against a new and all-powerful opponent the bania civilisation of the capitalist West. It will succumb to this newcomer, for the West brings science, and science brings food for the hungry millions. But the West also brings an antidote to the evils of this cut-throat civilisation – the principles of socialism, of cooperation, and service to the community for the common good.

PRECIS

Comparison of strengths and weaknesses of India vis-à-vis the west is the thrust of the given piece of writing. India has been similar to Italy in terms of being an ancient country with a long tradition of culture, politically divided, yet with a strong force of underlying unity, and like Rome, a great Italian city, Benaras too is the external city, not only of India, but of the entire east. Benaras, however, unlike Rome, the dominant city and a symbol of unity, indulged into imperialistic practices and has never been the only centre of wisdom and culture in India. As Italy gifted culture and religion to Western Europe, so did India to Eastern Asia. As Metternich called Italy a 'geographical expression', so India has been articulated in terms of such anthropomorphic expressions including Bharatmata, Mother India, a beautiful lady, cruelly treated by aliens etc. However, the above conception and portrayal, India must not be oblivious of the fact that the country is mainly a land of the bare-bodied peasants working in the fields and bent workers sweating and slogging in factories crushed by poverty and heaped with cruel customs like untouchability. Inspite of its strength to resist the outside powerful influences and absorbing vital, internal forces by the conquerors, India could not preserve its political freedom and political unity. Undermining the importance of the economic society and the political independence, Indians have suffered a lot facing many storms and protests, the old Indian culture could keep itself only in terms of outer manifestations, losing its kernal and today the country is fighting against such powerful onslaught of western capitalism and globalisation. Possibly the nation may yield to the western science as the latter brings food for the hungry millions. However, the western scientific outlook and approach is fraught with its own limitations as cut-throat competition annihilating the foundations of socialism, service to community and the common good.

Q 4. (a) Fill in the blanks using the appropriate forms of the words given below : 10

burn, near, hard, perfect, invite, create, join, administer, spendthrift, skill

1. I did not accept the _________ because I was angry.

   Ans. *Invitation*

2. An honest man is the noblest __________ of God.

   Ans. *creation*

3. His father prevented him from __________ a dance school.

   Ans. *joining*

4. A judge should __________ equal justice to all.

   Ans. *administer*

5. He looks gentle enough, but he can be __________ at times.

   Ans. *harmful*

6. He has __________ his case to my satisfaction.

   Ans. *perfected*

7. Your opponent is too __________ to cope with.

   Ans. *skillful*

8. Despite suggestions to the contrary, he continued to be a __________.

   Ans. spendthrift

9. The __________ sun made the traveller thirsty.

   Ans. burning

10. Bombay is the seaport __________ to Europe.

    Ans. nearer

(b) Use each of following words in two separate sentences, first as a noun and then as a verb: **10**

1. present

   Ans. Noun: He gave her a beautiful present.

   Verb: He presented to the crowd a wonderful speech.

2. move

   Ans. Noun: He noticed every move of his opponent.

   Verb: They were just moving aimlessly.

3. issue

   Ans. Noun: Corruption is the most burning issue.

   Verb: A warrant was issued on his name in a murder case.

4. pain

   Ans. Noun: He suffered from acute back pain.

   Verb: It pained me to know about the untimely demise of my friend's father.

5. crowd

   Ans. Noun: A large crowd attended Kejriwal's rally.

   Verb: People crowded around the office of Congress for ticket distribution.

(c) Rewrite the following sentences as directed within brackets: **5**

1. He had to sign or be executed. (Turn in to a complex sentence).

   Ans. He was asked to sign, failing which he would be executed.

2. Gave the order. (Use the passive form).

   Ans. The order was given.

3. I was doubtful whether it were you. (Turn into a negative sentence).

   Ans. I was not sure if it was you.

4. He disgraced his family.(Use the noun form of "disgraced").

   Ans. He brought disgrace to his family.

5. He was so tired that he could not stand.(Turn in to a simple sentence replacing "so" by "too")

   Ans. *He was too tired to stand.*

Q 5. (a) Correct the following sentences: **10**

1. The rain was accompanied by hail and storm.

   Ans. *Hail and storm accompanied the rain.*

2. I cannot help but to think that he is a fool.

   Ans. *I cannot help but think he is a fool.*

3. I have never seen a clever man at engineering than him.

   Ans. *I have never seen a clever man in engineering than him.*

4. It is all the more better if he marries your daughter.

   Ans. *It is best if he marries your daughter.*

5. Objection to this proposal can be stated as thus.

   Ans. *Objections to this proposal can be stated as follows.*

6. He travelled from one corner of India to the other.

   Ans. *He travelled in India from one corner to the other.*

7. She could not make up the mind.

   Ans. *She could not make up her mind.*

8. They tried to wipe out the poor widow's tears.

   Ans. *They tried to wipe away the poor widow's tears.*

9. It is the best ideal each person may aspire for.

   Ans. *It is the best ideal for which every person may aspire for.*

10. You are not entitled for admission.

    Ans. *You are not entitled to admission.*

(b) Choose the appropriate words from those given in the brackets to fill in the blanks in the following sentences: **10**

1. She has a __________ appearance. (gracious, graceful)

   Ans. *graceful*

2. Our principal is a man of kind and __________ nature.(judicious, judicial)

   Ans. *judicious*

3. He is __________ to both praise and blame.(sensible, sensitive)

   Ans. *sensitive*

4. Gandhiji was the __________ head of the Congress party. (virtuous, virtual)

   Ans. *virtual*

5. I do not regard his scheme as __________ .(practicable, practical)

   Ans. *practical*

6. The Equator is an __________ line round the world.(imaginative, imaginary)

   Ans. *imaginary*

7. The ship sailed ashore in spite of __________ difficulties. (elemental, elementary)

   Ans. *elementary*

8. Acts of __________ negligence are punishable by law. (willing, wilful)

   Ans. *wilful*

9. He was offered a __________ job.(temporal, temporary)

   Ans. *temporary*

10. I am the __________ owner of the house.(rightful, righteous)

    Ans. *rightful*

(c) Use the following phrases in your sentences so as to bring out their meaning: 5

1. to call forth

   Ans. *The Prime Minister called forth an urgent meeting to discuss the issue.*

2. to fall through

   Ans. *Will the deal fall through?*

3. to get along

   Ans. *It is difficult to get along with people with dissimilar interests.*

4. to lay bare

   Ans. *He was asked to lay bare the explicit details of the case.*

5. to put up with

   Ans. *India was finding it difficult to put up with the ever increasing revenue demands of the British administration.*

UPSC (MAIN) EXAM – 2003
ENGLISH
(Compulsory)

Time allowed: 3 hours ***Maximum Marks: 300***

Candidates should attempt all questions.

The number of marks carried by each question is indicated at the end of the questions.

Answer must be written in English.

Q 1. Write an essay in about 300 words on any one of the following: 100

(a) The Need for Alternative Sources of Energy

(b) The Role of Judiciary in Indian Democracy

(c) Freedom of Expression

(d) My Idea of an Administrator

(e) Pleasures of Reading

ESSAY

Role of Judiciary in Indian Democracy

The Indian Constitution, the fundamental law of the land, had been drafted with the four-fold objective of securing justice, liberty, equality and fraternity to all Indian citizens. The constitution has allocated different, distinct powers and functions to the three organs of the state viz. legislature, executive and judiciary. These organs play an important role in the achievement of the said objective. Traditionally, the legislature makes the law, the executive implements them and the judiciary adjudicates and interprets the law. Even though there is no strict application of the theory of checks and balances in India, the constitution has drawn certain limits and boundaries in respect of the legislative, executive and the judicial powers.

The judiciary in India, specially the higher judiciary has been assigned a vital role in various areas like upholding the federal principle, interpretation of the laws made by respective legislatures, testing the validity of such laws and more importantly in protecting the fundamental rights of the citizens. The Supreme Court stands at the top of the hierarchy of the courts constituted under the constitution. It is the final arbiter as to the upholding to the federal principle, the validity of a law or executive action and as to the enforcement of fundamental rights of the citizens.

The Constitution of India contains a number of provisions that deal with the structure, function and powers of the judiciary. It introduced a unified system in all the states and Union Territories. It virtually introduced a three tier judicial system viz. The Supreme Court of India(the highest court of the land), the high courts, and a subordinate judiciary in every state and Union territory consisting of many hierarchies. Although the constitution contains specific provisions relating only to the Supreme Court and High Courts, it leaves the subordinate judiciary to the states.

In India, the judiciary has come to exercise vast powers of judicial review in respect of the legislative and executive functions of the state and of the judicial actions of the judiciary. The Supreme Court and the High Court not only act as the arbiters to determine disputes that may arise between the Centre and states but also protect and enforce the fundamental rights of the citizens against the arbitrary action of the states. They also interpret the laws made by the legislature and they have the final say in the validity of any legislative or executive action of the state if it contravenes or abridges the fundamental rights of citizens. It is a unique feature identified only with the Indian higher judiciary that it has the power to determine the validity of constitutional amendments which perhaps is seen nowhere under any other constitution, written or unwritten. This power of judicial review is also vested with the judiciary by implication, even in certain quasi-judicial bodies like administrative tribunals.

Thus, the judiciary performs these functions in constitutional democracies:

(i) Interpreting the Constitution in deference to the wishes of the framers of the Constitution

(ii) Upholding the federal principle of maintaining the balance between the various organs of Government and between the Centre and the states, by whichever name they are called, particularly in a federal constitution)

(iii) Guarding and protecting the fundamental rights of the citizens

(iv) Testing the validity of legislative, quasi-legislative, executive or quasi-judicial action of the state on the basis of the constitution and

(v) Applying and interpreting the laws of the legislature.

In recent years, the judiciary in India has shown itself up as the only functioning arm of the Constitution. The judges have helped magnify the majesty of law and have been instrumental in the process of the law adapting itself commensurate to the needs of the changing times. Many landmark decisions on matters of public interest, like those relating to environmental issues, greater transparency and accountability of administration, have made an enduring impact on the society. From corruption to crime, corporate disputes to human rights, and activating the law enforcing agencies to disciplining the public, the courts have played a pivotal role in all fields for achieving the goal of social cleansing. The courts are now seen as the last resort for the oppressed and the helpless.

In the context of the collapse of responsible government by the executive, the courts were duty bound to come forward in the interests of the people of this country. The judges have been anxious to ensure that social change in consonance with the philosophy of the constitution takes place without impediments from other branches of the government.

The founding fathers made the legislature trustees of the powers reposed in them, and guardians of the peoples' liberties. The judiciary was to be an auxiliary check on the powers of the state organisations when in legislative bodies, the legislative business is not seriously transacted and there is bureaucratic apathy to the problems of the people, the void is sought to be filled in by resort to courts. Thus, an enlightened, independent judiciary is vital for a vibrant democracy.

Q 2. Read the passage and answer in your own words the questions that follow:

15 x 5 = 75

This rule of trying always to do things as well as one can do them has an important bearing upon the problem of ambition. No man or woman should be without ambition, which is the inspiration of activity. But if one allows ambition to drive on to attempt things which are beyond one's own personal capacity, then unhappiness will result: if one imagines that one can do everything better than other people, then envy and jealousy, those twin monsters, will come to sadden one's days. But if one concentrates one's attention upon developing one's own special capacities, the things one is best at, then one does not worry over much if other people are more successful.

There are those again who are discontented with their own job and complain of drudgery. But there is no job in the world which does not contain a large element of drudgery. Do you imagine that a Prime Minister has no drudgery to do, or an artist, or an author? I loathe drudgery as much as any man; but I have learnt that the only way to conquer drudgery is to get through it as neatly, as efficiently as one can. You know I am right when I say that. A dull job slackly done becomes twice as dull; a dull job which you try to do just as well as you can becomes half as dull. Here again effort appears to me the main part of the art of living.

Have I any other, and less disagreeable, hint to suggest? I believe that every man and woman has somewhere tucked away inside them a sense of beauty. Without this sense, life on this earth is veiled in dim grey clouds. It may be that you do not care, or think you do make the least effort, you may find that some or all of these things will cause you sudden delight; and once you catch that delight, it will never leave you. Because, if life as I believe, is a constantly renewed effort, then the human frame and nerves require some relaxation.

1. When does ambition lead to unhappiness?

   Ans. *As long as ambition acts as a source of inspiration, it is good. However, when one allows ambition to drive one to attempt things, which are beyond one's own personal capacity, then it becomes a source of unhappiness.*

2. How can a person avoid envy and jealousy?

   Ans. *The twin masters, namely envy and jealousy can be avoidable, if one concentrates one's attention upon developing one's own special capacities. One should do things one is best at, and not worry much if other people are more successful.*

3. How can we avoid the feeling of drudgery?

   Ans. *There is no job which does not contain some element of drudgery. However, we can escape the feeling of drudgery if we do our job efficiently and earnestly. Our sincere effort makes our work less boring.*

4. Should we avoid ambition?

   Ans. *No, we should not avoid ambition as it acts as a force of inspiration for our work. However, we should not allow ambition to become our master.*

5. What does the phrase "to get through it" mean?

   Ans. *The phrase 'to get through it' means doing the work thoroughly, accepting the challenge and not just go on sulking about it.*

Q 3. Make a précis out of the following passage in your own words in about 230 words. Mark will be deducted if the précis is not written on the separate précis sheets provided and the length of the précis exceeds or falls short of more than 10 words of the prescribed length. State the number of words used by you in the précis and securely fasten the précis-sheets inside the answer-book. 75

Some wars in past were quite as disorganizing and as destructive of the civilization of devastated areas as was the Second World War. North Africa has never regained the level of prosperity that it enjoyed under the Romans. Persia never recovered from the Mongols nor has Syria from the Turks. There has always been two kinds of wars, those in which the vanquished incurred disaster, and those in which they only incurred discomfort. We seem, unfortunately, to entering upon an era in which wars are of the former sort.

The atom bomb, and still more, the hydrogen bomb, have caused new fears, involving new doubts as to the effects of science on human life. Some eminent authorities, including Einstein, have pointed out that there is a danger of the extinction of all life on this planet. I do not myself think that this will happen in the next war, but I think it may well happen in the next but one, if that is allowed to occur. If this expectation is correct, we have to choose, within the next fifty years or so, between two alternatives. Either we must allow the human race to exterminate itself, or we must forgo certain liberties that are very dear to us, more especially the liberty to kill foreigners whenever we fell so disposed. I think it probable that humanity will choose its own extermination as the preferable alternative. The choice will be made, of course, by persuading ourselves that it is not being made, since (so militarists on both sides will say) the victory of the right is certain without risk of universal disaster. We are perhaps living in the last age of man, and, if so, it is to science that he will owe his extinction.

If, however, the human race decides to let itself go on living, it will have to make very drastic changes in its way of thinking, feeling, and behaving. We must learn not to say: 'Never ! Better death than dishonour'. We must learn to submit to law, even when imposed by aliens whom we hate and despise, and whom we believe to be blind to all considerations of righteousness. Consider some concrete examples. Jews and Arabs will have to agree to submit to arbitration; if the award goes against the Jews, the President of the United States will have to ensure the victory of the party to which he is opposed, since, if he supports the international authority, he will lose the Jewish vote in New York State. On the other hand, if the award goes in favour of the Jews, the Mohammedan world will be indignant, and will be supported by all other malcontents. Or, to take another instance, Eire will demand the right to oppress the Protestants of Ulster, and on this issue the United States will support Eire while Britain will support Ulster. Could an international authority survive such a dissension? Again: India and Pakistan cannot agree about Kashmir, therefore, one of them must support Russia and the other the United States. It will be obvious to anyone who is an interested party in one of these disputes that the issue is far more important than the continuance of life on our planet. The hope that the human race will allow itself to survive is therefore somewhat slender.

But, if human life is to continue in spite of science, mankind will have to learn a discipline of the passions which, in the past, has not been necessary. Men will have to submit to the law, even when they think the law unjust and iniquitous. Nations, which are persuaded that they are only demanding the barest justice, will have to acquiesce when this demand is denied to them by the neutral authority. I do not say that this is easy; I neither do nor prophesy that it will happen; I say only that if it does not happen the human race will perish, and will perish as a result of science.

PRECIS

Reflecting on the devastating and disorganising consequences of nuclear war and hence science, as a curse to the human civilisation, the writer states that a war in which the defeated is heaped with disaster is more fatal than the one wherein the beaten only suffers discomforts. In all likelihood though unfortunately, humanity is entering an era in which wars are waged in the former mode. Such inventions of science as atom bomb and hydrogen bomb have caused fears that all life on the earth may come to an end, as apprehended by Einstein. Keeping in view the destructive effect of science on human life, people must learn to suppress their urge to kill other humans. Otherwise, we are moving towards the extermination of human race. In other words, the proliferation of the right-wing ideologies should be suppressed or man will owe to science his extinction. This requires a radical change in our thinking, feeling and behaving. Life must be saved even at the expense of dishonor. We need to submit to the authority of the law even when imposed by some foreign authorities. To settle disputes between India and Pakistan, between the Jews and the Arabs, the affected nations will have to evolve a consensus to submit to arbitration. They must realize that the continuance of life on the planet is more important than sticking to vested interests and issues. To save humanity, we must learn to discipline our passions and submit to the law even if the later seems unjust and a discriminating and inegalitarian. Otherwise, we will perish because of science.

Q 4. (a) Fill in the blanks using appropriate forms of the words given below: 10

offensive, imagination, psychological, conceive, vacation, entire, enthusiasm, lacerating, deify, margin.

1. I do not believe in the __________ of an ordinary politician.

   Ans. *deification*

2. She could not bear to look at his __________ hands.

   Ans. *lacerated.*

3. Most people do not have any clear __________ of judicial activism.

   Ans. *conception*

4. Who can dare to __________ the boss?

   Ans. *marginalize*

5. A sensible person can __________ the plight of others.

   Ans. *imagine*

6. You have to consider the matter in its __________.

   Ans. *entirety*

7. It is difficult to __________ such dullards.

   Ans. *enthuse*

8. We can no longer __________ the poor and the suppressed.

   Ans. *offend*

9. You will have to __________ the house.

   Ans. *vacate*

10. __________ is an interesting subject.

    Ans. *Psychology*

(b) Use the each of the following words in two separate sentences, first as a noun and then as a verb: **10**

1. help

   Ans. Noun: *He is virtually of no help to the family.*

   Verb: Your advice helped me a lot.

2. nurse

   Ans. Noun: *She is a permanent nurse at PGI.*

   Verb: The child was nursed by her maternal grandmother.

3. judge

   Ans. Noun: *The judge awarded capital punishment to the murderer.*

   Verb: It is very difficult to judge from their behaviour.

4. pillory

   Ans. Noun: *Pillory was used in the past for punishment.*

   Verb: He was regularly pilloried by the press for his radical ideas.

5. round

   Ans. Noun: *The next round of peace talks will commence soon.*

   Verb: The boat rounded off the tip of the island.

(c) Rewrite the following sentences as directed within brackets: **5**

1. No metal is as costly as gold. (Use the comparative degree of "costly")

   Ans. *No metal is costlier than gold.*

2. I doubt you have done it. (Change into a negative sentence without changing the meaning)

   Ans. *I think you have not done it.*

3. He was elected leader. (Change into active Voice)

   Ans. *People elected him leader.*

4. She confessed that she was guilty. (Turn into a simple sentence)

   Ans. *She confessed her guilt.*

5. She said, "Can you write a poem?" (Change into indirect speech)

   Ans. *She asked if I could write a poem.*

Q 5. (a) Correct the following sentences: **10**

1. Each of the scholars, belonging to various countries have spoken about it.

   Ans. *Each of the scholars belonging to different countries has spoken about it.*

2. All were present except he and his sister.

   Ans. *All were present except his sister and himself.*

3. I wonder if ten thousand rupees are large sum.

   Ans. *I wonder if ten thousand rupees is a large sum.*

4. She lay the table an hour ago.

   Ans. *She laid the table an hour ago.*

5. He was absented from class for no reason.

   Ans. *He was absent from the class for no reason.*

6. He is untidy boy.

   Ans. *He is an untidy boy.*

7. All his plans fell out for lack of help.

   Ans. *All his plans failed due to lack of help.*

8. Of milk, coke and coffee, the latter is my favorites.

   Ans. *Between milk, coke and coffee, the latter is my favorite.*

9. All this happened prior 1971 war.

   Ans. *All this happened prior to the 1971 war.*

10. Scarcely had she gone that he arrived.

    Ans. *Scarcely had she gone, than he arrived.*

(b) Choose the appropriate words given in the brackets to fill in the blanks in the following sentences: **10**

1. Nehruji made a __________ speech in Parliament on this occasion. (historical, historic)

   Ans. *historic*

2. Such heavy responsibilities cannot be __________ easily. (born, borne)

   Ans. *borne*

3. The doctor visits him on __________ days. (alternative, alternate)

   Ans. *alternate*

4. I do not know why he is __________ towards me. (contemptuous, contemptible)

   Ans. *contemptuous*

5. To work for more than eight hours is quite __________. (exhaustive, exhausting)

   Ans. *exhausting.*

6. Democracy does not allow the __________ of the minorities. (prosecution, persecution)

   Ans. *persecution*

7. No meeting of the __________ of ministers has been scheduled for tomorrow. (council, cabinet)

   Ans. *council*

8. All worldly pleasures are considered to be __________ by saints. (momentary, momentous)

   Ans. *momentary*

9. Any __________ of secret documents is punishable by law. (tempering, tampering)

   Ans. *tampering*

10. He is an __________ person to work with. (amiable, amenable)

    Ans. *amiable*

(c) Use the following phrases in your own sentences so as to bring out their meaning: **5**

1. to come across

   Ans. *In U.S.A. one comes across various ghettos of Afro-American people.*

2. to be cut out for

   Ans. *He is perfectly cut-out for a job in the armed forces.*

3. over head and ears

   Ans. *He is over head and ears nowadays because of his hectic season.*

4. to see eye to eye

   Ans. *After a bitter quarrel, the two friends could not see each other eye to eye.*

5. to draw the line

   Ans. *The Indian National Congress drew the line for discussion, of only those issues that were of national importance.*

UPSC (MAIN) EXAM – 2002
ENGLISH
(Compulsory)

Time allowed: 3 hours **Maximum Marks: 300**

Candidates should attempt all questions.

The number of marks carried by each question is indicated at the end of the questions.

Answer must be written in English.

Q 1. Write an essay in about 300 words on any one of the following : 100

(a) The ways to enrich our regional languages.

(b) Whither Indian democracy today?

(c) Terrorism in India

(d) Science and Religion

(e) If I were the Prime Minister of India.

ESSAY

If I Were Prime Minister Of India

India is a democratic republic. It has its own supreme and fundamental law of the land i.e. the Constitution: which envisages separation of powers among three different organs; legislature; executive and judiciary. Assigning the task of making laws to the legislature and their interpretation by the judiciary, the constitution bestows the most important task of implementation of laws and execution of policies on the executive with the President being the dejure head, and the prime minister being the defacto head.

So, in the Indian parliamentary democratic set up, the real head is the prime minister. He is main task master. He is the leader of the party in the Lok Sabha and defacto head of the government and captain of the ministry. He is primus inter pares. Prime minister is the channel of communication between the President and the Council of Ministers under article 78 of the constitution.

If I were the prime minister of India, I would first attempt to tackle the issues of corruption, criminalisation, inflation, black money, poverty, illiteracy and the day to day problems of the common man like water, electricity, road, railways, communications, administrative red tapism and police excesses.

To address all these issues, I need to form a ministry of ministers with clean image. An efficient and effective public friendly bureaucracy will be the other top most priority. Framing and implementation of policies without delay and making them reach the grassroots level will also be a big priority. The participation of intellectuals in their respective areas of expertise so as to make best optimum use of their experience for the welfare of the people will be the other innovative initiative. To root out corruption and weed out criminalisation from politics to make Indian politics free from them, I would implement strict laws without delay.

Power generation to handle power crisis, development of infrastructure to boost industrialisation resulting in generating employment leading to eradication of poverty, illiteracy and ignorance will be addressed without delay.

My concern for the farmers' problems like subsidies, MSP, cheap seeds and fertilizers, supply of water and power, diversification of agriculture, development of organic farming will be real, immediate, serious and close to my heart. Then the in the words of Nehru, "to build a secular state in the most heterogeous society," will be the most formidable task for me.

I will make relentless efforts to bring social malpractices like female foeticide, female infanticide, child labour, child abuse, harassment of women, rape, molestation, and other such crimes against child and women to an end.

I will have zero tolerance for 4 Cs; corruption, criminalisation, casteism and communalisation and I would crush the entry of three MPs; muscle power, money power and mafia power.

In order to make a vibrant, rejuvenated, resilient and self-reliant India, I will leave no stone unturned to make its presence felt at the global level and convince the world to accept us a fast rising global economic player.

Q 2. Read the passage and answer in your own words the questions that follow:

15 x 5 = 75

The scientific and technological revolution has brought about fundamental changes in the socio-economic sphere. The use of diesel engine and electricity and the beginning of the application of atomic energy have changed the modes of production. These things have led to the concentration of capital in a few hands. Great enterprises are replacing cottage industries and small firms. The working classes have certainly benefited economically. The miracle of production has necessitated the miracle of consumption. Better amenities are available at a lower cost. A man can buy anything he wants today, if he can only afford. But what kind of men are needed today for our society? Men who can co-operate in large groups, men whose tasks are standardised, men who feel free and independent and at the same time are willing to fill in the social machine without any friction.

Modern man is faced with a sort of moral and spiritual dilemma. The crisis of values yawns before him. Today the old values are in the melting pot, and the new values have not found their foothold. Man has become the automation he has contrived; he has lost ownership of himself. The discord between the development of positive science on the one hand and the dehumanisation of man on the other is the worst crisis of the modern age.

Apart from the economic sphere, the socio-political sphere has not escaped this stratification and the congruent crisis of values. Since the Renaissance, man has been striving for individual rights and self-dignity. But under the present set-up, only two types of men are found– the conditioner and the conditioned. The propaganda offices and the planning bureaus have almost crushed the 'individual self'. Due to this pressure, the personality fulfillment or its all-round development is denied to many.

Questions:

(a) What has changed the modes of production today?

Ans. *The scientific and technological revolution, for example, expedited by the use of diesel engine and electricity and the beginning of the application of atomic energy has changed the modes of production.*

(b) What things are being replaced by great enterprises?

Ans. *One of the adverse effects of technological revolution has led to the concentration of capital in a few hands. As a result, great enterprises are replacing cottage industries and small firms.*

(c) What kind of men are needed today for our society?

Ans. *The capitalistic mode of production and society need such men who can cooperate in large groups, men whose tasks are standardised, men who are willing to fit in the social machine without any friction.*

(d) Why has man become the automation of his own creation?

Ans. *On account of the crises in the old values created by the contemporary advancements and the new values not finding their foothold in the fast changing society, man has become the automation; he has lost ownership of himself.*

(e) Is modern man able to attain personality fulfillment?

Ans. *The contemporary social set-up supported by bureaucracy, stratification and mechanization of life, has led to the rise by the 'social self' and the crushing of the 'individual self'. As a result, man is not able to attain personality fulfillment.*

Q 3. Make a précis out of the following passage in your own words in about 230 words, on the special précis-sheet provided. The précis-sheets should be securely fastened inside the answer book. Indicate the number of words used by you in your précis.

N.B. : Marks will be deducted if your précis is much longer or shorter than the prescribed length. **75**

"What is the use of a house if you haven't got a tolerable planet to put in on?" asked Henry David Thoreau. More than a century later, the Earth seems to be literally falling to pieces. Recent environmental set-backs include billions of tonnes of ice-shelves breaking off in the Antarctic and unusually warm temperatures in different parts of the world. Panic reactions range from predictions of sinking islands to the lamenting the ill-effects of global warming induced by release of green house gases into the atmosphere. The trouble is that we are too much obsessed with the problem of climatic change to even acknowledge the fact that the state of the planet hinges on much more. Climatic change is at best a symptom of a far more complex malaise, just as fever is most often only an indicator of something that's gone awry in our body. It is time for a complete and comprehensive planetary health check that will examine the impacts of change in land use, loss of biodiversity, use of fertilizers and pesticides and consistent pollution of water bodies. This would overcome the limitations of evaluating how ecosystems work by reacting to just one major environmental concern as is happening in the case of global warming. These considerations have been responsible for the Millennium Ecosystem Assessment. Financed by four major international bodies, including the UNO and the World Bank, the eco-panel was set up without much fuss last June (2001), and is expected to determine, over a period of four years and at a cost of $21 million, the state of the Earth's ecosystems.

The eco-panel will have source inputs from more than 2,000 natural and social scientists the world over. Put simply, the Earth will go through the equivalent of a through physical analysis, so that biological, economic and social information can be collated to help scientists arrive at a final diagnosis. What is crucial, says one of the scientists, is that "no one has previously tried to work out how all of these conflicting pressures interact." The other important factor is how well we can orchestrate trade-offs and interactions in order to maintain ecological balance. Scientific bodies like the International Panel on Climate Change (IPCC) have access to vast amounts of baseline data relating to the subject – although critics points out that the information available is mostly from the North, leaving the concerns of the South largely unrepresented. The newly constituted eco-panel will have to take all these aspects into account. For instance, it will have to ensure that data collection is more representative of the regions of the world. Today, we have the advantage of sourcing data from remote sensing satellites as well. The information thus gathered would have to be sorted out and analysed by specialists and also by generalists – before the panel comes out with specific periodic predictions, prescriptions and warnings. The healing process can begin only if all the scientific evidence and direction is made available to a wide audience and not just restricted to policy makers. Rather than depending solely upon governments to listen to and take corrective action, the focus should now be on convincing or individual action will eventually make the difference between regression and recovery.

PRECIS

The write-up highlights the extremely bad shape and deplorable health of the earth, rendered almost unlivable. Rampant anti-environmental activities of the inhabitants of the planet have caused such ill-effects and setbacks as the melting of Antarctic ice shelves, rising temperatures in different parts of the world, sinking of islands and depletion of the ozone layer induced by release of greenhouse gases into the atmosphere. Our panic with the problem of climatic change, which is merely a symptom of a far more complex ailment, will lead to nowhere unless a full pause is given to activities leading to loss of biodiversity, use of fertilizers and pesticides and consistent pollution of water-bodies. To assess and protect the Earth's ecosystems, a major international panel, financed by the UNO and the World Bank, was set up in June 2001. Setting of the eco-panel, comprising of 2000 natural and social scientists, the world over, aims at a comprehensive physical analysis of the earth and reaching a diagnosis keeping in view all the social, biological and economic obstacles and doing all the needful to maintain ecological balance. Collecting data representing all regions of the world though remote sensing satellites, analysing the same and making periodic prediction, prescriptions and warnings are other key concerns of the eco-panel. However, the healing process can begin only if the direction of the panel is in the reach of wide audience and not just remain restricted to the policy makers. Above all, collective corrective efforts are required to be initiated for the recovery and healing of the earth.

Q 4. (a) Fill in the blanks using appropriate forms of the words given below: 10

ride, diminish, devotion, shout, watch, contest, disastrous, pleasure, philosophizing, finance.

1. Mohan is ___________ to his father.

   Ans. *devoted*

2. None seems to have been ___________ with his speech.

   Ans. *pleased*

3. She __________ at the peon when he sat down.

   ***Ans.** shouted*

4. His __________ condition is at a low ebb now.

   ***Ans.** financial*

5. Several candidates are __________ the panchayat elections.

   ***Ans.** contesting*

6. The boy was frightened to __________ the movie.

   ***Ans.** watch*

7. What does Sankara's __________ teach us?

   ***Ans.** philosophy*

8. Hariharan's suspicious moves herald a __________.

   ***Ans.** disaster*

9. In the circus show, I saw a bear __________ a bicycle.

   ***Ans.** riding*

10. The chances of starvation deaths have __________ today.

    ***Ans.** diminished*

(b) Use each of the following words in two separate sentences, first as a noun and then as a verb: 10

1. race

   ***Ans. Noun:** Everybody is running a rat-race nowadays.*

   Verb: Race fast to hit the jackpot.

2. hit

   ***Ans. Noun:** PK was a great hit.*

   Verb: He hit me on the head with a rod.

3. play

   ***Ans. Noun:** Shakespeare's plays are all-time classics.*

   Verb: Children play in the evening in the nearby gardens.

4. touch

   ***Ans. Noun:** Dhirbubhai Ambani had a Midas touch.*

   Verb: He touched the pinnacle of success.

5. experiment

   ***Ans. Noun:** Life is an experiment.*

   Verb: Keep experimenting with life.

(c) Rewrite the following sentences as directed parenthetically: **5**

1. "Do not make a noise," said the teacher to his students. (Change into Indirect Speech)

   Ans. *The teacher ordered his students not to make a noise.*
2. Hari is so short that he cannot touch the ceiling. (Replace 'so be 'too')

   Ans. *Hari is too short to touch the ceiling.*
3. I gave him a ten-rupee note yesterday. (change into passive voice)

   Ans. *A ten rupee note was given to him by me.*
4. She bought a house last year. The house is white. (change into s simple sentence)

   Ans. *She brought a white coloured house last year.*
5. Hard as he worked, he failed in the examination. (Use 'though')

   Ans. *Though he worked hard, he failed in the examination.*

Q 5. (a) Correct the following sentences: **10**

1. He boasts his achievements now and then.

   Ans. *He boasts of his achievements now and then.*
2. She is living in this flat since 1995.

   Ans. *She lives in this apartment since 1995.*
3. The Principal was angry upon the boys.

   Ans. *The Principal was angry with the boys.*
4. Character is more preferable than intelligence.

   Ans. *Character is preferred to intelligence.*
5. Krishna hanged all the pictures on the wall.

   Ans. *Krishna put up all the pictures on the wall.*
6. The sceneries of Kashmir move me most.

   Ans. *The sceneries of Kashmir allure me most.*
7. Cattle is grazing in the field.

   Ans. *Cattle are grazing in the field.*
8. Hari is going foreign next month.

   Ans. *Hari is be going abroad next month.*
9. She knew that I am leaving the place.

   Ans. *She knew that I would be leaving the place.*
10. His elder brother gave him many good advices.

    Ans. *His elder brother gave him many a good advice.*

(b) Of the words given in the brackets, choose the one you think appropriate to fill in the blanks: **10**

1. The road accident proved to be ___________.(fateful, fatal)

   Ans. *fatal*

2. He got a __________ opportunity to qualify in the tests. (gold, golden)

   Ans. *golden*

3. Faridabad is an __________ city.(industrial, industrious)

   Ans. *industrial*

4. An ashram is a __________ place. (quite, quiet)

   Ans. *quiet*

5. Sohan's handwriting is __________. (eligible, illegible)

   Ans. *illegible*

6. We should not disturb the __________ of his mind.(piece, peace)

   Ans. *peace*

7. You should __________ an example to strengthen your viewpoint. (site, cite)

   Ans. *cite*

8. Akbar was the __________ to Humayun. (hair, heir)

   Ans. *heir*

9. Rajasthan is a well-known __________. (desert, dessert)

   Ans. *desert*

(c) Use the following phrases in sentences so as to bring out their meaning: 5

1. bring about

   Ans. *This administrative policy will bring about a sea change in the political scenario.*

2. call names

   Ans. *She called out names of those who were selected for the interview.*

3. run out

   Ans. *In the midst of the desert, my car ran out of fuel.*

4. by leaps and bounds

   Ans. *After the success in the Civil Services his popularity increased by leaps and bounds.*

5. lame excuse

   Ans. *"Such lame excuses shall not be tolerated.*

UPSC (MAIN) EXAM – 2001
ENGLISH
(Compulsory)

Time allowed: 3 hours **_Maximum Marks: 300_**

Candidates should attempt all questions.

The number of marks carried by each question is indicated at the end of the questions.

Answer must be written in English.

Q 1. Write an essay in about 300 words on any one of the following: 100

(a) Knowledge is power

(b) Consequences of globalisation

(c) Value of yoga

(d) Science and human happiness

(e) Tourism in India

ESSAY

Knowledge is Power

Knowledge distinguishes man from animals. Knowledge is power and it is a great strength of man. Knowledge makes us aware, informed and educated. Knowledge empowers, enlightens, enthuses us with confidence and capability. Man's inquisitiveness and insatiable thirst for it has enabled man to use and utilise it for the welfare of mankind. But at the same time, knowledge has been many times abused and misused for destruction of mankind.

Francis Bacon said Knowledge itself is power. Knowledge is the awareness of a fact or a situation. It is a rich and a unique possession that cannot be stolen or plundered. Knowledge doesn't decrease when it is given. In fact, knowledge increases its strength when it is disseminated. Our knowledge is the amassed thought and experience of countless human beings. Those who have wide-range of knowledge and experience can capture power and influence. The possession of knowledge gives them a distinct advantage over the semi-educated people. Half knowledge is regarded as 'the curse of god' and also it is worse than ignorance. The growth and survival of humankind depends upon knowledge. From the Stone Age until date, man has struggled to know the unknown. He explored land, water and space by virtue of his knowledge. Man has made progress in all fields starting from science, technology to arts etc. through his quest for knowledge.

At the dawn of civilisation, man was at the mercy of nature. He lived the life of a nomad. He then invented tools and weapons for hunting. Verbal communication also developed. He discovered fire and the wheel. These were the initial steps taken by man by utilising his brain.

The successful discoveries and inventions encouraged man to contemplate on new ideas. His ability to rationalise, analyse and store the events in his memory enabled him to achieve success.

Knowledge gave him the power, confidence and courage to make life worthy of living. He began to use the forces of nature for his own benefits. Thus, life became comfortable. He utilised his knowledge to improve his own life.

Man has been able to eradicate a number of diseases like small pox, plague etc. from the face of the earth. The human body can be operated upon for removal of cancer or for an open-heart surgery. The discovery of a number of antibiotics and drugs has reduced the suffering of mankind. Agriculture has also developed through the use of high yielding crops. The invention of the devices of communication has transformed the world into a global village. Computers has changed human life altogether. All these have been the fruits of man's quest for knowledge.

Knowledge gave man the feeling of strength and power. It leads to the nourishment of the mind. It enables one to give sound judgment. Education and knowledge are desirable for democracy. We should try to spread the level of knowledge in all fields. In rural India, the knowledge levels about family, problems of woman, child rearing and other social issues are very poor. Illiteracy and social backwardness combine to put the rural masses at the receiving end. A lack of knowledge leads to poverty and absence of methods of productivity and economic prosperity. This vicious cycle continues. Restraint, tolerance, understanding and capacity to manage affairs come with knowledge. If knowledge is imparted to our rural children, youth, women and men, they would emerge as a major empowered society.

Sadly, with the passage of time, man started misusing knowledge. He started using knowledge to destroy the very forces that provided him sustenance. He interfered with nature and disturbed the ecological balance. He has polluted air, land and water. He has thus created unfavourable conditions for himself and others. Man has developed destructive weapons that can destroy the whole of mankind. The bombing of Nagasaki and Hiroshima proves the fact. Man is posing a threat to the existence of flora and fauna.

Knowledge should not be misused. Nuclear power should be used for useful purposes. Man should find solutions to control and check pollution. The conventional sources of energy are depleting at a fast rate. He should try to find out sources of economical power generation.

Knowledge must be acquired and shared as a collective effort. It should be used only for peace, prosperity and growth.

Q 2. Read the passage and answer in your own words the questions that follow:

15 x 5 =75

The world we live in presents an endless variety of fascinating problems which excite our wonder and curiosity. The scientific worker attempts to formulate these problems in accurate terms and to solve them in the light of all the relevant facts that can be collected by observation and experiment. Such questions as 'What', 'How', 'Where' and 'When' challenge him to find the clues that may suggest possible replies. Confronted by the many problems presented by, let us say, an active volcano, we may ask: 'What are the lavas made of'? How does the volcano work and how is the heat generated? Where do the lavas and gases come from? When did the volcano first begin to erupt and when is it likely to erupt again?

In terms of chemical compounds and elements, the question 'How' refers to processes the way things are made or happen or change. The ancients regarded natural processes as manifestations of energy acting on or through matter. Volcanic eruption and earthquakes no longer reflect the erratic behaviour of the gods of the underworld; they arise from the action of the earth's internal heat and through the surrounding crust. The source of the energy lies in the material of inner earth. In many directions, of course, our knowledge is still incomplete, only the first of the questions we have asked about volcanoes, for example, can as yet be satisfactorily answered. The point is not that we now pretend to understand everything but that we have faith in the orderliness of natural processes. As a result of two or three centuries of scientific investigation, we have come to believe that Nature is understandable in the sense that when we ask questions by way of appropriate observations and experiments, she will answer truly and reward us with discoveries that endure.

Questions:

(a) How does the author describe the task of the scientific worker?

Ans. *The scientific worker attempts to formulate problems of the world faced by human beings in accurate terms and solve them in the light of all the relevant facts that can be collected by observation and experiment.*

(b) Why does the author speak about volcanoes?

Ans. *The author speaks about volcanoes because the eruption of these pose a big challenge to people and at times their lives are rendered difficult on account of volcanoes.*

(c) What does the equation 'How' refer to?

Ans. *The question 'How' refers to processes – the way things are made or happen or change.*

(d) How did the ancients look upon volcanoes and earthquakes?

Ans. *The ancients looked upon volcanoes and earthquakes as the erratic behaviour of the gods of the underworld.*

(e) What does the author say about our knowledge of the world?

Ans. *The author says that our knowledge of the world is still incomplete and there are thousands of questions yet to be satisfactorily answered. However, science has affirmed our faith in the orderliness of natural processes. By taking recourse to scientific investigations, we can discover enduring and rewarding solutions and to the problems faced by human beings.*

Q 3. Make a précis out of the following passage in your own words in about 230 words, on the special précis-sheets provided. Marks will be deducted if the précis is not written on the précis sheets. Marks will also be deducted if your précis is much longer or shorter than the prescribed length. The précis-sheets should be securely fastened inside the answer book. State the number of words used by you in your précis. 75

No amount of improvement and reconstruction in education will bear much fruit if our schools and colleges are undermined by indiscipline. An impartial examination makes it clear that students and teachers alike need more of the spirit of discipline. If proper education is to be given, acts of indiscipline prevalent in our educational institutions have to be checked.

Indiscipline may take the shape of group indiscipline or individual indiscipline. Group indiscipline is the worse of the two. While as individuals many of our students are as good as students elsewhere, the tendency to group indiscipline has increased in recent years. Many causes have led to this group indiscipline. For various reasons, under a foreign regime, acts of indiscipline became frequent, often necessitated by the political activities, which were launched against a foreign government. While there may have been justification for such indiscipline under different political circumstances, we feel that there is no justification now for such acts of indiscipline after the attainment of independence. The democratic constitution which the country has adopted permits the redressing of grievances through democratic machinery. It would be against all principles of democracy if such acts of indiscipline were to continue.

The real purpose of education is to train youth to discharge the duties of citizenship properly. All other objectives are incidental. Discipline, therefore, should be the responsibility of parents, teachers, the general public and the authorities concerned. There are some positive factors promoting discipline. The Indian student's natural tendency is to be disciplined. It is only when forces act strongly on him that he may sometimes be led astray. He appreciates rules and is normally inclined to abide by them. Much can be done to encourage this trend in school and college life. Personal contact between teacher and pupil is essential. Emphasis is also to be laid on the role of the class teacher or tutorial guide in promoting general discipline and the welfare of the pupils. Further, a greater responsibility should devolve upon the students themselves in the maintenance of discipline. Nothing is more calculated to develop a proper sense of self-discipline and proper behaviour than their enforcement. Not by any outside authority with any symbol of punishment but by the students themselves. They should choose their own representatives to see that proper codes of conduct are observed.

Another important method of bringing home to pupils the value of discipline is through group games. It is on the playing fields that the virtue of playing the games for its own sake and the team spirit can be cultivated. Such extracurricular activities as Boy Scouts, Girl Guides, the National Cadet Corps, Junior Red Cross and Social Service activities will promote a proper spirit of discipline. The building up of a truly harmonious and united form of community life should be the endeavour of all progressive educational institutions.

Beside these positive factors, certain negative factors also promote discipline. The discipline of the youth of any country depends upon the discipline that is exercised by the elders. It is a well-known fact that in all democracies election time is a time of feverish activity not always conducted in the most healthy spirit, and the utilisation by politicians of immature minds like students for purpose of electioneering campaigns, with or without slogans attached thereto, is not calculated to promote sound discipline among students. It should be considered an election offence for any member or party to utilise the services of pupils under the age of 17 in political or civic campaigns. Besides, while the educative value of leading politicians addressing our students from time to time may be readily admitted, the tendency often is for the leaders not to speak to the audience before them but to a wider audience whose attention they wish to attract through the press. It is not necessary that every speech made by a politician should be a political speech.

Lastly, discipline among students can only be promoted if there is discipline among the staff. The teacher and the educational administrator should realise that their activities are all being watched by their pupils. To what extent therefore, both in their personal conduct and in their general attitude to all problems concerning their country, they have to realise that there are limitations within which they must act for the best interests of education. Ultimately, it is the school or college atmosphere and the quality of the teachers there that ensure proper codes of conduct and discipline among our students.

PRECIS

The spirit of discipline is indispensable for the improvement and reconstruction of education. The major stakeholders of education – students and teachers – must take recourse to discipline, if schools and colleges are to be transformed into efficacious and efficient education institutions. The group indiscipline – more dangerous than the individual one – may have prevailed, necessitated by political activities against the foreign regime during the struggle for independence, however, the same environment of indiscipline must not be allowed to persist when we have built up the democratic and constitutional mechanisms, to the redressal of our grievances. The discharge of citizenship duties by the youth, the real purpose of education, will remain a distant dream, unless the teachers, the parents, the general public and authorities realise the value of discipline, practice and promote the same. Above all, the students themselves must develop a proper sense of self-discipline and appropriate conduct to realize their goals. The sense of discipline must not be merely enforced upon them. Group games and the social service activities including Boys, Scouts, Girl Guides, the N.C.C., Junior Red Cross etc. along with the fostering a sense of value of harmonious and united form of community life by the progressive educational institutions, are the various other methods of promoting discipline. During the election campaign, the time of feverish activity, the political parties and leaders must stick to self-restraint and be mindful of not indulging into any offensive activities, which may affect the sensitive and budding psyche of the students. On top of it, teachers and educational administrators must realise the value of the great Gandhian saying: "Be the change you want to see". They must present themselves as models to their students through their personal conduct and through their general attitude to all problems concerning the country.

Q4. (a) Fill in the blanks using appropriate forms of the words given below: **10**

value, offend, strike, jealous, put, grant, disturb, lead, fly, economic

1. The man __________ into a rage and tore away his garments.

   Ans. *flew*

2. A sensible man never takes everything for __________

   Ans. *granted*

3. No one seems to have taken ________ of her manners.

   Ans. *offence*

4. When are you __________ out to sea again?

   Ans. *putting*

5. I have no mind to trespass upon your ________ time.

   Ans. *valuable*

6. Try to rise above petty personal __________.

   Ans. *jealousies*

7. The officer __________ through one paragraph and accepted the rest.

   Ans. *struck*

8. The report I have received is very __________ indeed.

   Ans. *disturbing*

9. She has sent her paper to a __________ journal.

   Ans. *leading*

10. These new measures will give a boost to our __________.

   Ans. *economy*

(b) Use each of the following words in two separate sentences, first as a noun and then a verb: **10**

1. turn

   Ans. ***Noun:*** *Now its your turn, please.*

   Verb: Turn to your right.

2. spell

   Ans. ***Noun:*** *Spelling and writing practice is a must.*

   Verb: He could not spell even the most common words.

3. part

   Ans. ***Noun:*** *He spent a major part of his life at hostels'.*

   Verb: *She and her* husband have parted and have filed for a divorce.

4. contact

   Ans. ***Noun:*** *He came in contact with a superstar.*

   Verb: *Where can he be contacted?*

5. meet

   Ans. ***Noun:*** *The next NAM meet will be held in Kathmandu.*

   Verb: In his paltry salary, Ram found it very difficult to make both ends meet.

(c) Rewrite the following sentences as directed: **5**

1. You are too early for the show. (Use "enough")

   Ans. *You are early enough for the show.*

2. The Mahanadi is not so long as the Ganges. (Use the comparative degree)

   Ans. *The Mahanadi is not as long as the Ganges.*

3. Varsha readily complied my request. (Fill in the gap with a preposition)

   Ans. *Varsha readily complied to my request.*

4. We are sure of his honesty. (Change into a complex sentence)

   Ans. *His honesty is what we are very sure about.*

5. Sarita said, "Don't open the window." (Change into the indirect form)

   Ans. *Sarita said not to open the window.*

Q 5. (a) Correct the following sentences: **10**

1. May I now take your leave?

   Ans. *May I take your leave?*

2. The soup will taste better if it had more salt in it.

   Ans. *The soup would taste better if more salt is added to it.*

3. Is he used to come late everyday?

   Ans. *Does he come late everyday?*

4. Your daughter is twelve years old, isn't it?

   Ans. *Your daughter is twelve years old, isn't she?*

5. We must be true to our words.

   Ans. *We should be true to our words.*

6. Datta is living here since 1998.

   Ans. *Since 1998, this has been Datta's residence.*

7. A twenty miles walk is really very hard.

   Ans. *It is very hard to walk twenty miles.*

8. We watched the man to disappear in the woods.

   Ans. *We watched the man as he disappeared in the woods.*

9. Kalidas has written Meghadutam.

   Ans. *Kalidas had written Meghadutam.*

10. Let's have coffee.

    Ans. *Let us have coffee.*

(b) Of the words given in brackets, choose the one you think appropriate to fill in the blanks: **10**

1. He seems to be __________ to hard work. (adverse; averse)

   Ans. *averse*

2. The building does not __________ to safety regulations. (conform; confirm)

   Ans. *conform*

3. Asharam was accused of __________ the workers against the management. (exciting; inciting)

   Ans. *inciting*

4. Rescue workers rushed to the site of the plane __________. (crass; crash)

   Ans. *crash*

5. Gagan uses expensive __________ for his letters.(stationery; stationary)

   Ans. *stationery*

6. The factory __________ making toys. (seized; ceased)

   Ans. *ceased*

7. Shakil is __________ at solving difficult crossword puzzles. (ingenuous; ingenious)

    Ans. *ingenious*

8. I wish you a __________ recovery. (fast; speedy)

    Ans. *speedy*

9. Everybody said that her decision was __________. (judicious; judicial)

    Ans. *judicious*

10. You will have to ________ your afternoon tea as we have no more sugar. (forego: forgo)

    Ans. *forego*

(c) Use the following phrases in sentences so as to bring out their meaning: 5

1. deal in

    Ans. Mr. Gupta deals in imported cars and bikes.

2. prime of life

    Ans. Andre Agassi bid farewell to international tennis in the prime of his life.

3. above board

    Ans. PM Modi is really above board.

4. dwell upon

    Ans. Let's not dwell upon your earlier mistakes.

5. in full swing

    Ans. With the start of the Second World War, the armour manufacturing companies worked in full swing.